Unplanned Passage

*The Autobiography and Illustrations
of a London Marine Pilot*

Captain Peter J D Russell FNI

en Press

First published in Great Britain by Pen Press
All paper used in the printing of this book has been made from wood
grown in managed, sustainable forests.

ISBN13: 978-1-78003-058-6

Pen Press is an imprint of Indepenpress Publishers Ltd
25 Eastern Place
Brighton
BN2 1GJ

Printed and bound in the UK

A catalogue record of this book is available from
the British Library

Cover design by Adrian Trimble

The Author

Peter Russell was born in Folkestone in 1934. Educated during the Second World War and the austere years immediately afterwards; he was to spend a lifetime at sea starting in 1950. This is the story of his life, the people, ships and events which influenced it. Starting with his WW2 experiences, it follows his progress from Sea Cadet via the Merchant Navy and Royal Fleet Auxiliary Service to Master Mariner and Cinque Ports Trinity House Pilot. He finally retired as Senior Pilot in the Port of London and President of the Nautical Institute in 1999.

In retirement he retains his maritime interests as a Fellow of the Nautical Institute, a member of the Younger Brethren of Trinity House and Member of the Honourable Company of Master Mariners. A Life Member of the Marine Society and Sea Cadets and member of the RFA Association, he has also served as a member of Rotary International for more than forty years.

The illustrations, including the *self-portrait* above, are his work.

Dedication

To Sally who not only saved my life
But without whom....

Foreword

by

Julian Parker OBE FNI

The difference between a diary and an autobiography is the way events are put into context. To make script interesting and enticing, the background needs to be explained, the opportunities articulated and the reasons why exemplified. We are people of our time and there is real skill in bringing to life, episodes which took place decades earlier. It can be fun when you know the person, to ruminate on the bits which do not appear. What is fascinating about Peter Russell's life story, told with charm, and a certain self-deprecation, is that it comes across with a noble air. The unfolding drama has a depth to it which is uplifting.

Peter was bought up in Folkestone under the threat of aerial bombardment during the Second World War, survived this and coped with evacuation and different schools to start work in a tailor's shop in preparation to earn enough money to enable him to fulfil his dream of going to sea as an officer in the Merchant Navy. He became apprenticed to a company operating a heavy lift ship in the unglamorous world of ocean tramping. What a rich grounding that experience provided. He learnt seamanship where life and death depended upon rigging the derricks correctly. He learnt how to gauge people and observe behaviour when faced with hard work and difficulty. He also learnt to savour the run ashore and enjoy the good times, even more for their rarity. Almost out of the vocabulary today we can see how Peter acquired 'back bone'

So here we have an account which reveals an intelligent practitioner who could discern good from evil, luck from risk, laziness from exhaustion and who was not afraid to make the most of what life had to offer. After gaining his first certificate of competency Peter transferred to the Royal Fleet Auxiliary and became engaged in naval support, sometime monotonous, other times scary, and spiced with a level of social interaction which was to be an asset when applied to responsibilities of higher office later in his career.

Having married in the meantime and successfully passed his Master Mariners certificate of competency Peter transferred to the Trinity House London district pilotage service. We come to realise how luck can be turned to good fortune and how important it is for seafarers to keep a network of friends and acquaintances particularly when away at sea.

A pilot has the task of bringing ships safely into port and in the Thames estuary the channels are limited and navigable waters are determined by the state of the tide and the unpredictability of the weather. Large light tankers and ships with containers stacked seven high on deck can be affected more by the wind than the pulse and vortex of the currents. When these two environmental influences reach their strongest impact the pilot has to exercise a judgement where experience may be the only touchstone for a safe landing. The intensity of emotion when manoeuvres do not go as planned or the interaction with shipmasters as tensions rise and fog obscures a needle eye approach makes this section compelling. Always just behind the cloud is that burst of humour radiating like the sun lifting the mood to turn adversity into accomplishment with nothing lost except a bit of dented pride.

But what of Peter's personality? Has he concealed it behind the immediacy of the events unfolding or air-brushed the embarrassment that ship mates love to exploit for their own amusement. I have had the pleasure of working with Peter over many years and delight in the openness of his smile, his generous nature and irrepressible urge to make a contribution. This book holds no dark secrets for me because it has in its roots the belief that life is not about dominance but interaction. It does not always flow in the right direction, but then if you are open minded, people understand.

His character comes out in his willingness to lead on matters like pilotage reform and safe working practices, to activate the local community through Rotary, and to inspire the profession through his involvement in The Nautical Institute where he was elected President. We see this generous giving to help others but I cannot help wondering how all this outside activity impacted on family life and the strange emotional turmoil between settling for security and taking on a challenge. It is in a way a balance which has no fulcrum, one that can only be resolved through shared values.

Peter's wife Sally comes across as a loving companion, unprepared for the unpredictable nature of life married to a seafarer but who was equally determined to see things through, raise a family provide hope through adoption, manage the home and support Peter in his chosen career. No sign of dependency here, but we come to realise just how dangerous it was to be marooned in a hostile encampment in Singapore or to cope with emergencies when Peter was away at sea. This is a story seldom told and we need some literature to engage the land-locked populous in the domestic struggles which often have to be overcome alone. Times can be unbearably lonely and so being a seafarer's wife calls for huge spirit, a comfortable self-sufficiency and a resilience to keep positive. What an exceptional lady.

Part of the fascination when turning the pages are the illustrations, mostly Peter's atmospheric paintings. Many are ships, big brutes made of steel, solid and overbearing. However to seafarers they are not like that. They are more like objects for 'overcoming'. They are home, awkward to manoeuvre, difficult to maintain, wet or sea kindly, provided with spaces into which cargo will not quite fit, always needing attention, never comfortably on time and always somewhere to be lost. Perhaps not as capricious as sailing ships but we still retain our affectionate 'she' to describe them.

Peter does not do draughtsmanship, but in his painting he somehow conveys an instinctive feel for the nature of the way we seamen come to view our place of work. These artefacts are imbued with the soul of the artist and that makes them original.

I would like a wide audience to share the experience of *Unplanned Passage* There are so many lessons to pass on. It is too personal to be a novel. The characters in a novel are imagined and do not have to be believed. Here however we have a real person, a family man, a mariner who reached the top of his profession, a charitable Rotarian who believed in enriching the local community and a creative artist. This is also the story of how rewarding a life at sea can be.

Acknowledgements

This story could not have been told and would not have appeared in print without the help and encouragement of many people to whom I am deeply indebted. Firstly the book could not have been written without the rich blend of characters of the Merchant Navy and Royal Fleet Auxiliary with whom I had the privilege to serve with deep sea over the first seventeen years of my career. Then the Masters and crews of the thousands of ships I subsequently served over thirty two years as a Port of London Pilot and of course my irrepressible and stalwart colleagues.

I am deeply indebted to Julian Parker OBE, FNI the long-time Secretary and First Publisher of the Nautical Institute for his continual encouragement, advice and his kindness in writing the Foreword together with his friendship and inspiration over many years.

For giving me the opportunity to achieve my potential, I must thank the Elder Brethren of Trinity House and particularly so Captain Peter Mason for his continual support for all pilots and of course all my colleagues over many years. I was particularly lucky to serve in the Port of London Authority with Rear Admiral Bruce Richardson CB, RN, as Chief Harbourmaster and remember with gratitude Richard Carr and Mike Belsey as Manager and Deputy Manager of Pilots, together with all the Pilotage Co-ordinators and boats crews operated by Trinity House, the PLA and ESL at Ramsgate and Harwich Harbour Haven at the Sunk for their support, good humour and respect over many years. I am also indebted to Tom Drennan and the many Tug Masters of Howard Smith Towage who gave me valuable service over the years and often kept me out of trouble; when the weather and tide or mechanical failure contrived to make things difficult. Many thanks are due to the Thames Watermen, working from open boats in all kinds of weather running lines to exposed dolphins, at all hours of the day and night. I remember particularly the continued support of Allan and John Barker and Stan Clifford and their teams, who worked with me at Shellhaven and Coryton refineries for some sixteen years.

I am also particularly indebted to my colleague Jim Francis for sending me to view his reports of his near fatal accident and giving me the opportunity to quote from them and for his stalwart and successful efforts to enhance pilot safety; resulting from those personal experiences.

So much for the story which once told, needs publishing and here I came to entirely new waters with some trepidation. I need not have worried for I have found in the publishing and printing world amazingly friendly and helpful people willing to guide me on a course beneficial to the project, without always seeking personal advantage. At this stage I would like to thank once again Julian Parker for his initial advice and then Bridget Hogen, the current Nautical Institute Publisher for giving me further useful contacts and much valued advice. I would like to thank Patricia Eve of Seafarer Books for her kind words of encouragement and her careful consideration of the original manuscript. Among the printers Ian Fiander, Roy Skinner and Tony Chapman have been particularly helpful and I am really indebted to them all for their time, patience and advice. In the publishing partnership world I am indebted to Lynn Ashman, Grace Rafael, Claire Spinks and the staff of Indepenpress Publishing for their patience and real cooperation in introducing this old sailor to the intricate world of publishing. Huge thanks to my grandson, Adrian Trimble, for his cover design and to Jacqueline Abromeit also, who finalised the layout measurements.

Contents

List of Illustrations

slope of his drive, which was covered with ice and a dusting of snow before coming out to help.

Following the angiogram I was sent back to my room to be prepared while arrangements were made to include me on the afternoon list for the Consultant Surgeon. The young nurse from Hong Kong, surprised to get me back requiring further treatment that day, was instructed to get me ready for major surgery. Explaining quietly to me that she was not really used to this particular procedure, she produced a large cut-throat razor and grabbed hold of what I had always considered to be a valuable part of my anatomy. My mind rapidly focused on her shaking hands as she roughly scraped away the pubic hair and for a while I concentrated on the immediate threat to my manhood.

An elderly grey-haired gentleman who, I took to be another patient, wandered into the room dressed in what appeared to be green pyjamas and a dressing gown. He peered at me closely and was, I thought, about to wish me well when he introduced himself as the Consultant Cardiothoracic Surgeon.

"Doctor Bucknall tells me that we really need to operate on you this afternoon and if he says that I am sure he is correct," he said. "What do you think about that?" My eyes took in his rubber boots and I wondered just how much blood they expected to be sloshing about the operating theatre.

"Er… well, I'm not too excited about the prospect but I suppose if it has to be done it would be better to get it over and not have to think about it," I replied shakily, studying the reassuring and experienced face of the consultant with new interest.

My wife Sally, poor girl returning from shopping and expecting me to be the routine four hours for an angiogram, returned to bravely face the news of my imminent surgery. She was advised to return home to the south coast for it would be many hours and late at night before I would be likely to recover from the operation. She poor girl was horrified at events and was further faced with a problem getting home, for as it was raining I had dropped her off at the entrance to Ashford Railway station while I went off to park among the several hundred cars in the giant car park. She now had to find my car and drive it for the first time, something she managed very capably despite her fears.

Things happened from then on very quickly. I arrived at the entrance to the operating theatre noting two other trolleys patiently waiting with recumbent gentlemen gently sleeping.

The Theatre Sister looked at me in horror and demanded to know where I had come from?

"Postling," I replied brightly, curious at her interest.

"No," she said, "I do not have you on my list for today."

Somebody stuck a needle into me and I was gone before I could ask if perhaps tomorrow would be more suitable.

Well of course I was very fortunate that Sally had insisted my Doctor give me a Stress Test instead of just an ECG and that subsequently I received the very best treatment. I quickly recovered, although I have to say it was not exactly an experience I would ever like to repeat. In three days I was up and walking and in six days was sent home. I felt many years younger, took up walking and returned to work piloting ships on April Fool's Day three months later. I suppose I could have taken early retirement but I loved the job and I think in retrospect if I had not driven myself to get fit enough to work again I would not have achieved much that I was later proud to have done.

When I came out of hospital I was advised to walk every day increasing the distance by at least 100 yards which I far exceeded, being up to eight miles a day, by the time I attended the cardiologist six weeks later.

Having lost a couple of stone and been passed fully fit by my own surgeon and the company's medical experts, I returned to full-time piloting including that of the very largest tankers using the Thames Estuary. I felt at least ten years younger.

Shortly after returning to work I entered a 6000 metre charity race, something I had never attempted before. I had intended to walk but looking around the other competitors in their Lycra shorts and running vests with famous athletic club's logo on them; I began to feel somewhat inadequate. I must confess I was not totally unprepared; I had done the course a couple of times earlier in the week but had been surprised by the speed with which my calf muscles tightened up. This time I sought advice prior to the start from a friend who had run in both the New York and London Marathons. He demonstrated the exercises and movements he used to warm up while awaiting the start. I moved to the back of the throng and tried to look as though I knew what I was doing. It was a mistake. When I turned around it was to find that the starter – who must have had a very quiet voice – had let the rest of them go! As they disappeared around the corner at the end of the street, I set off in pursuit but I have to tell you... it was a somewhat lonely race!

It did have its compensations however... I did win the sympathy vote... "look at that poor old man"..."come on Granddad" and a respectful "keep going sir" from the police constables at the street corners.

By running in front of the crowds in the High Street and walking when out of sight in the back streets; my appearance was somewhat better than my performance! I am pleased to say that I did complete the course, my arrival being greeted with considerable relief by my wife but also by the officials – the St Johns Ambulance staff and the policemen – who were waiting to go home to lunch!

Well, all that was 13 years ago, since when Sally and I have both retired and travelled the world. Following the scare in 1996 I thought I would try and record the more interesting experiences of my somewhat unplanned passage through life while I still had the time and the memory. Thirty-two years of my life was spent piloting ships in and out of the Thames Estuary, a career I initially never set out to follow but one which by chance came my way, it was a most rewarding experience allowing considerable personal satisfaction; truly a 'lovely job'.

You will find here no great deeds of 'daring do' but mainly humorous anecdotes and reflections of fifty years of a life spent at sea.

First trip Apprentice

Chapter 2

Earliest Memories

I was born on the 31st October 1934 in a small nursing home in Chart Road, Folkestone. My mother, who was eight years older than my father subsequently, told me repeatedly that she had gone through a very difficult time giving birth, an experience which she never wished to duplicate. Apparently it had something to do with the size of my head; but whatever, I was to grow up the only child of loving parents. I have often considered in retrospect just how unappreciative but lucky I really was, not to be an only child because of course that does have disadvantages but to be born an Englishman of caring and loving parents who remained constant throughout their lives.

My earliest recollections were of the kitchen and the back garden at a house called "Little Warden", at Capel-le-Ferne, a village perched on the extreme seaward end of the North Downs overlooking the Dover Straits, the English Channel and the lovely old Edwardian town of Folkestone. The house was newly built and had been purchased by my parents and named after my maternal grandfather's public house, the "Lord Warden", a popular establishment adjoining the Royal Marine barracks at Deal and the home in which my mother had spent all her early life. My father, who never in his life drunk more than the odd sociable glass, presumably went along with the name to please my mother who he worshipped through the fluctuations of life for the following fifty-two years.

The kitchen, I recall, smelled of new paint and cabbage, while the garden consisted of heavy bright-red earth, in the midst of which I remember the figure of my father struggling to remove the last of the builder's rubble and turn the plot into some form of garden. Of course I had no idea what he was doing at the time but the sunshine was warm and from across the green fields there were the white butterflies to attract my attention, as they waited in anticipation of his labours. I must have spent some time sitting in a pram in that spot outside the kitchen for the memories are still vivid a lifetime away.

My parents were heavily involved in a concert party raising funds to build the village hall at Capel-le-Ferne but mother really did not settle in the village, hating having to push the large pram up the hill from Folkestone after visiting my grandparents or shopping. With my arrival and the loss of my mother's income and my grandfather's loss of tenancy of the "Lord Warden" at Deal, my parents soon ran into financial difficulty. Unable to sell it, "Little Warden" was rented out and soon we were to move down the hill to Folkestone where my parents rented a house in Morrison Road.

The war was on the horizon when we moved into the small terraced house, 27 Morrison Road, which abutted The Tram Road. The Tram Road was an exciting street for small boys because alongside it ran the branch railway line to Folkestone Harbour, a busy route up a gradient which required the boat and freight trains to be pushed and pulled by four small frantic little engines gushing smoke and steam as they struggled up the hill from the harbour to join the main line from Dover to London.

Two things I remember at Morrison Road; the first being nearly poisoned when my mother gave me the wrong medicine from one of several identical green bottles which were used in those days. The doctor, a Scotsman with a surgery next to the railway arches at the end of the road, was quickly on the scene and dosed me with salt to induce nausea. It worked but I still remember being the star of that particular family drama.

The other were the evacuees, but more of them later.

Further memories of those early days are of receiving my gas mask at a hall in Wear Bay Road and walking to St Mary's Primary School down Grove Road, a street parallel to Dover Road, with the large square cardboard box and heavy gas mask strung around my neck; for by then World War 2 had begun. I also remember being told to alternate on which shoulder to wear the gas mask, for if I did not then surely I would grow lopsided.

The hall in Wear Bay Road Folkestone I recognised instantly when, together with an over friendly puppy, I was to visit many years later in the 1970s to take our unmanageable bloodhound "Placid" for dog-training classes, a procedure she found far too boring and distasteful. Quite obviously Placid considered such classes a necessity only for inferior bred dogs and not for such grand hounds as she, registered with the Kennel Club.

Chapter 3

World War 2 – The Evacuees

During the weeks of what was called the phoney war of late 1939, not a great deal seemed to happen but there was much preparation throughout the country. Air-raid shelters were built and many sensible defensive precautions such as tank traps were gouged out along the North Downs above Folkestone; white scars that can still be seen today. However in retrospect some very odd decisions were made at the time, not least the evacuation of children from the London Boroughs to Folkestone and other south coast towns, soon to be in the frontline of a very real war. South East England as a result of bombing and long range shelling was soon to become known as "Hell Fire Corner".

I was just five years old and I imagine something of a soft spoilt only child living with my parents at 27 Morrison Road, Folkestone, not far from the railway line which linked the potential target of Folkestone Harbour with the main line to London and the north, when we had billeted with us two large tough boys (or so they seemed to me) from Bromley as evacuees. They seemed large to me anyway, although I remember they did wear short trousers.

Today I cannot remember what they looked like or how long they stayed with us, although it cannot have been for long but I do vividly remember one of them stepping from the staircase onto a very precious model lead coach and horses of mine, which I was playing with in the hallway. It folded flat under his relatively large foot. Whether he did it deliberately or whether it was an accident I never did know, but I was distraught and made the suitable commotion which might be expected from a spoilt five-year-old; while he protested his innocence.

Now if he got into trouble or not I cannot tell you but I certainly hope not, for following Mother's death at the great age of 92 years, I came across a very sad little letter written to my father at the time by the boys' own father, a Mr T J Halton, on the 6th September 1939. In it he expresses "heartfelt gratitude" for the fact that my parents have taken in George and John but fearful that such kindness and generosity might be abused; he asks my father to correct the boys if at any time they were to misbehave.

I'm sure my father would have done no more than speak quietly but sternly to them, for he never raised his voice or a hand and hopefully he was in the house when the coach and horses met their demise. I cannot remember, but feel sorry for the culprit if retribution was in the hands of Mother!

They were sad lost years for both parents and children, years that could never be replaced. A few of the evacuees were happy and many from the slums and poorer industrial areas of London found themselves living in the countryside with clean air and better food than they had at home, but the vast majority were unhappy. They heard the radio reports of bombs dropping on London and of course many, while safe in the countryside, lost their parents and grandparents to the destruction of war. I wonder what happened to the Haltons, they must have returned to Bromley when the bombs started to fall on Folkestone in a matter of weeks.

Going through my late mother's possessions I came across a letter from the late Queen Mother thanking my mother for taking in evacuees. I imagine it was a standard letter sent to all who opened their homes but it certainly looks original and gives the impression that it is signed in ink by the Queen herself. I can imagine at that busy and worrying time such thoughtfulness was gratefully appreciated and was one of the many reasons the late Queen Mother was so popular with elderly people who lived to remember those difficult days.

Battle of Britain

One beautiful summer Saturday afternoon in 1940 my father and I had just left Sandgate Road, the main shopping thoroughfare in Folkestone, to walk down via the harbour area and up to our new home on the east cliff at 21 Foreland Avenue, a relatively newly built semi-detached house, my mother going on ahead on the bus to prepare tea. I don't recall where we had been, but probably it would have included a quick visit to see my maternal grandfather, by now an ex-publican who ran the bar in the restaurant at Bobby's, the large department store which dominated the high street.

We were just approaching the steps down to the Parish Churchyard when my father shouted, "Run quickly."

He had heard the unmistakable roar of a Messerschmitt FE109 diving out of the sun to make its presence felt among the shoppers that pleasant Saturday afternoon. 'Burning up', the town was probably no more than sport for the young man who had obviously come in from France at sea level before climbing to dive again on the town, hoping possibly to draw the RAF from Hawkinge out into a trap waiting somewhere up sun over the channel. The RAF undoubtedly won the Battle of Britain because Air Marshal Dowding insisted the battle be fought over England where our pilots had the advantage of time in battle and survival if shot down. There was to be no pursuit out over the English Channel and France, much to the frustration of the Luftwaffe who continually tried to draw our fighters into traps. Obviously there had been no warning; the air raid siren had not gone off for the streets were full of people.

Immediately down the steps on the left in the Parish Churchyard, there remains to this day a large rectangular tombstone in memory of a lady who had died in Colombo three days before Christmas 1819. It was down behind this that my father threw me as the aircraft came down in a screaming dive. I remember hearing the machine guns and the shouting of people but, despite my endeavours to see exactly what was going on, I could not move the bulk of my father who had me firmly pinned down in safety. It was soon past however and people talked excitedly in the sunshine of their narrow escapes.

Shortly we heard rumours that a bus had been caught on the Dover Road. We set off for home rapidly, my father concerned that it might have been the bus with my mother on going home, although of course he did not let on to me his fears. I never learnt whether in fact a bus had been hit for happily my mother was at home completely unaware of the excitement my father and I had experienced together, she was more interested that we wash our hands and sit down for tea.

The large rectangular tombstone is immediately on the left as you go down the steps from West Cliff Gardens to the Folkestone Parish Church Yard.

The inscription on the tombstone reads:

To the memory of Ann,
Daughter of William & Ann Cullen,
The beloved wife of James Stuart
After 25 years residence in Ceylon she died at Colombo
on the 22 December 1819

The Spy

My mother was working as the fur buyer in Bobby's the leading department store in Folkestone when war broke out. It was a job she was not to keep for long as demand and stock fell and eventually we were evacuated for a year or more to Cumbria. Mother had a vivid imagination and I remember an incident when she was convinced she had overheard a German spy in the store enquiring of a Battle of Britain fighter pilot where he was based.

It was of course a time when there were large signs up on the buses and in public places warning that "walls have ears". A time when street signs were removed together with road signs, indicating the directions to towns and villages, and I believe even the signs were taken off railway stations. It must have been horrendous travelling and total confusion for the general population, never mind the spies.

Well, Mother of course reported her suspicions and was taken seriously by the police, for I vividly recall as a small boy travelling in a large black Wolsley car underneath the skew railway arches on the Dover Road and along Canterbury Road, as we toured the poorer area of town in company with Mother and two large sinister looking men from Special Branch wearing trench coats and trilby hats. We searched in vain on a couple of days for the "spy" but to no avail although Mother was sure she had recognised him in that area.

My Father thought it all a waste of time and even I as a small boy was not convinced, although the thought that we were actually on a real spy hunt was incredibly exciting. In retrospect I feel sure that Mother, to whom all foreigners were the same, had perhaps mistaken one of the Polish aircrew who were based at Hawkinge aerodrome and seen frequently around the town for a German. Was he just a fellow flier with a professional interest in just where his RAF colleague was based perhaps, rather than a real spy... I wonder?

Chapter 4

1939 Hospital Carrier Maid of Kent

The Family at War

When war broke out my paternal grandfather was serving as a 'quartermaster,' that is a helmsman rather than somebody in charge of stores, on the cross-channel ferries based at Folkestone and Dover. During the First World War he held a similar position on a ferry *HMS Empress* which had been converted to a seaplane carrier and took part in the battle of Jutland, a ship which must have had some success for his records show that he was paid some Prize Money. Once again he quickly found himself in the front line with the evacuation of France where he served in the hospital ship *Maid of Kent*, clearly marked and painted white with large red crosses on the sides and upper decks. Grandmother must have felt a sense of false security that this time he was serving on a ship which would not be attacked, but sadly that was not to be the case.

There is a picture of the bombed and completely destroyed *Maid of Kent* alongside a quay with a burnt-out hospital train in what the *Illustrated London News* wrongly described as Dunkirk, although both my cousin and I distinctly recall our grandfather telling us they were bombed in Dieppe.

Word had arrived home with the news of the loss and for a while my grandfather was missing as were many of the crew but the country would live through the losses at Dunkirk before there was news of my grandfather.

Hospital Ship Maid of Kent after bombing at Dieppe

I have since discovered that the *Maid of Kent* was taken out of service in Boulogne on the 2nd September 1939 and sent direct to Southampton, having been requisitioned for service as a hospital carrier. Arriving two hours after the outbreak of war she was quickly fitted out and painted white with the broad red crosses of a hospital ship, sailing just a week later to pick up a schedule running between Newhaven and Dieppe. All went well for eight months, the ship returning with around 250 sick and wounded troops on each run to Dieppe. However by the 14th May 1940 Dieppe was under air attack and had become a very dangerous place. On the 18th May just after 2200 hours, the ship had been berthed less than an hour when nine bombs fell around her. Another air raid damaged the port the following night, and both the Masters of the *Maid of Kent* and the hospital carrier *Brighton* felt particularly vulnerable moored in the inner basin to load the wounded and requested permission from the authorities to move to a tidal berth for a quick getaway. Although permission was given on the 21st May, by that time the lock gates had become jammed and late that afternoon at 1710 hours in broad daylight, the *Maid* was hit by four bombs aft and set ablaze. The ship was immediately abandoned and sank. Fortunately all but nine of the officers and crew escaped and began another adventure to get home.

Happily I remember standing outside 29 Dudley Road in Folkestone, my grandparent's home with my grandmother, when grandfather appeared unexpectedly walking around the corner from the Tram Road with a kit bag on his shoulder. My grandmother was naturally overcome with joy but shocked to see that his hair had turned completely white.

I had not been told that he was missing and never really learnt of the horrors he had experienced because my grandfather like many people who have been really exposed to terrible experiences in war, tended to keep those experiences to himself, not wishing to relive them. A quiet gentle man with a twinkle in his eye he had been through hell but survived. He had escaped from France in a fishing boat together with others and landed further down the coast I know not where. He survived the war serving in the old two-funnelled ferry *Biarritz* but luckily, although he experienced many adventures and was at the Normandy landings on D Day the 6th June 1944, nothing was quite as horrific as the loss of the hospital ship *Maid of Kent*, loading allied wounded soldiers, to German Stuka dive bombers during the fall of France in 1940.

The Unexploded Bomb

Our family did not seem to live in Morrison Road for long before moving into a brand new house, 21 Foreland Avenue, which was no more than a couple of streets away but in a road of new semi-detached houses of the 1930's style. With people moving away from the town to escape the bombing and shelling, many houses had become vacant. It cannot have been easy to sell a house but with luck the owner could let it out for rent; my parents, unable to sell their house at Capel-le-Ferne, now had tenants while they in turn became tenants. At the back of the house I remember was a builder's yard full of stacks of white bricks, ideal for building castles but sharp and heavy for a five-year-old and inclined to pinch your fingers. The weather was warm and beautiful, the air pungent with the smell of the flowering shrubs and weeds full of butterflies.

In the dining room which opened through French windows onto the back garden we had what was called a Morrison Air-raid Shelter. It was basically a large steel table supported by very strong girders at each corner acting as the four legs, under which fitted the mattress from the double bed. The sides were fitted with strong wire mesh to keep out flying debris while, the strength of the table was designed to withstand the weight of the whole house collapsing onto it.

My father was based at that time in a fire station at the lower end of Dover Road, working nights. Folkestone was being regularly bombed, the first bomb falling just down the road from our house in a cul-de-sac just off Warren Way.

To this day I can vividly remember waking up in the middle of the night in the Morrison shelter to the sound of anti-aircraft guns and the unmistakable droning sound of German bombers overhead. My mother and I lay awake expecting the worst and then we heard it – the whistling noise of a bomb falling, a bomb which seemed to be coming directly at us. The sound grew closer and closer and then, when our final moments seemed to be upon us, there was a terrific thump which shook the French windows and the whole house... and then an eerie silence.

Eventually, like an electrical storm does, the raid passed over and the all-clear siren sounded allowing us to relax and fall asleep; completely unaware of the live monster buried deep in the rhubarb patch at the bottom of the garden.

Later that day my father found the crater at the back of the house still complete with unexploded bomb. Naturally the people in the street and area were evacuated while the bomb disposal team risked their lives to successfully defuse the bomb. I seem to remember I was sent to my grandmothers in Dudley Road and never did see it or even the hole which had been filled in by the time I was allowed back in the garden; however I can still hear the sound of that falling bomb as clear as if it were yesterday.

Alston and Evacuation

With the bombing in Folkestone intensifying, my father decided my mother and I would be safer moving away from the coast. Our first move for a few weeks was to the police headquarters in Maidstone where we were billeted with an uncle, who was a police sergeant, and his family but the house was not large enough and in any case the Battle of Britain was reaching its most severe period right overhead. It was decided that together with some friends we would be evacuated to Alston in Cumberland to share a large house owned by relatives of the Rye family, who ran an ironmonger's shop in Folkestone.

I remember my father came up on the train to Maidstone Station to see my mother and me off, not knowing when or even if he would see us again. The trains were full of people in uniform and particularly so the train from King's Cross to Newcastle, but I remember little of the journey – until we came to a shuddering halt on the railway bridge outside Newcastle-upon-Tyne railway station. It was dark, the air raid sirens whined and the anti-aircraft guns opened fire. We could hear the droning of enemy bombers and the sounds of exploding bombs and the occasional rattle of falling shrapnel. Even as a very young boy I sensed the tension in the air as we huddled there helpless on a stationary train above the River Tyne in the middle of an air raid. I was curled up underneath the bar counter in the Pullman car; it never occurred to me to wonder why we were there rather than in an ordinary carriage until much later in life. When I questioned my mother she conveniently could not even recall the event. Eventually the "all clear" sounded and the train steamed slowly through the fine drizzling rain into the station. My mother and I were directed to a hotel fairly close nearby, the dark unlit streets were wet and the still air smelt of smoke and cordite.

The following day we crossed the Pennines in the sunshine through beautiful countryside in a small train with slam doors and windows which were pulled closed by long leather straps and had the glass criss-crossed with brown sticky paper. The engine puffing smoke and steam, wheels spinning, rushed energetically at the gradients as we crossed to Cumberland and our destination... a large country house which was to be home for the next year. It was a very old house just outside Alston, a house which we boys all thought haunted, a house with a secret passage down to a dungeon hidden behind the wall in the billiard room and a moat around the front door, large Elizabethan chimneys which looked like towers and a drive surrounded by thick undergrowth and rhododendrons.

My memories are of being taken by a large boy on arrival to see the upper tributary of the River Tyne which was the river running through the grounds. I remember the icy cold water coming over the top of my Wellington boots and then falling from the slippery wet stepping stones and floating some distance on my back in the shallow water before being dragged cold, miserable and frightened from the river by my very embarrassed custodian. I was pulled squelching and tearful back to the large house where my mother ensured a great deal of fuss ensued, resulting in my being thrust protesting into a large steaming bath which was already occupied by a mass of pink flesh who, through the steam turned out to be a family friend known to me as "Auntie Madge".

I quickly recovered and the next day was enrolled in the local school which I attended for a year, travelling into Alston in the mornings on the farmer's milk float together with Barry Rye and churns of milk. We had a bitterly cold winter with snow drifts ten feet high according to the old newspaper cuttings my mother kept. I remember those cold walks home from school as it got dark, the clogs we wore and the dark clouds racing across the sky and driving rain, the sore chapped bare knees and the roaring wood fires when we reached home. We were a long way from the war although occasionally night raids could be seen off on the distant horizon towards Newcastle beyond the Pennines and towards Barrow-in-Furness. Unfortunately my mother became ill at the end of the first year with jaundice and we returned to Kent where I was to become a boarder at "Goudhurst School for Boys" now known as "Bethany" today. I cannot recall the journey back south; it obviously was uneventful.

Chapter 5

Elements of War – Long Range Shelling

Dover was subjected to more long range shelling from France than was Folkestone, but still both my paternal and maternal grand-parents were to survive two near misses when the houses in Dudley Road and Radnor Park Crescent directly opposite their homes were completely destroyed without warning. They were the only houses to be damaged in those streets throughout the war. Unlike air raids when the approaching enemy aircraft or doodlebugs could be identified and the Air-Raid sirens sounded, the first shells arrived unannounced.

The shelling does not appear to have been very accurate in the main, missing most military and industrial targets, although I do remember seeing an enormous shell hole right through the base of a large chimney at Henry Tolputt's timber yard close to the harbour. Despite the hole, the brick-built chimney stood for some time before being demolished.

Whether the Germans used very large guns on railway lines or whether they fired from fixed reinforced concrete bunkers, I do not know. We certainly had a number of very large guns which were used to fire at the enemy ships or coastal fortifications and these were kept in railway sidings off the main Dover to London Railway, one of which I remember seeing was in a wood on the south side of the track near Pluckley. One can still make out the level ground and path of the old track in the woods to this day.

Bananas

Sometime in 1942 or 1943 there was great excitement at Bethany School, Goudhurst, for one day a small aircraft did a couple of circuits low over the school, waggled its wings and approaching into the wind dropped almost silently onto the playing field. A man in a crumpled khaki military uniform got out, carrying a canvas bag, and walked through the gathering throng of excited small boys into the school buildings to see the Headmaster, the Rev. E. E. Hayward. Meanwhile we boys tried to get close to the aircraft which I seem to recall was an Auster, somewhat battered, travel-worn and stained. It sat patiently on the grass, its engine cooling, amid the fumes of aviation spirit and hot oil wafting about the idle propeller. There was the curious ticking sound of contracting metal coming from the obviously overworked little aeroplane, and I wondered just where it had come from.

The mysterious stranger turned out to be the father of one of the older boys who dropped in to see how his son was getting on at school and bring some presents from somewhere foreign. It was a time of hard rationing; sweets and chocolate were rare although being in the garden of England we had lots of fruit and unofficially the local farmer's apples to eat. Fruit from abroad was just not seen, but this military gentleman had brought his son at least one banana among other things. We younger boys did not get to see the "other things" but after the banana had been eaten I can vividly remember being allowed to smell the skin and recalling the smell of bananas from before the war. It was however a long time before I recalled that a banana should have been yellow and not black.

American Survivors

Bethany School was not on the main routes between the major bomber airfields in East Anglia and Germany and we seldom saw RAF bombers either outward or on their return mainly because they bombed at night and had returned by dawn long before we got up at school. The American Flying Fortresses and Liberator bombers however carried out daylight raids and these were a common sight over Kent, returning from Germany, often flying very low as they struggled to remain in the air and perhaps desperately sought an airfield large enough to put down their damaged aircraft.

Sometimes they would have an engine on fire but more often the fire would have been extinguished but one or two of the engines would be stopped and useless and feathered. Limping home they would often be so low we could see the crew members waving to the boys cheering them homeward bound from the playing fields below. We could see large holes in the wings, tail fins and main body and wondered how they could remain in the air and whether once they passed out of sight they ever made their home bases. I remember seeing a column of black smoke arising somewhere in the direction of Tonbridge not long after a Flying Fortress had limped over and wondering if the crew had managed to get out before the aircraft had crashed. We never knew of course, and while it was exciting to watch those brave men flying past one was often filled with a terrible sadness after the excitement. The aircraft we saw were of course the survivors, single aircraft showing their scars of battle, we rarely from our position saw them flying out in formation to bomb the enemy.

However I do remember the Dakotas and Lancaster going over towing large Horsa gliders for Operation Market Garden, the enormous airborne attack on the Rhine bridges and Arnhem. We had never seen so many aircraft outward bound in broad daylight, the sky was full from horizon to horizon with aircraft moving slowly and carefully in long lines. We had never seen gliders being towed and had no idea how many men and even small vehicles were being carried. Little were we to know of the successes and failure of what was to become a horrendous battle later to be depicted in the film *A Bridge Too Far*. At the time one could not help but feel certain the Germans would be terrified of this demonstration of power.

Doodlebugs

At Bethany in the middle of Kent, I was very much aware of Hitler's first secret weapon – the V1 flying bomb or doodlebug – from the very first day it was fired at London, for its path from the Calais area to London took it right over the school.

I vividly remember that first night the 12th June 1944, just six days after D Day and the allied landings in Normandy, a night before a defensive strategy had been developed. However it was just a short time before three lines of defence were established. Anti-aircraft guns along the south coast were the first line of defence after which fast fighter aircraft such as Typhoons, Mustangs and Mosquitoes chased those escaping the AA guns, shooting them down with cannon fire into the Kentish countryside before they reached the string of barrage balloons ringing the south of London and visible from the school. That first night was a new experience of the sound and sight of war to cause fear and excitement to rows of schoolboys standing in lines in their dressing gowns and pyjamas.

The school didn't have air raid shelters and in fact I can remember that we rarely had an air raid in the middle of the countryside; but on this particular night, not long after we had all gone to bed in the dormitories, we were all turned out and formed up in the lower asphalt playground slightly below the ground level of the main school buildings. We stood there in long lines wondering what it was all about until we heard the first of the flying bombs approaching overhead. It was a unique noise like no other but one which we were to become familiar with during the next few months. We soon learnt that if you could hear the engine then you were not in danger, but as soon as the engine cut out the bomb came down with devastating effect. The lines of boys looked up in wonder to see a sheet of flame from the exhaust moving low and rapidly across the sky to be followed by several more droning past before we were allowed to return to bed unable to sleep because of the excitement.

Over the coming months we were to experience far more excitement as we witnessed the chase and destruction of many doodlebugs by fast-moving fighter aircraft most of which were shot down mainly harmlessly into the fields, while the boys in their excitement recovered hot cannon shells and cartridge cases from the playing fields following a sortie.

The closest I came was one afternoon when coming out from the side entrance in the main school building onto the tarmac playground; I hurried to see the doodlebug I could hear approaching. In the door entrance I heard the engine cut out above my head to the left and almost immediately the duck egg blue underside of a V1 appeared from above the large oak tree in the centre of the playground. It lazily rolled onto its side and dived into the playing field a hundred yards away behind a block of wooden classrooms. It was very close and exploded with a tremendous bang. I was immediately thrown backwards through the door into the passage on my backside by the blast, ending up at the feet of a member of staff who quickly grabbed me by the collar to prevent my curiosity causing me further danger.

There is the last time I visited the school still a copse in the playing field which today is thought by some to have developed on the sight of the doodlebug. Actually the copse was there long before, and on that hot summer day the small wood had been surrounded by a flock of sheep. Sheltering sleepily from the blazing hot sun in the cool leafy and peaceful shade under the oak and ash trees their world came to an end. The sudden violent explosion turned that idyllic scene into chaos filling the air for what seemed like hours afterwards with smoke, wool and falling leaves and the very unpleasant smell of slaughtered sheep.

On another occasion somewhere over the school a twin-engine Mosquito chasing a V1 either came to grief when too close to the doodlebug as it exploded in the air. Once again the air smelt of death as the pieces descended around the school, and that was when we learnt that Mosquitoes were actually made of plywood and their very brave fighter pilots were extremely vulnerable.

That summer school holiday I went home to Folkestone, to find landing craft in the harbour and a great deal of anti-aircraft activity from guns all along the cliffs attempting to shoot down the approaching V1s. According to the local Folkestone *Herald* Newspaper who later produced a map of fallen doodlebugs, 593 were shot down in the sea off Folkestone and Hythe. My parents decided the town was too dangerous for me and took me on a week's holiday to Herne Bay which turned out to be a real stroke of luck; for while we were away a new and very inexperienced American anti-aircraft gun unit set up business at the end of the road. Their inexperience meant that in their first attempts they failed to bring the V1s down in the sea but hit them when almost overhead. One fell opposite our home, completely destroying the houses on the south side of the road and causing considerable blast damage to ours. I didn't get home again that holiday but after an extra week in Herne Bay was moved to a farm of a school friend near Canterbury before returning to Bethany. I have subsequently come across an invoice which tells me that my parents were compensated by the government with the vast sum of £147 and a few shillings. Doodlebugs were horrible but at least you could hear them coming, unlike the V2 ballistic missiles which fell on London causing severe damage, until their launch sites were overrun by the allied armies.

1945 The Aftermath of Returning POWs

In 1945 I was eleven years old and was to leave my boarding school and return to Folkestone to attend the Harvey Grammar School having successfully passed the entrance examination. The war was nearly over but still the casualties occurred. I vividly remember that while doing an interim summer term at Harcourt School while I waited for the Grammar School Year to commence, being told that we had lost a pupil or a couple of pupils on the hills above the school and just above the newly carved white horse of today. The children had found some unexploded ordinance which had gone off when they moved it. As we stood in the playground in animated groups we could see the position of the accident marked by a small white tent and sombre black police cars attending the investigation. We were all warned of the dangers, but I remember a small group of us boys still could not resist floating across a very deep pond at the base of Caesar's Camp on aluminium wing fuel tanks discarded by long- range Mustangs and other aircraft. The water was very deep and dangerous but most of us were good swimmers and had no fear.

I was, however, to become a casualty of my swimming; for it was a time when our surviving POWs started to return from their long forced marches across eastern Europe through Germany to reach the British and American lines, together with those from the Japanese POW camps in the Far East. They had suffered terribly and many died on the marches from starvation and illness.

Strange very gaunt sick-looking men, many like living skeletons with all their ribs and bones clearly visible, began to appear on the beaches that summer in Folkestone and particularly so the beach at Sandgate Riviera, which was fairly isolated from the general public. It was the nearest beach from Morehall in Cheriton that my friends and I used to frequent at the weekends and after school, going down the steep paths and steps from Coolinge Lane on our bicycles. These poor men I guess must have been soldier ex-POWs recuperating at St Helena, the military hospital at Shorncliffe barracks nearby. I was also a keen member of the Folkestone Swimming Club which used a large open-air swimming pool on the sea front.

One lovely summer's day, at our home in Harcourt Road, I was to be hit by the most excruciating stomach pains which quite quickly turned to uncontrollable bowel movements. The doctor was called and fortunately suspected that I had caught dysentery. Tests were taken and proved positive but the illness I remember lasted for some six weeks. I had become a war victim, for it was concluded that the disease had been passed from the ex-POWs through the water of the swimming pool which I believe was closed for some time. In isolation I never did learn whether I was the only casualty but probably not.

Dysentery is a most unpleasant condition but fortunately I had avoided amoebic dysentery which would have prevented my sea-going career. However it is an experience and condition which one never forgets and one which was to affect me some nine years later when serving as third officer on a ship on the Japanese coast, a country where human excreta used to be employed as fertilizer on the crops. The ship was of all places in dry-dock when the bug struck me once again, which meant that while we were living on board we had to use a bath house and toilet on the dock side requiring a key. I soon acquired a personal key and spent some time running backwards and forwards between ship and bath house while I awaited my watch relief and the Master to return from a run ashore.

The Master on his return was somewhat scathing about my self-diagnosis and suggested it was no more than Montezuma's revenge, but I have to say once you have suffered from dysentery there is no mistaking the symptoms. Ignoring the Master I called a taxi and set off for the Bluff Hospital in Yokohama where the illness was rapidly confirmed and I was isolated. In all fairness to the Master he was most apologetic when he came to visit me the next day. This time with the aid of the new antibiotics which had been discovered I quickly recovered and have managed to avoid a further outbreak in the last 50 years.

As a young Sea Cadet

Chapter 6

Going to Sea

From my earliest recollections I had always wanted to go to sea, I avidly read sea stories mainly by Percy F Westerman about Deck Officer Cadets, Apprentices or Midshipmen of the "half-deck," depending on which commercial company the characters in the book served. Sadly, much like today, none of the schools I attended appeared to be interested in my dreams or offered any encouragement; how wrong they were.

I joined the Folkestone Unit of the Sea Cadet Corps at the earliest opportunity, immediately after the war, with its Headquarters based in the property immediately to the west of Sandgate Castle. In 1947, aged 13 years old, I went off with another lad to join my first ship for the summer holiday aboard *HMS Modeste* a frigate moored up alongside the cruiser *HMS Royalist* in the middle of Portsmouth Harbour. Apart from actually living on a ship, the most exciting part of the holiday was when the coxswain of our 32-foot sailing cutter was given a reprimand for hitting the old WW2 aircraft carrier *HMS Illustrious* just below the quarter deck while teaching us the rudiments of sailing and rowing. Sleeping in a hammock was a new and uncomfortable experience but one I was fortunately not to repeat when I finally got to sea, but the first sounds of continuously running machinery humming through the night and the distinct oily smells of a working ship were to become a familiar part of my life.

The following year I travelled alone aged 14 years up to Scotland on the overnight train, for some reason up the east coast to Edinburgh and then across to Glasgow where, I reported to the Royal Naval Routeing Officer for onward transport to Faslane and a Tank Landing Ship *HMS Hunter*. I remember the early morning runs up the mountainside, deck hockey on the tank decks and the icy cold water of Helensburgh Council open air Swimming Pool, built into the River Clyde. Travelling north on the train I met what was known as a Bevan Boy, these were young men recruited into the coal mines instead of the services. This particular chap, who had an electric flashing bow tie, and wore large horn-rim spectacles and entertained me with a continuous banter of funny jokes, had just been for an audition as a comedian in London. I have often wondered in retrospect whether I was entertained by a young Eric Morecambe, probably not but I like to think I was so privileged.

Folkestone SCC Remembrance Day 1949

I had great experiences as a young sea cadet, shooting Lee Enfield .303 rifles on the Army's indoor ranges at Shorncliffe camp, boxing, swimming, sailing and learning of things maritime. In the Guard we wore white gaiters and white belts which required the careful application of Blanco, while on the belt hung a huge eighteen-inch bayonet which I polished with Brasso until you could see your face in it. I thought I looked the cat's whiskers with the seven folds in my bell-bottom trousers and deliberately battered cap on parade in the town on Remembrance Day with fixed bayonets. It was in those days that I learnt to wash and press my own uniforms, using the kitchen sink to wash by hand and an iron heated on the stove and a damp cloth to press in the seven folds in my bell bottoms, representing the seven seas because my mother either could not find the time or, more likely, could not manage to turn me out in the manner I desired. The ability to look after myself was an attribute to serve me well when I eventually went to sea and had from day one to do just that. In my last year at Folkestone as a Sea Cadet some kind person gave us musical instruments and I was to find myself the base drummer for a few months, the entire extent of my musical career.

We did not have many real adventures but one day while out sailing off the Folkestone Headquarters in a 27-foot Montague Rigged Whaler we became becalmed and, despite our rather feeble efforts at rowing and what I now realise were rather inept instructions to row initially against the strong Spring Tide, instead of directly for the beach, we were rapidly swept down channel towards Dungeness landing eventually in the dark without lights on the Hythe Beach near the Redoubt. As there had been loss of life of some Sea Cadets in rather different circumstances some time earlier in a different part of the country, panic had begun to ensue ashore when we failed to return from our jolly in beautiful fine weather. Apart from being exhausted from trying to row the heavy boat in and pull it clear of the water, we were ravenous on landing. Thus we were taken to what was known as a "British Restaurant" in Hythe for fish and chips before being returned by lorry to some anxious parents in Folkestone.

Leaving School

I left school at 15 years old having done reasonably well at the Harvey Grammar School Folkestone in the subjects required to complete a General School Certificate, but I had to wait until I was 16 years old before I was allowed by the authorities to work aboard a ship. Sitting at home for a few months was not an option I considered or in fact my parents could afford; I had to find a job.

That was in fact not difficult with my qualifications and therefore not telling of my future plans in the summer of 1950 I got a job as a junior salesman in a Military Outfitters called "Allkits" in Sandgate Road, Folkestone. I was 15 years old and waiting impatiently to reach the ripe old age of 16 and start a career at sea, something I did five days after that long awaited birthday. Each morning my first job after making the tea, together with most other shop juniors, was to wash down the pavement outside the shop. Sandgate Road was a smart shopping area and sparkled first thing in the morning in those days.

"Allkits" made to measure officers' uniforms for the many Army Officers based at Shorncliffe Camp and for the young ladies of the WRAF Officer Cadet Training Unit at RAF Hawkinge. An interesting job for a young man, although as I recall the little Rolly Polly Jewish manager never let me handle the tape measure on our visits for fittings. However I was paid commission and found, when given the opportunity, I was fairly successful making more money than the six pounds five shillings per month I was subsequently to earn during my first year at sea. As well as the military clothing the company also retailed civilian clothing and was just one of a number of first-class gentlemen's tailors established in the town. These were "Walter Moncrief's", "Broadleys", and "Bobbys" (which became Debenhams) and finally "Wallace Hale" the last one to survive but now sadly gone leaving the town currently without a quality tailor.

During the next few months I was desperate to find a shipping company that would employ me without the advantage of pre-sea training and was fortunate that the local chairman of the Sea Cadet Corps, the late Commander Neate RN, had good connections in the shipping world and City of London. I was initially offered two ships: the passenger ship *Monarch of Bermuda* running out of New York to the Caribbean, an attractive proposition in the austere food rationing days of Britain; and the *Empire Byng*, a specialist heavy lift tramp ship built under licence during the war from Christian Smith of Norway and at that time on a Clan, Hall, Harrison charter running railway and other heavy equipment to East Africa.

I did not know which to choose and went again for advice to see my school friend's father Captain A. Walker DSC the Senior Master of the Southern Railway Cross Channel Ferries. A great character who had earned his medal for gallantry taking off thousands of refugees on many trips prior to the evacuation and more than 12,000 troops from Dunkirk during six trips in his ship *Biarritz*, while under almost continuous air attack. Despite his harrowing experiences he lived to be over 100 years old.

Captain Walker reminded me that he had already advised that my father could not afford to send me to one of the famous pre-sea training schools, such as "Worcester", "Conway", "Warsash" or "Pangbourne" and that to get an apprenticeship; I needed to accept either one of these two offers. He did not in any case believe that expensive pre-sea training was necessary and although he could well afford it, he did not plan to send his own son Neil anywhere except straight to sea with the Royal Fleet Auxiliary Service.

He pondered on the matter and reminisced for a while about his own apprenticeship in a tramp company, telling me some story about being so cold and wet that he had to wrap newspaper around his feet to keep warm; it should have put me off. Finally he suggested on the *Monarch* I would be nothing but a "glorified bridge boy", whatever that was, while on the tramp ship I would thoroughly learn my trade and he thought I would benefit from the latter appointment. I greatly respected his opinion and thought there is little point in seeking advice if you then go and ignore it but I sometimes wonder how my career would have developed had I chosen the posh passenger ship. Certainly my career at sea could not have been better as it developed but as a working class lad, who I was, although my mother always insisted we were something else, I was at that time probably sociably vulnerable although fairly well house-trained. Without a doubt old Captain Walker knew me better than I knew myself at that age and gave me sound advice, although there were to be many occasions in those first years when I doubted his wisdom.

SS Biarritz off Dover, wind against tide

First Days at Sea

I was sixteen years and one week old; it was November 1950 with crisp cold sunny weather and at last my dream had come true – I was actually going to sea as a deck apprentice and the first step on the ladder to Master Mariner.

On the 10th November 1950 I had joined at Huskisson Dock in Liverpool the heavy lift ship *Empire Byng* of the Dalhousie Steam and Motorship Company, one of seven ships run by a London Greek ship owner by the name of Nomikos. I had travelled the afternoon before from Folkestone on steam trains, via London to Lime Street station Liverpool, in my brand new navy blue apprentice's doeskin uniform. My parents had kitted me out at Tourneys, a marine tailors in Snargate Street, Dover, according to a list supplied by the Shipping Federation. Sadly it had cost my father far more than he could afford and was to put him into debt for several years to come with my grandparents; who were only too pleased to be able to help.

Life is full of lost opportunities which at the time one does not often recognise, but in retrospect I wonder now why we did not buy my uniforms and kit from "Allkits" the military outfitters in Folkestone, where I had worked for several months since leaving school and where, as an employee, I would have been able to buy at a considerable discount. I do not recall whether we even thought about it at the time. Maybe I did not want to warn my first employers of my imminent departure. Once at sea I soon found that at least half of the expense which had caused my father so much anguish could have been avoided, for much of the uniform on the Shipping Federation recommended list was more suitable for those about to begin a career in the finest passenger ships and was to be useless for the likes of me; beginning four years of cheap labour aboard a heavy lift tramp ship.

I had sufficient kit to fill a large metal sea chest which we had managed to find second hand in one of the local auction rooms. Painting my name and the name of my ship on it with pride I travelled in style using porters to help me with the chest at the railway stations and crossed London in a black taxi to catch the train for Liverpool, feeling rather important for the first time in my life.

The excitement grew as it got dark early that cold November afternoon and the train pulled steamily but slowly into Lime Street Station where there was a mad scramble for porters. I thought I was out of luck but happily a cheerful fellow came to my rescue. I explained about my large sea chest in the guard's van and suddenly realised with horror that my cheerful new friend only had one arm. I need not have worried, he was more than up to the task which was probably more than I was with my gratuity but he seemed happy enough and grinning at this shiny new apprentice, he wished me well with my first ship.

The taxi soon deposited me at the foot of a very steep gangway leading up to what appeared to be an enormous riveted ship towering high up above the rubbish-strewn quayside and I wondered how I was going to manage the chest. I need not have bothered, for the Bosun seeing me arrive soon had some large ABs chuck my precious possessions into a cargo net, and using a derrick lifted the chest aboard the ship where, unbeknown to me at the time, it was to remain for the next five years empty in the Mates locker.

The ship which was as we say "bung light" had just returned on a Clan, Hall, Harrison Line charter to East Africa, taking general cargo and heavy railway equipment exports out and bringing home copper ingots, coffee and ground nuts from the new Ground Nut Scheme just established in Tanganyika. The holds were completely empty and stunk of ammonia, stale urine and strange fetid tropical aromas which badly needed cleaning before the next cargo could be loaded; and this was, I discovered, where I came in. The senior apprentice, a tall Scandinavian looking quietly spoken Geordie by the name of Jimmie Clark, soon turned me out of bed on that first morning enquiring whether amongst all that wonderful shiny new gear I had any working clothes such as a boiler suit or working trousers and shirt and rubber boots? I had a pristine white boiler suit which I hurriedly put on but which was never to be pristine again.

My job, carefully supervised, was to clean the strum boxes in the bilges in number two hold, known as "bilge diving". Most of the water had been pumped out but the residue of rotting ground nuts, stinking native excrement, rats' nests and general muck still needed to be cleaned from the strum boxes. My job was to get into the bilge and clean this mess out by hand into buckets provided by Jimmie Clark, who then arranged for them to be hauled out of the empty hold to somewhere out of sight on deck.

I suppose I could have been desperately discouraged that first day but somebody had to do the job and who but the junior minion on board? Besides I knew from reading many Percy F Westerman books about the adventurous life of deck apprentices that life for the junior apprentice was not supposed to be exactly a bed of roses. However something was about to happen that made that day worthwhile and gave me an anecdote to recount through many years of swinging the lamp with other old seafarers.

The empty hold was 83 feet long, the double-bottom tank tops had a thick timber sheath ceiling and the hold had very heavy side frames which went right up to the main deck. It was just one big hold without tween decks. We had removed the side plates on the bilges and cleaned to the very after end when Jimmie reacted very quickly on seeing a large rat disturbed by my activities run the length of the hold to escape us. Picking up a small shackle from some of the 10-ton derrick working gear on the ceiling, he hurled it the length of the hold and, as I watched in fascination and incredulity, the shackle arched through the air to land squarely on the terrified rat, squashing it flat.

Jimmie turned slowly to me and remarked:

"When you're a senior apprentice and have been at sea
as long as me, you'll be able to do that!"

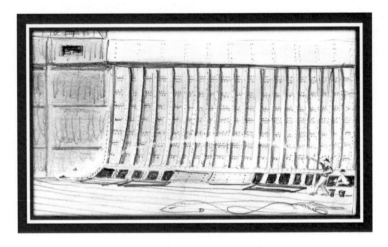

Death of a rat

What an exciting adventure going to sea actually was already turning out to be, never mind the muck and the rotten jobs; this was the life for me. I learnt a lot from Jimmie Clark but unfortunately we lost him to his continued career elsewhere after just one voyage to East Africa and I never saw or heard of him after that one hilarious voyage.

Off to sea – November 1950

Mombasa 1951

Home on leave – 1951

Chapter 7

My Apprenticeship Days

Life at sea in the turbo-electric heavy lift tramp ship *Empire Byng* in 1950 was to be a real adventure visiting exotic places around the world, places that had been but dreams for so many of my earlier years. What was so striking in those days was the number of British ships to be seen in every port, the canals we were to visit in transit, and the number of British pilots working in ports from Abadan to Zanzibar. There were just so many British Shipping Companies; most with large fleets but of course somewhat smaller ships than the much larger ones of today. The British Merchant Service dominated the commercial maritime world with ships manned by British, Indian and Hong Kong Chinese seamen but all with British Officers.

The other impression I had was that nearly all the British and Dutch Colonies we visited in Africa and elsewhere were kept so neat and clean by comparison with the Colonies of other European countries. That may appear a bit Imperialist and patronising but I am sure those of you who travelled the world in those days must have observed that this was a fact.

The work was hard and the hours long and the heavy lift cargoes challenging and interesting, but I thrived and I imagine I matured fast, learning rapidly to live in a small community, sharing the good and bad experiences with my fellow shipmates. During those years I learnt to splice rope and wire, rig and man derricks, both General Purpose ten-ton derricks, as well as the three Heavy Lift Jumbo Derricks each capable of lifting 120 tons. I was taught to sew and repair canvas hatch covers and boat covers for which I bought a left-handed palm, rig painting stages to paint over the side and to use a Bosun's chair to wash and paint down the masts, the stays and other upper works. Scaling rust with a small hammer or electric chipping hammer was a dirty, noisy and common occupation which probably did my long-term hearing no good. While washing from one bucket of cold water, pumped by hand at the end of the working day on a long ocean passage, left one with a healthy respect for water.

The *Empire Byng* did not have automatic steering gear and was always steered by a helmsman which was not only one of the most interesting jobs I was to learn but one which gave me considerable experience of subsequent value for when I became a Pilot much later in my career. Whether this was a common practice in tramp ships I never knew, but when I became Senior Apprentice for a number of years I was always expected to take the wheel both going into and out of port no matter what time of day or night. I always thought it an honour to be trusted at such a young age with the wheel during the most interesting parts of the voyage. I not only learnt how to handle the ship in different weather conditions but at different speeds, in rivers and strong tidal conditions. I learnt to work with Pilots of all different nationalities and had a healthy respect for their abilities, although at that time to become a Pilot myself was far from my planned career which was something of, and remained, an unplanned passage.

My longest voyage out from home was just twenty days short of four years mostly spent in the Far East during the Korean War. I spent my last teenage years based in Japanese ports, at that time a sailor's paradise, on a shuttle service to Korea with equipment for the US Army, but more of that later.

After joining in Liverpool as the ship completed her discharge we signed on Articles of two years' duration, a new 'scouse' crew of sailors easily identified by the caps they were to personally hand-sew from either old blue jeans or white linen sheeting, similar to the style of those worn by the pop singer Donovan some years later. Come to think of it, they also sang a lot wherever we were in the world the favourite being the unabridged version of 'Maggie May' and one called 'Eskimo Nell'. They were a friendly capable crowd, good at their work and particularly good at football; although their language and strange dialect took some understanding and tolerance.

Prior to loading the ship we proceeded to Glasgow for dry-docking and de-fumigation to kill the millions of cockroaches and the multitude of rats which had bred well on the previous voyage to the east African ground nut scheme. We were all put ashore for 48 hours into some kind of hostel among the grim tenement buildings of Govan while the gas did its work. We soon found when outward bound that it had not been very effective on either species.

Leaving dry-dock on the 26th November 1950 we moved to King George V Dock in thick fog, a very eerie first experience, where we commenced loading for East Africa before moving to Victoria Dock Birkenhead for further cargo; finally sailing on the 10th December 1950 for my first deep-sea voyage. I was very sea sick for twenty-four hours entering the Bay of Biscay but fortunately discovered my sea legs on the second day and was to be little troubled for the remainder of my career.

We proudly passed the magnificent stately Rock of Gibraltar late on the 14th December 1950 for the first time before steaming along the superb Barbary Coast in flat, calm, glassy seas with the backdrop of the blue and mauve distant Atlas Mountains. The multitude of twinkling lights on a particularly dark bible black night marked the presence of the busy city of Algiers silent on the southern horizon, while on the bridge wing all that could be heard was the sounds of the sea rushing past and quiet muttered conversation between the officer of the watch and the helmsman emanating from the darkened wheelhouse, the quiet of that night broken occasionally by the sound of a bell clearly being struck three times from the forecastle head as the lookout indicated yet another ship appearing on the invisible horizon dead ahead.

It took us ten days to reach the Suez Canal at Port Said, a manic place full of bum boats with persistent Egyptian salesmen, each small boat loaded with drawers stuffed with bargain shirts, shorts and socks. There were camel stools (or seats), birds in cages, shite hawks in free flight, boatmen trying to sell to the innocent sepia coloured dirty postcards of naked plump Victorian ladies, and there was constant noise and the bustle of boats and continually the slow graceful movement of large ships of all nationalities leaving the canal and arriving for transit.

The Suez Canal Searchlight was hoisted on the forward davit designed and fitted for that purpose and two canal mooring boats were lifted aboard before the Suez Canal Pilot embarked and we were off in convoy southbound. The Pilots in those days were British, French and South African Master Mariners who remained servicing the canal up until the time it was nationalized by General Nasser, after which the job was carried on mainly by Russians and Egyptians some with the vaguest maritime experience. I was to meet in the 1960s both an Egyptian Professor of Oceanography and a former Naval Attaché working as pilots and there were doubtless many other strange hands drafted in to pilot the convoys of ever larger ships.

Christmas saw us in Aden for bunkers before we headed around the Horn of Africa and down the east coast of Africa to a new port to be built at Mtwara, Tanganyika for the now infamous Ground Nut Scheme. We were carrying on the fore deck a small tug and three barges to establish a new port because the equipment for the scheme had to be transported from the port of Dar-es-Salaam to the inland site selected for cultivation at Kongwa in central Tanganyika, using the only available transport; a single-track railway with a steam locomotive. Unfortunately, a sudden flood of the Kinyansungwe River wiped out the rail tracks, leaving a dirt road as the only means of transport; an alternative was needed and Mtwara came about. The Ground Nut Scheme was typically one of many projects doomed to failure in Africa as a result of inadequate planning and the harsh conditions; ironically we had arrived much too late, for the project was to be abandoned that same year at a loss of some £49 million.

The port, we were to discover, was no more than a large natural lagoon with incredibly clear water in which swam sparkling shoals of barracuda and the occasional large menacing shark. The lagoon was surrounded by jungle and, when we arrived, the British pilot mysteriously appeared from nowhere in what I am sure was a canoe. The same voyage we were to load giant yellow Caterpillar tractors and earth movers the best of the ruined equipment being returned to the UK for refurbishment having been wrecked by a combination of weather, hard ground and considerable misuse.

Two jobs I remember vividly from that voyage were cement washing the inside of a small freshwater tank as we rolled southwards down the African coast in the humidity of the north-east monsoon and bailing out by bucket one of the barges which, being on the top of number one hatch, had taken in water in the earlier bad weather. Running parallel southwards at exactly the same speed and in sight for several days was the sparkling white silhouette of the Ellerman liner *City of Karachi* on her maiden voyage, a ship which was to be one of the very last to take her Trinity House Cinque Ports Pilot many years later at Dungeness when the Pilot Station was moved to Folkestone. The other was taking the wheel as we left Aden late on Christmas Day 1950 with too many people the worse for the celebrations.

My first two voyages out from the UK were to East Africa and of about 5 months' duration each. The first, out via the Suez Canal, we had Christmas bunkering in Aden and then down the coast to Mtwara, Tanganyika and then to Beira, Mozambique to discharge Rhodesian Railway coaches and some general cargo before returning to the British Protectorate of Zanzibar and Mombasa, Kenya. We discharged as we went the remains of our general cargo and loaded spices, copper ingots, groundnuts, coffee and on deck military equipment for Adabiyah in the Gulf of Suez; and then home to Plantation Quay Glasgow to commence discharging and loading around the coast once again for East Africa. After part loading general cargo, which I remember included a consignment of grey flannel trousers for Zanzibar of all the odd places, the ship completed loading back on the Mersey with eighteen railway carriages for the Rhodesian Railways to be landed at Beira. We spent 42 days in the anchorage off Beira awaiting a berth together with a host of other ships many of whom were to spend even longer there. The only entertainment there was listening on the radio to the General Election when Winston Churchill was re-elected to power.

The African Spice Islands

Zanzibar, which had been the centre of the slave and ivory trades the previous century, was a magical place of waving palm trees golden beaches and endless blue skies. The distinctly Arabian looking town was attractive,

Stevedore, Mombasa, 1951

but an area we were told to be avoided. The community was then mainly Arab and Indian while the harbour was in those days full of Arab dhows still trading with the Arabian Gulf. We had some general cargo to discharge but the ship mainly took on water and loaded spices, cloves and nutmegs for the United Kingdom. The dhows traded heaven knows what. History had ensured that the Arabs and Indians lacked popularity and subsequently in 1964, just a month following independence from Britain, thousands of Arabs and Indians were killed by genocide and thousands more expelled when the islands became part of Tanzania.

Heavy Lifts

The discharge of the heavy lift cargo of Rhodesian Pullman Railway carriages, working during the day at Beira using only one of the three jumbo derricks at a time; was a slow job which required all the deck hands. Initially to rig and attach the steam guys which would be used to haul the lift over the side and back, suspended from one of the three 120-ton lift jumbo single swinging derricks, to which was attached the dolly and hook. Then to break out the derrick and pick up the 9-ton steel spreader secured on the main deck before one could start to lift the first carriage.

Kilindini, Mombasa, Kenya in 1951

The Chief Officer with the Bosun assisting took charge of the operation while the Second Officer drove the heavy lift topping lift and the Third Officer the heavy lift purchase. The working wires were of 5¼ inch and 5 inch circumference respectively rove through large six-fold steel blocks on the derrick to two large individual revolving grooved drum ends in the housing below. The Bosun's Mate drove one of the steam guys and the lamp-trimmer the other, although these positions were often taken by the more experienced apprentices. The large range in the tide meant that discharging could only be carried out when there was sufficient height of tide for the suspended railway carriage hanging below the derrick and spreader to clear the wharf, despite the subsequent list engendered as the load was worked over the side with the steam guys.

It is amazing to recollect that within just over eighteen months I was to be working two holds simultaneously on my own, discharging 32 ton Sherman tanks and other heavy equipment with Korean stevedores. Well it was not safe but it was expedient.

The First Man-made Fibre Mooring Ropes

Before leaving the UK on that second voyage the ship had been supplied with what we believed to be the world's first man-made fibre mooring ropes made of nylon. Being light and much thinner than normal manila and hemp mooring lines, they caused much derision outward in the Suez Canal on the 30th April 1951 when passed to a large tug to help us manoeuvre out of the waiting and bunkering basin for entry into the canal. The Tug Master refused to believe we were serious and had nothing, in his opinion, more suitable. Deciding he would demonstrate the inadequacy of our pathetic tow line, he went Full Ahead on it with his tug and indeed he did demonstrate that nylon ropes stretch. It not only stretched but eventually parted with a flash like a bolt of lightning and recoil which dangerously swept the forecastle, scattering the Mate and sailors for cover. It was fortunate for the Tug Master that the rope did part, for by that time he had virtually girded and was so far over on his side that the water had begun to flood through the engine-room skylights. The tug however came upright again and was quickly replaced by somebody more tolerant of our modern mooring equipment.

Stevedore, Mombasa, 1951

In Durban, South Africa, in 1951 we were able to buy at the Mission to Seamen ready prepared parcels of tinned fruit to bring home to the UK, where of course they were a real luxury with food rationing still in existence after the war. We had some delay waiting several weeks at anchor for a berth at Kilindini, Mombasa before we loaded for home via the Suez Canal. During that time at anchor we ran the ship's motor lifeboat as a liberty boat and I was fortunate to be paired up with the Second Mate, Bill Thomas, who allowed me to act as coxswain while he acted as deckhand, thus allowing me to gain considerable boat-handling experience; I gather my colleagues were not so fortunate. At Mombasa, as a guest at a party when as entertainment we all had to sing solos, I managed to swim into a coral-encrusted buoy, part of a shark defensive barrier for the sea water bathing pool at the Royal Naval Armament Stores Depot. An incident that left me with a permanent scar on my left shoulder and for which the loss of a miniscule of my blood excited some underwater activity outside the net.

The main entertainment at Mombasa for us was at the Mission to Seamen where we were to enjoy film shows, play billiards, table tennis, and go on organised days out to a wonderful beach further up the coast. I recall cutting across some rough land between the quays and the main street, the entrance to which I seem to recall was decorated by what appeared to be a couple of giant elephant tusks; rough land which when going ashore in the daylight I felt might contain snakes, hyenas or other wild creatures, but if it did I never saw any.

Coming back to the ship at night was a different matter, for the path caused us to run the gauntlet past a ramshackle little shanty bar called the 'Anchor' with an illuminated blue sign which cast an unearthly glow upon a line of highly painted big black whores looking like a row of ugly witches standing on the stoop. They called out to us offering their services in a most memorable way as we hastily walked uncomfortably past.

"Hey Johnny you like Jig-i-jig? We black girl outside but inside all same Queen Victoria."

I guess it was a traditional chant probably going back to the turn of the century, as indeed by the look of it, so did some of the ladies of the night. At sixteen I was horrified that anyone of my colleagues might take up the offer, if a combination of alcohol and historical interest did get the better of them. Fortunately even the roughest of our crew looked with great distaste on this particular group and their offers were a source of great derision, particularly among our Royalists.

After serving several ports on the East African coast we returned to the United Kingdom via Aden for bunkers and the Suez Canal. Arriving at Avonmouth on the 11th August 1951, we discharged our African cargo and loaded around the UK coast at Glasgow, Birkenhead and Liverpool and then across to Antwerp, picking up a Cinque Ports Trinity House Pilot off Dungeness where 17 years later I was to be licensed as a London Pilot. The pilot was not compulsory but was employed to take us through the heavy traffic and the few remaining minefields to the pilot station for Antwerp at the A1 buoy. Ships in those days bound through the Dover Straits from the west invariably ran along the English coast using the superior navigational aids established there and convenient relatively straight coastline before crossing the Dover Straits to the southern North Sea.

Death on Deck

While loading in Antwerp for East Africa with cranes at a riverside berth the deck crew were re-rigging the topping lift on one of the 10-ton derricks housed upright at No.3 hold, when the gallows strop parted and down came the large steel block and wire tackle striking the winch man working the electric winch on the deck immediately below. The Able Seaman, who I recall was named Brown, was struck on the back of the head and shoulders and mortally injured to die in the ambulance before he reached hospital.

The winch and deck had become a gory mess and as soon as the casualty had been removed the Mate sent for the three youngest apprentices who were washing the bridge paintwork with lumps of cotton waste dipped in a bucket of warm water and soda; a cold unpleasant job with bare hands on a winter's day in Europe. Not half as unpleasant as cleaning up the gory consequences of the accident with sand and water which, when tipped into the River Schelt, turned the fast-flowing water pink as it flowed past the ship to the sea. A popular man Mr Brown left, I believe, a widow and two children for whom we managed to collect from the ship's complement of about fifty, the grand sum of £95 – a most generous amount in those days, amounting to nearly four months' pay.

Off Charter and into Tramping

Our third voyage of seven months, we circumnavigated Africa clockwise this time to East Africa bunkering at Las Palmas before commencing discharge at Durban, Beira and Mombasa where completion of discharge saw us come off charter to Clan, Hall and Harrison Lines and from whence we proceeded tramping. First loading salt by basket in Aden where it was loaded from barges for Osaka, Japan bunkering on the way at Pulau Bukum, Singapore from a Shell tanker which looked remarkably cool under spotless white awnings in the humid tropical heat. Osaka was cold, grey and war-damaged with few cars and little to sell except highly decorative china tea sets, little Kokeshi wooden dolls and beer – I bought some of each at an exchange rate of £1 to 1000 yen. As the bitterly cold January days passed slowly, the Japanese stevedores laboriously discharged the salt for £15 per month by using buckets and pairs of derricks rigged as union purchase, the yard derrick suspended above the crowded wooden sampans where families with innumerable small smiling children sat around their warm charcoal cooking stoves, waving chopsticks at us. Once again we received no mail from home, but after eight days we were empty and sailed on the 8th January 1951. It was to be a horrendous passage pounding along in ballast in thick fog across the North Pacific to Vancouver Island, to load sawn timber for Avonmouth and home. Navigating by dead reckoning (to the lay person pure guesswork) and the occasional radio bearing, not knowing when exactly or how accurate would be our landfall; it was a miserable uncomfortable passage.

The ship had radar of sorts but it rarely worked and certainly did not work that voyage. Fortunately we made a clear and reasonably accurate landfall and picked up the Canadian pilot before proceeding through the islands and inland waterway in thick falling snow to Vancouver itself. The pilotage was impressive the pilot requiring a stopwatch to record the time it took, not only between turns but for the return of the echo of the ship's whistle bouncing off the rocky pine-covered islands, his only method in such poor visibility of estimating how close he stood into danger. Thank God that in my subsequent career I was never called upon for such ability.

It was daylight with visibility down to nil in the heavy falling snow when, standing on lookout cold and frozen in my duffle coat and heaviest clothing in the eyes of the forecastle head, peering into a white void and feeling very vulnerable and somewhat isolated, being well aware that if we ran into anything I would hit it first, I was suddenly startled to hear directly above me a booming voice; a voice from heaven above demanding.

"What ship? Where bound?"

It was, I was to find out, not God but the voice of the duty watchman perched in a small wooden office in the middle of the Lion's Gate Bridge at the entrance to Vancouver Harbour. He had been speaking through a loudhailer but he certainly gave me a fright before he quickly shut the window again and picked up the telephone to warn the tugs, watermen and immigration officials of our imminent arrival; carefully entering the time and name of ship in his logbook before putting another log on his wood burning stove.

Chapter 8

An Unnerving Experience

Over the years as an apprentice I had many experiences, but here are a few of the more memorable and printable that I recall.

I suppose it was a rotten trick to play on anyone, but *Paddy* (we will call him that to disguise his identity) had already struck the junior apprentice during a drunken episode on one occasion and was genuinely disliked by all the apprentices and his peers amongst the hard-working Liverpool crowd. He was gross, dirty, and lazy, foul-mouthed and, as it later transpired, a homosexual to boot; unfortunately he was usually the AB of the next watch to take over from me as the first lookout on the eight to twelve watch.

The apprentices manned the four-to-eight watches with the Chief Officer, keeping a lookout on the forecastle head during the hours of darkness or in poor visibility and taking turns of two hours at the wheel. This was of course before the days of automatic helmsmen and when the lookout was kept from the eyes of the forecastle unless the sea was actually breaking over it.

The ship was rolling quite heavily as she ran before a large following sea and the moon occasionally broke through the dark clouds racing past, the night I decided to put the fear of God into the good Catholic *Paddy*. Having secured a pair of gloves to the arms of my duffel coat and long sea boots to the tail of the coat which I had stuffed with a canvas ventilator cover, I checked my watch as I stood on lookout between the anchor cables ahead of the windlass. It was nearly time for my relief; so carefully I secured the head of the duffel coat to the halyard of the Suez Canal davit and hoisted my improvised dummy aloft, where it swung violently as the ship dipped her bows between the rollers.

I waited in anticipation hidden behind the windlass for the arrival of the unsuspecting *Paddy* to relieve the watch, as did the apprentice on the wheel and the standby cadet peering forward from his cabin port hole to see what happened. I saw the large shadow of *Paddy* pass the shaded deck lights of the bridge house as he descended into the well deck before climbing up the port side ladder to the forecastle where he paused. Something had obviously caught his eye but then on he came, somewhat cautiously, to stop dead when the moon broke through to reveal a macabre sight; what appeared to be the body of the apprentice swinging from the Suez Canal davit. *Paddy* turned and ran shouting something incomprehensible and lost in the wind. As he made for the bridge I quickly lowered the dummy, stowed away the spare kit under the windlass, and pulled on my duffel coat.

Keeping lookout

I was pacing up and down on the forecastle looking for ships, when the foredeck was illuminated by a quivering Aldis light as the Mate probed the darkness in response to screams from *Paddy* that:

"The cadet has ung imself surr"

Unfortunately for *Paddy* his breath smelt strongly of cheap Japanese whisky and I quite obviously had not departed this world. The fact that the apprentice on the wheel casually dropped the thought into the Mate's ear on hearing the cries from forward cannot have helped the situation.

"I expect *Paddy* has been at the hard stuff again"

The episode cost the poor man a day's pay when he was logged for being drunk on watch. Well, yes, I suppose it was unkind but he was drunk and revenge can be sweet. *Paddy* never mentioned the event to me so I guess he just didn't believe his own eyes!

An Error of Judgement

The heavy lift ship Empire Byng was renamed *Peter Dal II* in 1951. When not carrying heavy lift cargos she was very popular in the timber trade and carried a number of record-breaking cargoes from British Columbia to South Africa and to the United Kingdom.

The stevedores in British Columbia were the hardest working stevedores I witnessed in our worldwide tramping. Of course the method of stowing the timber was slow as the layers of timber were built up much like a dance floor, each piece of the jigsaw being moved into place by two men using long-handled hooks. No space was left as the timber of different lengths was built up from the tank tops until some fifteen feet above the main deck. It took several weeks and a number of ports around Vancouver Island before topping off in either New Westminster or Vancouver itself.

The stevedores often had to drive some considerable way to the more isolated ports on the island but they were usually on deck at 06:45 to start work at 07:00 and then they kept going right through to lunch time refreshing themselves with ice cold water from a freshwater urn which moved up with the subsequent layers of timber. The break for lunch was brief before they worked on through the afternoon but fortunately there was no night work.

The smell of the freshly cut cedar and pine and the clean air was invigorating. They were idyllic days, I was young and British Columbia is a beautiful country; the fact that a timber deck cargo was nearly to be the end of me is another story for this is a further anecdote about being relieved by *Paddy* as lookout at the end of yet another four-to-eight watch.

Finally loaded with some eighteen feet high deck cargo above the main deck on numbers 2 and 3 holds between the bridge and the after accommodation and fifteen feet on number 1 hold forward of the bridge; we sailed for Avonmouth from New Westminster. Across the after holds had been built a wooden catwalk complete with guard rails for the safe passage of the crew to and from the bridge house, while forward of the bridge man-ropes had been rigged on either side with wooden ladders leading down onto the forecastle. Because the ship was to pass through the Panama Canal, spaces around the Panama leads had been left sufficiently clear in order to work the leads.

The first night out was dark as we rolled steadily south, I paced the forecastle deck waiting to be relieved by the large familiar fat figure of *Paddy*. I saw him pass up onto the deck cargo around the port side of the bridge housing and start forward. I had turned to scan the horizon when the air was filled with expletives.

Making my way carefully to the break of the forecastle head I discovered that *Paddy*, who had himself rigged the man ropes on the port side, had walked up the outboard side instead of inboard and stepped into space falling down onto the Panama bits.

I asked possibly a silly question,

"What are you doing down there, Paddy?"

He replied in his usual uncouth manner,

*"Well I'm not f*****g well learning to fly, that's for sure!"*

Naturally being concerned for his health I enquired,

"Well have you broken anything?"

To which the reply came,

*"Well to be sure there is nothing here to f*****g well break!"*

Slowly and painfully he climbed up the ladder to the forecastle, insisting on taking his watch but pleading with me not to tell 'the crowd' what had happened. He was a tough hard character, but had he been a more considerate man I might have saved him considerable embarrassment on that long voyage home but I have to plead guilty to telling everyone on board the story with some small embellishments just as soon as I could.

A Close Call

This same deck cargo from which *Paddy* fell was nearly to be the death of me as some three weeks later we crossed the North Atlantic rolling sluggishly with a heavy swell on the port quarter. It was just coming on six thirty in the morning on a cold and windy day when my task that particular morning, as standby man on the four-to-eight watch, was to make my way aft across the timber to the after accommodation and call the Bosun and the day workers from their sleep. The ship which had three holds, one forward of the bridge and two between the bridge and after accommodation, was much like a tanker of that era except for the two large Sampson posts, winches and four derricks sited midway between number two and three holds. The block of accommodation amidships housed the deck officers and apprentices, hospital, heavy lift gear and of course the navigating bridge. Everyone else, the engineers, all the ratings, galley, officers' salon, mess rooms and stores was housed in the after accommodation above the engine room.

It was just getting light when I left the shelter of the bridge housing and climbed onto the catwalk built of timber over the 18 feet high deck cargo. For the standby man to call the day-workers was routine and something which was done automatically without reference to the mate on watch. I had not been warned of anything untoward and the weather conditions were no worse than we had been experiencing for several days as we rolled homeward bound from Vancouver towards Avonmouth.

I was halfway across number two hatch when the port quarter was lifted by an enormous heavy swell. The ship rolled particularly violently and there was a loud bang, followed quickly by another as two of the substantial chains securing the timber deck cargo parted at number two hatch. The heavy sodden timber suddenly started to move sideways beneath me with the roll, dragging the catwalk with it as the timber started to cascade into the sea on the starboard side. I started to run aft as the catwalk broke up behind me and luckily I just made it to the Sampson post on the port side where I leapt clear of the rush of timber and climbed above the devastation and maelstrom of spinning timber below me. I clung on to the vertical ladder on the outside of the post as the wind howled and the spray drove across the deck. Every time the ship rolled to starboard, more and more timber slid over the side from number two.

I shouted in vain as my cries were swept off to leeward and I looked unsuccessfully to see if the mate had seen me. Unbeknown to me he was still working out the ship's position from the few stars he had managed to take as dawn broke. The lookout another cadet was on the forecastle despite the weather and hidden from me by the bridge structure.

It was now decision time. There was no way I was going to get back to the bridge to report the loss, which had obviously gone unseen or unheard and therefore I would need to get back down onto number three hold where the catwalk and timber appeared to be secure. As a young apprentice however, I was probably influenced by the fact that the galley and food was all aft and it was coming on breakfast time. Waiting for a quiet or relatively quiet moment in the heavy rolling I slid down to the top of the deck cargo, made it to what remained of the catwalk and ran like hell for the after accommodation where I kept going until I reached the telephone at the after mooring station, turning the telephone handle frantically until I heard the disgruntled voice of the Mate. He was not pleased to hear he had lost several hundred tons of prime British Columbian pine and cedar over the side and certainly not concerned about my close call with death, which he was sure I was exaggerating.

Running for my life

I called the Bosun with a large steaming mug of tea and the cheerful message that, "by the way the Mate wants you to get all hands out on number two and re-stow the timber, there's been a spot of bother!"

Turning onto a more southerly course we steamed all that day with the ship pitching heavily as all the sailors and the three apprentices worked to re-secure and re-stow the heavy wet timber. Timber which had been so carefully worked into position by those skilled and experienced stevedores in New Westminster. It never looked quite the same but "chippy" the carpenter made a proficient job of re-building the catwalk and the voyage was completed without further loss. I was never party to exactly how much we lost in mid Atlantic but undoubtedly someone somewhere, probably in the Leeward Islands, was eventually pleased to have it washed ashore; I was just pleased not to be still clinging to it.

Chapter 9

The USA in the 1950s

After discharging the remains of our timber cargo at Avonmouth, the *Peter Dal II* was chartered to the United States Military Sea Transportation Service (MSTS) as a heavy lift ship to carry mainly Sherman tanks to battle in Korea; but first we had to get there. We started off on the 14th March 1952 with a nine-day passage across the North Atlantic in ballast to New York, to berth at Staten Island and commence loading military stores of all kinds.

It was a time when the giant Cunard liners *Queen Elizabeth* and *Queen Mary* would steam majestically up past our berth to Manhattan. King George VI was on the throne but Senator McCarthy was at his most influential period in the United States and certain individual members of the US Immigration Service, not known even today for their sense of humour, thought they had extra powers of authority legal or otherwise. To be allowed ashore we all had to sign a declaration that we were not communist agents or even sympathisers, and our poor very anglicised Liverpool born Chinese Chief Steward was not allowed ashore under any circumstances, the company having to pay a bond to ensure he remained on board.

However the greatest personal indignity perpetrated against the cadets was carried out by the Port Health officials, not just in New York but every port we visited where the US had jurisdiction after the war. This occurred when the four of us were regularly lined up in the Officers' Smoke Room for what I later learned was something called a 'short-arm inspection'. This involved exposing ourselves by opening the fronts of our dark navy-blue doeskin uniform trousers and being sprayed upon our appendages with a thick white powder which I believe to be DDT. The mess it made of our uniforms was not funny. The aim of the exercise was I believe to kill Pediculosis Pubis, 'crabs', something we had heard about but had little opportunity to acquire or any desire to get. Whatever it was supposed to kill, I believe it is now beginning to work and I am seriously considering suing the US Government for personal deprivation and injury.

In the early 1950s the exchange rate gave us 4.5 United States Dollars to one Pound Sterling. In our time off duty, we were to enjoy New York and the hospitality of some very generous Americans through the facilities of the British Apprentice Club. The BAC opened in 1921 by King Edward VIII when Prince of Wales was based in the famous Chelsea Hotel, an establishment at 222 West 23rd Street. The club had been started by two wealthy ladies – Kathrine Mayo and M. Moyca Newell – who wished to reciprocate the hospitality they had witnessed given to American Servicemen in the UK during the First World War. The facilities were for the use of British Apprentices and Cadets of ships visiting the several ports of New York.

The ladies rented a number of rooms on the third floor of the hotel where the cadets could relax in a home like environment or take part in organised activities such as, theatre visits or picnics or even home hospitality over the weekend in the country and dances, where the girls had all been carefully vetted by the BAC. There were no rules and cadets could come and go as they wished, helping themselves to ice cream or Mrs Spaulding's famous chocolate cake. Mrs Lucile Brisbane Spaulding was the manager and organiser for thirty-one years, retiring shortly after our visit, her long service being recognised by the award of an Honorary OBE.

At the time of our visit it was customary for every Cadet arriving in New York to receive a written invitation to use the Club by name via the ship's agent. There was always a warm welcome and, apart from Mrs Spaulding's home-made chocolate cake in the refrigerator, there was television which was a new experience for most of us to watch. There were social events, visits to the many places of interest and organised theatre trips; I remember three of us being taken to dinner and then on to the premier at the Radio City Music Hall of the film *Singing in the Rain.* There were undoubtedly some really kind and generous people in New York at that time.

The Chelsea Hotel was a place with a tremendous history; several survivors of the Titanic stayed for some time in this hotel as it was just a short distance from Pier 54 where the Titanic was supposed to dock. The hotel had been or was to become over the years the residence of many of the world's most famous writers, musicians, actors and directors. Writers such as Mark Twain, Dylan Thomas, Arthur C. Clarke, Arthur Miller, Quentin Crisp, Gore Vidal, Tennessee Williams, Allen Ginsberg, Robert Oppenheimer and Jean-Paul Sartre to name just a few. The hotel has been a home to actors and film directors such as Stanley Kubrick, Lillie Langtry,

Eddie Izzard, Kevin Elliot Gould, and Jane Fonda, Some of the most prominent musicians include Édith Piaf, Bob Dylan, Janis Joplin, Jimi Hendrix and Sid Vicious.

Sadly Charles R. Jackson, author of *The Lost Weekend,* was to commit suicide in his room at the Chelsea on September 21, 1968. It is also known as the place where the writer Dylan Thomas was staying when he died of alcohol poisoning the year after our visit on November 4, 1953, and where Nancy Spungen, girlfriend of Sid Vicious of the Sex Pistols, was to be found stabbed to death on October 12, 1978.

Two experiences I further recall of New York were the finding of the bloated body of a white man floating right alongside the ship berthed at Staten Island, a body which had surfaced after what the police told us from experience must have been at least a week in the sea. Not a pleasant sight before breakfast.

The other memory concerned the painting of the ship's side. We had eleven seamen on deck; good hard-working experienced ABs, but using paint brushes and rigging painting stretchers to lower themselves down the side, it took them the whole day to paint one side of our riveted ship. At Staten Island an American Liberty Ship, a WW2 welded ship of much the same size, berthed astern of us and a couple of sailors produced two long aluminium poles, to the head of which was attached at right angles what turned out to be rollers about two feet long. Filling a metal trough with grey paint, the two men then proceeded to paint the whole of the side of their own ship in the one day by walking along the quay. We were witnessing early use of the paint roller, common now in all DIY stores.

By contrast to the cosmopolitan experience of New York we were to complete our loading for South Korea in Charleston, South Carolina. Here most of the stevedores were huge but gently-spoken black Afro-Americans. We found them easy to work with but the attitude of the white supervisors difficult to tolerate; arrogant 'red-necks', men who spoke to their labour force as if slavery was still a fact of life, to which I suppose economically so it remained. After a run ashore to the movies we got into trouble on the segregated bus for sitting in the wrong part and refusing to move. It was only the bus driver threatening to throw us off and the kindly whispered advice of an old grey-haired black man patiently waiting to get home who said we, 'would only make the situation worse'; that got us to sit quietly fuming in the correct section of that bus.

Peter Dal II, loading in Charleston, South Carolina.

We finally topped off our cargo with 40 old street cars from Charleston, South Carolina, which were being sent as a gift to the people of Seoul, South Korea to replace the street cars destroyed during the invasion. The cars which appeared to have been originally built in Glasgow, or at least fitted with drive mechanism manufactured in Scotland, were extremely old and must have been replaced some years before but not scrapped. The only problem we had was that while a number of street cars were stowed fore and aft in the holds which were 83 feet long, those on deck were stowed athwartships and consequently hung several feet over each side of the ship and we were to transit the Panama Canal where we would have to lie alongside in the locks. We were initially delayed at the Canal but eventually passed through with the aid of large fenders and a dumb barge. We made a somewhat irregular track across the Pacific after bunkering in San Pedro, California, with diversions of course on several days to avoid rolling in heavy beam swells; to arrive finally in the anchorage at Inchon and join the war effort.

So what exactly was the Korean War about?

Chapter 10

The Korean War 1950 – 53

The Korean War was a war fought before the days of live television reporting and a full scale war which few people, unless they were directly involved, knew much about or really cared. It was a long way away on the other side of a world much larger than the world we know today, fought in a little country no larger than the area of England. It was a small country that few people in the UK had ever heard of until the North Korean Army swept over the border on the 25th June 1950. I spent over three years in Korean waters during that war and even I remained unaware of many of the aspects which have only recently come to light, facts which I thought might be of interest to this story.

North Korea and South Korea were two regimes imposed following the end of the Second World War when Stalin would not agree to general democratic elections for the whole of the Korean people. Prior to that Russian troops occupied the line north of the 38° parallel of latitude, the Americans to the south. Following elections in the South and the imposition of a communist state in the North, the two small independent countries emerged and the Russians and Americans forces withdrew except for a few advisors who remained to train and equip the growing armies of the new states.

The response to the invasion was swift, a resolution was passed in the UN just two days later and the United Nations went to war for the first time. The 16 countries who fought for the UN were Australia, Belgium/Luxembourg, Britain, Canada, Colombia, Ethiopia, France, Greece, Netherlands, New Zealand, Philippines, South Africa, South Korea, Thailand, Turkey and the United States and unofficially Japan. They were opposed by North Korea, China and unofficially Russia.

The North Koreans armed with Russian T34/85 tanks and working to a plan devised by Russian staff officers stormed down the Korean peninsula and in two months had forced the South Koreans and the rapidly arriving UN into a small perimeter only 38 miles wide around the port of Pusan. But General Douglas MacArthur, America's most famous soldier at that time serving as Military Governor of Japan, had been appointed overall commander of UN forces and you may say what you will about the man but his strategy on this occasion was exemplary.

Four days before he was appointed overall commander and only ten days after the invasion, he started his planners working on a counter invasion at Inchon, just south of the 38° parallel, to cut the North Koreans in two. On September 12/13 1950, just eleven weeks after the initial invasion, UN troops successfully landed at Inchon from 247 ships on the west coast of Korea and the breakout from the Pusan perimeter began. The North Koreans were driven out of South Korea and the UN advanced virtually right up to the mountain ranges on the Manchurian and Russian borders. The well-equipped army of North Korea had lost 50,000 men and been defeated in less than a month.

However, hiding in the mountains was a large section of a less well-equipped army but one of some 5 million men and on the 8th November 1950, in desperately cold conditions and I can tell you Korea is one of the coldest place I have ever been, the Chinese started their offensive. Despite horrendous casualties among the Chinese and tremendous battles by the UN, the Glorious Glosters defence of Hill 325 being one you may have heard about, the UN were gradually pushed back until they eventually held along the Han River, once again well into South Korea. The UN using carrier born aircraft and long-range bombers from Japan and Okinawa daily harassed the supply lines of the communists, while British Royal Marine Commandos and US Special forces made punitive raids along the coast. It was not long before the Chinese started to withdraw to a diagonal line drawn from approximately just south of the 38° parallel in the west to the 39°North in the east, conceding some territory. There the war was fought for the next two and a half years using huge tunnels and bunkers, much like the First World War with thousands of men being killed over the daily possession of a number of dirty brown battle-scarred hills, with names like the Hook and Pork Chop before eventually an armistice was agreed.

The Naval War had been one of complete dominance by the UN who always had at least six to eight aircraft carriers fighting while others rested in Japan. There were battleships and cruisers and a whole range of escorts and supply ships. HMS *Glory,* HMS *Ocean* & HMS *Theseus* were the British Carriers, HMAS *Sydney* was Australian while the Americans had more than a dozen carriers of varying sizes. One little known fact which has now emerged is that the Japanese supplied the minesweepers and crewed many of the landing craft used at Inchon in 1950.

Self portrait, winter 1952 aged 17 years, note American GI hat

The air war was very different. Initially the communist forces had superiority with over 400 MIG 15s powered by an engine whose design the UK had given the Russians. These aircraft could fly at 40,000 feet, some 10,000 feet higher than the initial US jets and, what is more, some were being flown by Russian pilots who have since been credited with shooting down over 1000 UN aircraft during that war. Most of the Russian fighter squadrons of that era were at some time given battle experience in the Korean skies and many aces developed with scores as high as our Battle of Britain pilots. Initially most UN fighters were propeller-driven Mustangs, Corsairs and Seafurys which were sitting ducks, although there were a number of credited claims of MIG 15s by propeller-driven US Mustangs and British-built Seafurys. Heavy UN losses meant the US was forced to send their latest Sabre Jet aircraft into battle and go into mass production of the aircraft; which proved superior to the MIG and was eventually flown by airmen of nearly all the UN countries. Despite the fact that the UN were not allowed hot pursuit into Manchuria and to attack the communist air bases, Chinese losses mounted to an unacceptable level due to better technology and, reluctantly, they came to the negotiating table.

Many people died in Korea including 710 British servicemen KIA (killed in action) and a further 1,263 missing in action that were never found. Many of these young men were doing their National Service which was extended from eighteen months to two years, others were volunteers. Several million people were casualties; there are no available figures for the communists but their ground troops out numbered the UN's by 18 to 1 and they died in their thousands for nothing. Korea remains divided today much as it was in 1950.

Korea – Inchon Air Attack

The Korean War was a hard fought and bitter battle in the air and on land but at sea we saw little of the hostilities, there being little opposition to the vast United Nation's Fleets around the peninsular. During my nearly four years running in new tanks and other heavy equipment from Japan, Guam and Taiwan we personally had little excitement and certainly no dangerous moments. There was some uncertainty one day off the east coast of Korea, north of the 38 parallel when, bound for Sok Cho Rhee to land a full cargo of Sherman tanks into landing craft unescorted, we were stopped by an American destroyer whose crew had obviously gone to action stations when we failed to respond to what they thought was the recognition signal for that particular day. Somebody had got it wrong and we were sure it was our allies. However, the sight of their own tanks on our decks convinced them we were really working for the US Military Transportation Service (MSTS) as we claimed and we were reluctantly allowed to proceed.

Another incident took place while we were anchored off Inchon one lovely summer's day, not far from the hospital ship *Repose* and scores of other merchant ships with the US Battleship *Missouri* and the British cruiser HMS *Belfast*; when a couple of Chinese MIG jet aircraft beat up the anchorage. The black American GI radio man on watch on the wing of the bridge with me dived for cover in the scuppers, the whites of his eyes wide with horror at this disturbance to his afternoon siesta in the sunshine. As I seem to recall only HMS *Belfast* returned fire. Flying at masthead height, the two Chinese jets were gone in a flash without, I think, causing any casualties amongst the crews sunbathing on the ships. That was really my only bit of real enemy action during the whole war but there were a number of interesting and dangerous or amusing incidents that took place in those years.

US Hospital Ship, Repose, Inchon 1952

Sherman Tanks

At the very outbreak of the Korean War a wise person in the US Military realised that there would be a need for some ships to be able to load, transport and discharge heavy equipment and especially tanks in the absence of sufficient large Landing Ship Tank (LSTs). The British had four wartime built heavy lift ships, each with three 120-ton derricks and the US Military Sea Transportation Service quickly chartered the SS *Peter Dal II* (ex *Empire Byng)* the *Empire Wallace* the *Empire Marshal and* the *Empire Viceroy* which together with the Norwegian sister ship *Belocean* loaded military cargoes in the United States and headed for Korean waters.

On arrival, *Peter Dal II* discharged in Inchon and Pusan her general military cargo plus street-cars for Seoul from the USA and headed for Yokohama to load Sherman battle tanks; for the fighting was relentless at that time and there was great need. We loaded a total of 83 tanks per voyage just one layer in the holds and another layer on deck, turning around in less than 24 hours. The tanks were then rushed across to Korea, up the east coast to a place just north of the 38 degree parallel called Sock Cho Rhee or to Inchon on the west coast; where we discharged them onto barges or individually into small LCTs. We did many such runs over the coming years, alternating with taking heavy bulldozers and large crawler cranes to Pusan and loading battle-damaged but expensive equipment brought back down the line to Masan. I know the equipment was expensive because the Americans at that time very oddly used to stencil paint on the side of each new piece of equipment going into battle a sign which read; *"This piece of equipment cost $........ take care of it".*

The Sherman tank was declared to us at 32 tons each, carrying some fuel and equipment and measured approximately 19.5 feet long, 9.5 feet wide and 9.5 feet high. This allowed us to stow 12 x 4 tanks facing fore and aft with two tanks in the middle athwartships, in each of numbers 2 & 3 holds, with one less in number 1 hold. They were secured with dunnage, wire lashings and bottlescrews and usually we had no problems with them moving in bad weather. However, one day we steamed past Moji and left the Inland Sea to cross the straits between Japan and Korea when we ran into a very heavy beam swell and the ship started to roll heavily. The rolling was soon accompanied by a tremendous crashing from number 2 hold and investigation revealed that the Sherman tank stowed athwartships in the middle on the port side had apparently not been lashed securely. With its brakes off and unsecured it was consequently on the move, rolling violently with considerable kinetic energy and weight directly on the riveted shell plating. Caterpillar tracks astride the main hull frames,; it careered up and down again to crash into its fellow bed mate.

The Mate sent the three Apprentices, by 1953 his most experienced seamen, together with Bill Oliver the Bosun to secure the brute. This turned out to be quite an exciting experience, for first of all we had to secure a heavy steel snatch block to one of the frames on the ship's port side above the rolling Sherman and another on the frames on the starboard side. Then rig wires from the two small fleeting winches inside the centre castle via the snatch blocks to secure to the large lifting lugs built into the four quarters of the tank. The most dangerous part was to jump on the violently moving tank and screw on large shackles to the end of the each set of wires. I seem to recall that I was to drive one of the winches but certainly the Bosun, who was not only a very fine seaman but also inclined to be a bit gung-ho, was the one to leap onto the tank. He quickly secured the slack wires and gradually we took up the weight until we had the tank under control and we manoeuvred it back into its correct stow and re-lashed it with wire and bottle screws. During the whole procedure the ship continued to roll heavily and I have often wondered in retrospect, and with the benefit of experience, why whoever was on the bridge at the time did not put the ship on a more suitable course to assist our efforts.

Chapter 11

Farewell to the Far East

Kure, a British Base, was one of the few ports in Japan that we did not visit while on charter for three years to the USMSTS, our cargoes being all American military ones; but by the end of the Korean War, the *Peter Dal II* was a familiar sight in all the major Japanese ports, which in turn were busy US Bases. Towards the very end of hostilities we did have a pleasant interlude away from the US Military, loading a full commercial cargo of wooden pit props for the mines in Korea – or were they perhaps railway sleepers? Whatever, we loaded them in the pretty anchorage off the town of Kagoshima in the south of the islands

Kagoshima – a delightful little ancient city built in a lovely fjord opposite the base of the active volcano Sakura Jima, set among fields of local Satsuma trees – was the place where British trading interests first landed in Japan setting up textile mills. Interestingly I found many people there spoke good English without a trace of an American accent unlike the rest of Japan where spoken English was common but Americanised. The people were also extremely honest and would run after one to return money or objects dropped in the street or left behind in a shop; it was difficult to relate the same people to those we had been brought up to despise during the Second World War. To get ashore from the ship in Kagoshima we had to use a boat, but I remember the Japanese super cargo in charge of the loading arrived in his own sea plane. He was a charming man, I believe a younger member of the one of Japan's major industrial families, who had been I recall in the Japanese Navy serving as liaison officer on a German submarine. He told us of his adventures when the U-boat was forced to surface after being damaged and he was captured; leading to his internment in Canada. He very kindly entertained the Captain and some of the ship's officers at a proper Geisha House. This turned out to be a real novel and classical experience for all of us rough sailors who, for two years on the coast, were more used to a less cultural and less accomplished experience than that of these refined young ladies serving us tea and playing weird instruments, unsettling to the English ear.

Yokohama was really our home base from where on occasion we were able to visit Tokyo and see the famous classical Kabuki Theatre, climb Mount Fuji, and swim in the sea at Kamakura below the wonderful cherry blossom trees in their April splendour surrounding the Giant Buddha. Mainly however we enjoyed the fruits of the sailors' paradise that Japan was to offer during those times. We were paid a 150% War Bonus while in Korean Waters up until the Armistice was signed; prices were low in Japan, the pound sterling had not been devalued and we were able to get US$4.25 or 1000 Yen to £1.00 and we lived well.

A number of lasting impressions; the slight unavoidable taste of fish in the eggs and bacon from the chickens and pigs fed on fishmeal, the strong smells from the countryside and particularly on the day the "honey cart" collected the contents from the primitive toilets for use as fertilizer on the farm crops. The taxis were in the early 1950s, almost without exception British-built Morris Cowleys or Oxfords. The exceptions were the occasional ex-US serviceman's large imported American personal cars. Japanese-built taxis did not appear until late 1953 and these were small poorly-built Daihatsu, not in those days our vehicle of choice.

Pre-WW2 the major Japanese shipping companies employed British Masters and Chief Engineers, of whom many finished their days in Japan and whose graves can or used to be seen in a Christian Cemetery on the Bluff Hill overlooking Yokohama Harbour. It was interesting for me, particularly in the light of my subsequent career, to note at the time that the best Japanese ships of the liner companies NSK and OSK always berthed in Yokohama with orders coming over the loudhailer in clear English:

"Send away the Headline"

or

"Send away the springs"

I imagine such nonsense soon disappeared as during the following years Japan's economy boomed; consequently I noticed by the time I became a London Pilot, English was not a strong subject on the Japanese ships I piloted.

Sinking of the *Toya Maru*

1954 was a bad year for typhoons in the Far East and Typhoon Mary was a particularly unpredictable beast. At 12:00 hours on September 26, 1954, it was proceeding north-east at a speed of more than 100 kilometres an hour and was predicted to reach the Tsugaru Strait at around 17:00 hours.

At 11:00 hours, the passenger ferry *Toya Maru* arrived at Hakodate after its first journey that day from Aomori. She was originally scheduled to return at 14:40 hours, to arrive at Aomori just before Typhoon Mary. However, due to the severe weather, another ferry the *Dai II Seikan Maru*, a somewhat poorer quality vessel, could not depart on its scheduled journey to Hakodate. Therefore, passengers and vehicles were transferred to the *Toya Maru* delaying departure. The captain of the *Toya Maru* decided to cancel crossing at 15:10 hours.

At 17:00 hours, following heavy rainfall in Hakodate, the weather cleared up and the outlook improved. The captain, presuming that the typhoon had now passed as predicted, decided to proceed with the journey for Aomori. However, by this time the typhoon had slowed and was predicted to stay over the strait for an entire day. Strangely, the typhoon was gaining strength over the Inland Sea instead of losing strength as would be traditional and therefore normal.

At 18:39 the *Toya Maru* departed from Hakodate with approximately 1,300 people aboard. Shortly after sailing the wind picked up rapidly coming from a SSE direction. The captain, seeking shelter, anchored on the lee side of Hakodate at 19:01 to await an improvement in the weather; however, the ship immediately dragged her anchor and heavy seas came aboard on the vehicle decks and entered the engine room causing immediate loss of power. A distress call was made to which we in the *Peter Dal II* responded racing up the coast with an enormous following sea and very strong winds.

At 22:26 hours, the *Toya Maru* beached and a further SOS call was made. However, the wind and waves were so strong that the ferry heeled over unable to remain upright and, at around 22:43 hours, the *Toya Maru* capsized and sank in the Tsaguru Strait several hundred metres off the shore of Hakodate. Of the 1,309 on board only 150 people survived, while 1,159 (1,041 passengers, 73 crew and 41 others) died.

By the time we arrived later in the night we could find nothing with our floodlights and without radar we were achieving little steaming in circles but put our own vessel in danger. We finally anchored, only to find on what turned out to be a still clear and calm dawn that we had narrowly missed the upturned hull of the ferry and had anchored virtually alongside what had become the tomb of so many people lying there, still and menacing in the early morning sunshine.

In 1954 the officers and crew came to the completion of our two-year Articles of Agreement and the company decided to send our good but somewhat boisterous Liverpool crew home and replace them with an Indian crew. We three Apprentices, not having come to the completion of our four-year indentures, were told we would be retained aboard until the ship returned to the United Kingdom on completing the voyage or completed another two years on articles, whichever was the shortest; such was the standard practice of the ship owner in those days when the Apprentices were exploited as cheap labour. Luckily as the senior Apprentice, although the youngest, I was promoted to un-certificated Third Officer in order to save the company the expense of flying another new officer out to the Far East.

I was happy but thought my two colleagues badly treated for they were to subsequently complete their indentures and remain in the ship for nearly another year, against their wishes, before the ship finally returned to the UK. *Peter Dal II* finally returned home on the 22nd October 1955 after circumnavigating the world once more by way of British Columbia, South Africa, Aden, India, Japan again, and BC again. David Hopkins, who was I think eighteen months older than me, was only a few weeks junior and was also promoted to third officer shortly after me as a day worker, I having bought the second mate's sextant for £4 being given the watch keeping and navigating experience which was to be of great benefit to me later. Colin Fowles, who was something like six months junior to us although older than me, completed his indentures on that final long voyage home in the *Peter Dal II;* which was to be not entirely without incident.

Tahsis, British Columbia

With the completion of the Korean War, the US Government finally released us from our charter to the Military Sea Transportation Service on the 19th March 1955, and in great spirits we headed across the Pacific to load a full cargo of lumber for South Africa. Passage across the Pacific on this occasion was idyllic once two days clear of the Japanese coast, smooth long swells and seas surmounted by blue skies by day and clear starlit skies by night, excellent star sights and never any doubt as to our position. This time we arrived with incredibly clear visibility to see the snow-capped mountains of Vancouver Island long before embarking the pilot for a large lumber mill owned by the Gibson Mills and East Asiatic Company at Tahsis. Situated at the head of the beautiful steep-sided Tahsis Inlet (part of the Nootka Sound and a place where in 1778 Captain James Cook sought shelter and landed on his voyage to find the North West Passage), this idyllic sheltered inlet is protected from the violent Pacific storms by its geography, making the docking facilities a valuable asset together with the deep water for ocean-going ships.

Not a large community, it consisted of a newly built lumber mill (the previous one having burnt down in 1948), some large dormitories for the mill workers, a few small houses for the managing staff, a church, and a bowling alley-cum-recreational hall and coffee shop. The only way in then was by ship or seaplane, the fjord being surrounded by impassable steep but beautiful mountains. Communication was by radio telephone and newspapers arrived twice per week by seaplane. The community was still and quiet, hidden among the snow-covered pine and cedar forest with little inlets in the fjord being fed by cascading mountain streams. The steep mouths of the streams were surrounded by thousands of large salmon waiting anxiously and impatiently their turn to climb the cascading fast running water to spawn. The fish were so thick on occasion the Pilot would stop the engines as we glided through the larger silvery shoals. The local lumberjacks were able to scoop a choice fish out of the water into small open canoes, rejecting and throwing back all but the finest fish. We had so much salmon to eat for the next few months we became blasé; I imagine such fine meat was somewhat boring for the long term inhabitants. The community of some 2,500 people was one of many cultures from Pakistani to Pole and other displaced Europeans following the Second World War, working in the mill and on the logs for about $480 Canadian per month and a five-day week.

About the time we were in Tahsis a cougar came down off the mountainside and grabbed a four-year-old child in the snow-covered backyard of one of the few company houses in the village. Bravely the fourteen-year-old girl acting as baby sitter while the parents partied in a neighbouring house saved the child by great presence of mind. Acting with tremendous courage she quickly wrapped a leather harness around her own arm and shouting loudly thrust that arm into the jaws of the cougar which, startled by her shouts and rapid approach, had dropped the small wriggling child bleeding into the snow. The parents and neighbours alerted to the attack came out rapidly and armed, shooting the cougar dead, but it had been a close call and a clear example of outstanding calculated bravery. I seemed to remember the heroine was small of stature and very wiry.

Not so brave were a party of apprentices and junior officers who went for a walk up into the pine forest one quiet Sunday afternoon during a rest day from their ship. One of Reardon Smith's of Cardiff tramp ships, possibly the *Indian City or* certainly one of her sister ships, she lay still and sleepily quiet alongside the wooden quay while emitting the occasional wisp of steam off into the still cool but sunlit crisp air. The party on exploration were walking noisily after lunch up the only trail at the head of the inlet laughing and fooling about among the tall elegant pine, beautiful smelling cedar trees and silver birch, free from the confines of the ship. Further up the long trail two students from the University of British Columbia continued, engrossed in a traditional task in a warm sunlit clearing, ignoring the sounds of jolly jack ashore as the party noisily approached.

Now it just so happens that the two students were full-blooded members of the First Nations tribes that had inhabited the Nootka Sound regions for some four thousand years. On vacation they had killed a bear and, stripped to the waist and somewhat bloodied and bent over at their task, were skinning the carcase with large hunting knives. Hearing the imminent arrival of the sailors they rose out of the bracken to their feet to greet them.

Shock, miscomprehension and terror swept through the party who, having perhaps been subjected by the Seafarers Education Service to too many Hollywood western films, took off in fright back to the ship at great speed. The story went at the time that the ship's radio officer even got into contact with the Royal Canadian Mounted Police to report his suspicions that the First Nations were on the warpath, but I cannot believe that although I seem to remember reading it in the newspaper *Vancouver Sun* (or was it *Post?*).

Bhandary – Long Beach California

Following the 1947 partition of the sub-continent of India and establishment of the republics of Pakistan and India, most of the seamen who were Moslems based in Bombay and Calcutta remained in India and continued their employment mainly on British ships. However after a while the Indian Government, at the insistence of the Hindu majority, brought in rules which meant that each ship employing an Indian crew had to take a mix of both Moslems and Hindus. This meant the employment of both Moslem and Hindu Bhandary or cooks usually sharing one galley, a recipe for trouble and strife.

By early 1955 I was still serving as Third Officer of the heavy-lift ship *Peter Dal II* on a passage from Vancouver, British Columbia with a full cargo of timber for Durban, South Africa. The ship had been out from the United Kingdom for over three years and was not in fact to return home until the following November. We had left the UK with a Liverpool crew but had, after the first two years on the Japanese and Korean coast, changed to lascars from Calcutta and an extra small galley had been installed in the redundant gunners' accommodation on the upper poop.

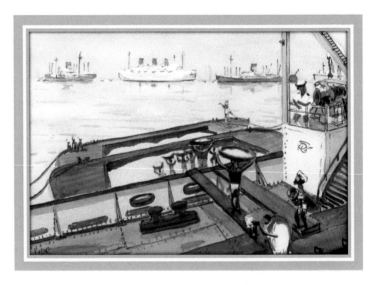

Loading salt in Aden for Calcutta

With delays at the Panama Canal and the extra cost involved, it had been decided to make the 12,125 mile 35-day voyage via Cape Horn instead of the shorter route via the canal which meant we put into Long Beach California for bunkers.

We were only there for the day and the mates shared the day on duty, starting of course with the junior officer – me! During my watch in the morning the Senior Electrician, a man in his early forties, came running across the top of the timber deck cargo from the direction of the after accommodation to where I was talking with the elderly American watchman at the gangway amidships.

"Quick get an ambulance," he shouted, "there's been a fight on the poop and the Bhandary is lying on the deck with his brains coming out."

"I'll call the ambulance," the watchman said I thought afterwards perhaps rather too eagerly.

"Tell the mate what has happened will you, while I go aft with the First Aid kit," I replied and started off at a run.

Arriving on the poop there was bedlam, angry voices shouting and screaming as the Moslems faced the hated young Hindus. Knives were out, being waved threateningly in the clear blue sky, and already I could hear the sound of distant sirens as the 'cavalry' came to the rescue.

The shouting stopped and the crowd opened on my approach to reveal the body of the Bhandary dramatically writhing and moaning in agony on the deck outside the new galley. His head was bleeding profusely, the blood mixed with a thick grey-brown substance flecked with small white pieces which presumably the electrician had imagined in his panic to be the poor man's brains. I scrapped some of it away with my hands and discovered a rather small cut in the scalp and realised the substance was curry and the white pieces were rice!

Somebody had not liked his early lunch, suspecting it to contain pork or something taboo to his particular religion, and promptly crowned the cook.

Another of many such disputes quick to escalate but soon calmed down by the appearance of the Serang and Donkey Man and several armed Long Beach Policemen. The Bhandary was taken off to the hospital to have some stitches, and the captain saw the funny side of the incident until he received the bill for the ambulance and medical treatment from the Agent just before sailing. The electrician as one can imagine had his leg pulled un-mercilessly all the way to Durban.

Chapter 12

RFA Eaglesdale – Suez

After studying at my own expense for my Second Mate's Certificate of Competency at King Edward VII's Nautical College in Stepney, I turned my back on what I had come to consider the sordid commercial world. Following an interview at the Admiralty in an office overlooking Horse Guards Parade, I was invited to join the Royal Fleet Auxiliary Service. I was glad to be going back to the fresh air at sea after smoggy London, having had several months during which I had cycled every day down the then cobbled stones of the Commercial Road to Stepney, having come through the City of London from Balham where I had been staying with my dear elderly Uncle Ernie and Auntie Gertie.

My first appointment was as Third Officer of RFA *Eaglesdale,* joining on the 3rd August 1956 in Swansea. Built in 1942 for the Ministry of War Transport, an average sized freighting tanker of 8,032 Gross tons and Deadweight of 12,040 tons, with a speed of ten knots, she had a steam 3-cylinder triple expansion engine. Built with steam engines because the UK's diesel engine manufacturing capacity was full, these ships were generally termed as 'troublesome'. Ending the war in the Far East Fleet Train it is interesting that her Chief Engineer was awarded the OBE, possibly for keeping the old girl going, surmounting difficulties at that important time.

I relieved an ex-naval Commander serving as Un-certificated Third Officer, a man who went on to take his "Merchant Service Certificate of Competency" because by that time the RFA no longer accepted the "Masters Certificate of Service" which appear to have been handed out to all and sundry by the Royal Navy at the end of WW2. This officer was eventually to command in the RFA. I had spent five years with dry cargo ships carrying everything from bulk salt, iron ore, lumber to very heavy lifts of locomotives and railway rolling stock, tugs, landing craft and barges, tanks, cranes and assorted general cargo, including grey flannel trousers to Zanzibar. But as I had never been on a tanker before I was to learn 'the basics' from the Chief Officer, a boisterous lively Irish man known as "Black Sam Dunlop"; an officer who went on to distinction as Commodore RFA

Captain S C Dunlop DSO, OBE, CBE at the time of the Falkland Campaign and who died in 2008.

'The basics' were that tankers such as RFA *Eaglesdale* in those days loaded at about 1000 tons per hour, usually by gravity, from large tanks ashore. It normally took only about 12 hours to load, while discharging was done by the ship's own steam-driven pumps at a maximum of 400 tons per hour, taking twice as long. Tankers were rarely in port for long and usually the oil terminals were miles from civilization; most of our time was to be spent at sea and there were few opportunities for visiting places of interest or socialising but good prospects of saving money. RFA *Eaglesdale* was to carry Furnace Fuel Oil for discharge at Naval Ports or into the new Fast Fleet Tankers or commercial chartered cargoes of crude oil between the oil producing countries and refineries in Europe.

Tankers were particularly dangerous in those years and frankly the equipment and training then was a bit 'hit and miss'. The heavy black fuel oil or volatile crude oil poured gravity fed into the ship at a steady rate, not being slowed down from on shore as each relatively small tank neared completion, as one might expect, because ashore there was just no way of telling when on the ship we were to change tanks; all they knew was the amount we were expected to load. Until that was loaded, the safe distribution among the tanks – divided into three across the beam of the ship and eight or nine fore and aft – was down to the Deck Officers.

Loading and discharging oil cargo was carried out to a plan devised by the Chief Officer taking care to maintain stability and avoid stress which might cause the ship's hull to become deformed through hogging or sagging. With the Chief Officer in overall charge and usually on deck during the whole loading process, the Second and Third Officers worked six hours on deck and six hours off. With the oil pouring in relentlessly, careful observation down through the open tank tops was needed as the oil rose rapidly to the top of the tank and manic manipulation of very large heavy valves on the main deck, was needed first to crack open the next tank and ensure all was well and then to rapidly shut down the completing tank and fully open the next centre tank or two wing tanks. This before the black oil shot under pressure like a fountain up through the narrow tank lids to cover everything and everyone around. Many a tanker was to wear the black scars of negligent watchkeeping in those days. I was fortunate in narrowly avoiding just such a catastrophe in RFA *Eaglesdale* myself when one of my lascar seamen, struggling with a manual task at the limit of his physical ability, was slow in opening a tank valve before I could shut off the nearly full tank. In an endeavour to load the tank to capacity, I had waited almost too long before changing tanks and watched in horror as the oil reached the underside of the deck below my feet and with a whoosh stopped two inches inside the tank lid before falling back with gravity as the adjoining tank valve was fully opened. Once again luck was on my side in life.

In loading to capacity we were aware that, particularly with crude oil, highly volatile gases would build up in the ullage – that gap between the oil surface and the underside of the deck. Fortunately this is a situation which has since been avoided by the insertion of inert gases from the main engine. However in the years before such a solution, the tanks loaded or in ballast prior to tank-cleaning on passage were a death trap to seamen. This was particularly so during the process of tank-cleaning itself, when the tanks were washed mechanically with hot water to remove the oil sludge residue clinging to the internal frames and ladders. A residue which often had to be finished off with hand-held steam hoses; for there often remained lethal gases sufficient to take the life of the unsuspecting seaman sent in to clean them.

I remember seeing, and have somewhere a small faded photograph I took a couple of years later when passing through the Suez Canal, showing the remains of a wartime built T2 Tanker the *Stanvac Japan*, lying at anchor in the Bitter Lakes with the whole of the main deck looking as though it had been opened with a giant tin opener. The tanker, which had left Bombay in ballast on a Saturday night for the Persian Gulf, was about 500 miles north-west of Bombay when on the Sunday 19th October 1958 a violent explosion occurred, blowing off the entire midshiphouse of the ship, including the bridge. The ship had a total complement of 70, including 54 Indians recruited at Bombay. I believe a number of the 51 survivors were badly injured.

Twenty of the crewmen, 10 British officers and 10 Indians, were killed including the Master but the 2nd Mate, who I believe was an officer by the name of Gordon Allely had a remarkable escape being in the wheelhouse at the time. He came to, finding himself trapped in the sinking bridge section with the hull of the ship steaming away from him. The wheelhouse doors were jammed and the story is that he managed to escape only by breaking the wheelhouse windows with his bare hands. How the engineers and those aboard the hulk managed to rescue him I have no idea. The Court of Inquiry held on 12th–15th Oct 1959, was unable to ascertain the probable cause of the explosion owing to the absence of any direct evidence, as all involved on the bridge and deck were killed.

Tankers were indeed unforgiving in those days.

RFA *Eaglesdale* was immaculate with a lascar crew but obviously my tramp ship uniforms did not pass muster with the Master, for as soon as we reached Gibraltar, he marched me ashore to the local branch of the naval tailor Gieves, later to become Gieves and Hawkes of Saville Row and insisted they open an account for me, make me a new superfine doeskin number one uniform and fit me out with a full set of tropical gear. When asked how much a month I would pay by banker's order for this privilege, my captain immediately announced that I should not be expected to pay more than £2 per month; and so it was for a number of years. I was astonished at their generosity but I suppose it paid off for I kept my account going with them through my days as a self-employed Trinity House Pilot and right up until pilotage was reorganised and I became a Port of London Authority Pilot and received rather different quality but free uniforms.

I spent nine months in RFA *Eaglesdale*, mainly running across the North Atlantic to the Mediterranean. On my 22nd birthday the 31st October 1956 the RFA joined the fleet for Operation Musketeer; the landing by British and French troops to retake the Suez Canal which had been nationalised by the Egyptians. RFA *Eaglesdale* arrived a few hours after the main landings and, being a freighting tanker, was left in the outer anchorage from where we topped up the smaller replenishment tankers with Furnace Fuel Oil. Nothing much exciting happened to us apart from the continuous air activity overhead, but a lot of souvenirs appeared as we topped up various ships and all the officers left Suez with brand new AK47 rifles which were not much use without the ammunition and which, because obviously we could not take them home, ended up somewhere in the ocean. I do remember the 2nd Officer of one of the Ranger Class tankers offered to sell me what he called a Maltese yacht for £24. The so-called yacht turned out to be a Suez Canal Bum boat complete with drawers and cupboards for all the sale trinkets. Naturally I declined the kind offer and hopefully the poor owner got it back eventually. Once empty of FFO we left for an unusual assignment but one which required considerable work cleaning the residue of thick black oil out of the tanks in order to carry fresh drinking water to Gibraltar.

Following three delightful weeks cleaning tanks and loading the fresh water in Casablanca very slowly through small canvas hoses, it was then discharged in Gibraltar and RFA *Eaglesdale* set out across the North Atlantic to load a commercial cargo of crude oil in Curacao for Rotterdam.

The Lone Canoeist – 1956

Rolling gently along at ten knots in the north-east trade winds, some six hundred miles north east of the Sombrero Passage between the Leeward Islands and the Windward Islands, we had not seen another ship for days. On the 12th December 1956, the second officer Dai Thomas and I had just taken a sun sight to obtain the noon latitude after which I went down for lunch in the saloon, situated in the after section of the ship. The Indian steward served me with a delicious curry and momentarily disappeared out the door onto the after deck to enjoy the cool breeze as I tucked in to my large steaming plate full, only for him to come flying back in shouting excitedly; *"Sahib come quickly, come quickly, small boat."*

The Lone Canoeist – 1956

I dropped my fork and ran out on the deck following the steward to the starboard side and looked to see where he was pointing. Sure enough, there rising and disappearing on the swell was a small boat rapidly being left behind. It was already difficult to see but the steward assured me it had one man in it.

I quickly ran back along the flying bridge to the navigating bridge to raise the alarm and, while the second officer put the wheel hard to starboard, I called the Master and warned the engine room to stand by for some engine movements. Sluggishly the old tanker came round and the second officer brought her back onto the reciprocal course. We scanned the sea with our binoculars as the Master asked unanswerable questions, but the second officer had not seen the boat and I had only caught a glimpse of it between waves a hundred yards astern. Now none of us could see it and to make matters worse a heavy rain squall came drifting down on the trade winds. The Master reduced speed and we all searched until at last we saw a small dot appear on the top of a big swell and altered course towards it.

The Master Captain Rowling carefully manoeuvred the ship slowly upwind of what we thought to be a casualty. The Deck Serang had prepared a cargo net for the side and the deck crew stood on the rolling main deck with heaving lines and lifebuoys as we drifted down beam on to a remarkable sight.

Here in the middle of the North Atlantic sat a fair-headed and red-bearded sunburnt European in a folding canvas canoe. Strapped across the canoe was a paddle with lifejackets secured to the ends to make an outrigger. Secured to what seemed another paddle was what looked like a shirt rigged as a sail. The man calmly sat there, smoking a cigarette while he took our photographs.

We shouted to him asking if he needed help; he stared back at us silently. We asked who he was and a variety of questions querying whether he needed rescuing or wanted food or water. He studiously ignored us staring across the rolling swell as if we were mad and not himself. He neither raised a hand to wave nor uttered a word.

The Master had a dilemma; we obviously could not take the man forcefully from the water for his own safety. He would have been difficult to catch anyway even if we had launched a lifeboat. He had ignored our offers of assistance, just what more could we have done? The decision was made we would leave him to his devices and proceed on our way, reporting by radio his presence to other shipping and the maritime authorities.

We slowly turned back onto a south-westerly course and with three prolonged blasts on the ship's whistle wished him farewell; he sat calmly in the canoe rising and falling on the swell ignoring us as we sailed away.

Arriving in Willemstad, Curacao we were to boiler-clean before loading when fire broke out in the engine room. In no time black smoke was billowing out through the engine room skylights and on somebody's thoughtless instructions a lascar fire party started pouring sea water from the boat deck through the engine room skylights on to the machinery below. Fortunately the Second Officer Dai Thomas had put on the breathing apparatus and organised the deck serang and I to back him up clearing his safety lines while he attempted to get below the fire with a fire extinguisher. Despite being soaked from the efforts of the excitable party above, he was successful in putting out quite a small fire very quickly. The water damage to the main electrical switchboard took much longer to resolve.

Daily sailing 27ft whaler from RFA Eaglesdale nr Curacao 1956

Whaler sailing, Willemstad, Curacao, 1956

Many weeks later after the engine room fire delayed us loading in Curacao and gave me the chance to sail in the steady NE Trade winds with the purser dozing forward, most afternoons in the ship's recreational 27-foot Montague rigged whaler that we were fortunate to carry, we eventually returned to the United Kingdom after discharging a full cargo of crude oil for Rotterdam. Here the Master received a letter from the *lone canoeist's* publisher enquiring if anyone had thought to take a photograph? Well in those days few of us carried a camera and certainly nobody had a video camera; they hadn't even been invented. The only photograph was a belated effort the Second Officer took but by that time the gallant doctor was drifting astern with his thoughts, a mere speck occasionally cresting a wave.

We did discover the man's name was I recall Doctor Lindmann, a German who had gone into a sports shop in Bavaria, bought a folding canoe, taken a ship to the Canary Islands, stocked up with canned food and paddled out of the harbour bound for the West Indies. He had not communicated with us, for he did not want to be rescued or assisted in any way and felt that any signal he made might have been misinterpreted. It appears he was pleased we left him to cross the North Atlantic without help but the following day he capsized in the heavy swell and lost his camera, fresh water and all his remaining tinned provisions. He survived the next six or seven weeks living on rain water and flying fish but eventually landed on a beach on, I think, St Thomas. He needed the photographs to publish in a book he was to write of his adventure.

After discharging her commercial crude oil cargo in Rotterdam, during the carriage of which we flew the red ensign rather than the blue ensign of the RFA, *Eaglesdale* crossed the North Sea to Chatham where she was to de-store her future unknown. I left for leave and to plan for marriage to Sally, the lovely girl I had become engaged to prior to joining the ship.

RFA *Robert Dundas*

Although in those days voyages with the RFA could be long, and officers and crew signed on for Two Year Articles of Agreement, the personnel staff did try on occasion to accommodate important family arrangements; but it was rare, with a shortage of officers, that one's plans worked out. It was with some luck therefore that, having told the Marine Superintendent that I planned to get married on October 5th 1957 at Holy Trinity Church in Folkestone, I was sent on the 20th July 1957 to Portsmouth to join the small coastal store carrier RFA *Robert Dundas* as Second Officer. Built in 1938 of 1124 Gross Tonnage and some 222 feet long, the ship was powered by a six-cylinder diesel engine and had seen better days and more dangerous days at Malta during the war and at the Normandy Landings.

Now she was engaged on a fairly relaxed peacetime routine, moving pieces of equipment and stores between various Admiralty Establishments circumnavigating the United Kingdom. The ship was in Portsmouth loading for Loch Ewe a beautiful large deep-water loch on the west coast of Scotland which had seen much service during World War Two as a convoy rendezvous and departure point. In the 1950s the Admiralty still kept the necessary buoys and anti-submarine net to protect the entrance handy on site. The cargo for Loch Ewe was replacement buoys and nets. We were to return to Portsmouth via the Pentland Firth to Rosyth, The Tyne and

Chatham. It was to be a pleasant two summer months with some idyllic weather for which I was truly thankful because my cabin, which smelt perpetually damp, had just the one door which opened onto what proved to be a very wet deck in anything over a moderate sea. I certainly would not have liked to have been on the same run in the winter months.

Sailing one beautiful quiet and still summer's afternoon, with the sea like glass and crowds of people enjoying the weekend sunshine, we approached the entrance to Portsmouth Harbour chugging along purposely through the home-coming yachts just about the time many people were sitting down for tea and cakes at the harbour side cafes. Now at the entrance to Portsmouth old town harbour there is a small hut on a long narrow pier which HM Customs used as a hailing station to establish where ships and other craft of interest were bound to or from. As we approached the hailing station Alec Bee the Chief Officer, seeing the small figure of a customs official coming scuttling out of the cabin along the pier with a megaphone, walked to the port wing of the bridge and waited.

Across the still calm air came the bellow, *"Where are you bound Robert Dundas?"* The Chief Officer Alec had what we used to call a North Atlantic voice; more used to being heard from the forecastle in the middle of a howling gale than in the genteel tea-rooms of Old Portsmouth. Raising his megaphone he bellowed in a broad Scottish accent *"Loch Ewe"* in reply.

Now I have to say the effect in 1957 of such a simple truthful delivery had quite a startling effect upon those on the shore watching the rough sailors going to sea. The heads came around, the tea cups went down and mothers covered the ears of their children. I cannot be sure what they imagined he had said but I think if today he had actually bellowed an expletive sadly not one head would have turned.

Service in the *Robert Dundas* worked out well for us, allowing me sufficient time at home to get married and set up our first home. However we had a disastrous honeymoon in an ex-Coastguard Cottage on the cliff tops at Prawle Point in South Devon, a cottage without electricity but lit by Tilly gas lamps where unfortunately both Sally and I were to succumb to the virulent Asian flu which hit the country in 1957. The working Coastguards in the neighbouring cottage, knowing we were on honeymoon, did not realise when we did not appear outside that we were both ill and imagined I think that we were too preoccupied with other matters as the milk bottles mounted up outside the door.

Chapter 13

Loading Ammunition

I joined the Royal Fleet Auxiliary Armament Store Issuing Ship *Retainer* on a cold wet day at Hepburn-upon-Tyne as Third Officer just before she completed her conversion at Swan Hunter's Shipyard in November 1957.

Originally built for the China Navigation Company's Hong Kong, China Coast – Australia service in 1950 and named *Chungking*, she was of 9,498 gross tons and had been a cargo passenger liner carrying 48 first-class passengers, 320 third-class and 265 passengers in the tween decks. Built at Scotts Shipbuilding Co Ltd at Greenock, and powered by them with a six-cylinder Scott–Doxford engine, she had a service speed of 15 knots but was capable of doing more. With dimensions of 477 x 62 x 35 feet and with a loaded draught of 25 feet she proved, due to the changing political situation in China, surplus to requirements and almost at once was sold with her sister ship *Changchow* to the Admiralty. Both were earmarked as Armament Store Issuing Ships but both had to wait for conversion and be chartered out until there was space available in the very busy British shipyards and the financial opportunity occurred. *Retainer,* as she was named for RFA service, had been chartered to Messageries Maritimes, Buries Markes and Montship to name a few but now finally she was ready to begin a long and valuable lifetime serving the Royal Navy around the world.

Prior to taking up station in warmer climes at Malta with the Mediterranean Fleet, we sailed for Portsmouth to load her cargo of naval armaments. These were loaded from barges with *Retainer* moored at buoys in the middle of Portsmouth Harbour. It seemed a strange place to me to be loading such a dangerous cargo and I recalled the devastation that had occurred in Halifax and at least two ports in world when earlier ammunition ships had exploded. However risk assessment was not in fashion then; and the port had considerable experience in handling ammunition to warships, didn't it?

Well we were loading anti-submarine missiles called "squid" into number 3 hold and about to cease work for lunchtime when I decided, as the duty deck officer, to watch the final sling of "squid" come aboard from the boat deck before joining the Chief Officer David Evans for an aperitif in the Wardroom (which overlooked number 4 hold). Standing with the after wardroom door open, I was horrified when the strop holding the "squid" parted and whoosh the missiles disappeared down the lower hold. The Chief Officer's spontaneous reaction I will always remember, for as quick as a flash he turned to the bar steward and said what might well have been his last words:

"Steward, a large pink gin quick and put it on the Third Officer's chit!"

RFA Retainer, Gibraltar, 1958

Ammunition was obviously safer than I imagined; the "squids" bounced harmlessly amongst the scattering armament store workers and we all breathed again; the only injury being to my personal bar bill.

The Admiral's Missing Barge

While at Portsmouth as Duty Officer of RFA *Retainer*, I was visited late one night by some highly indignant Dockyard Policemen who wanted to arrest some of our young deck boys who, it seems, while bored and waiting in the Dockyard for our liberty boat to bring them off to the ship; had discovered the Admiral's beautiful green barge in an adjacent berth with the ignition key still in place. Temptation, fuelled with a certain amount of Dutch courage imbibed earlier, got the better of them and they took off in grand style. Their noisy boisterous departure had however been spotted and the authorities took off in pursuit.

Fortunately for the culprits the Admiral's barge was much faster than the pursuing policemen who were soon lost during a wild circumnavigation of Portsmouth Harbour. Having led their pursuers a merry dance, the barge had been returned without so much as a scratch to its moorings just in time for the culprits to scurry into the routine liberty boat and back to *Retainer.*

The policemen however duly tracked the culprits down and they wanted blood. When I established how the alleged boat thieves had managed to start the barge and suggested to them that it had perhaps been somewhat irresponsible of somebody to leave the key in the ignition, I sensed the representatives of the law were on the back foot. When it became apparent that the barge had been returned without damage I knew the boys were off the hook, and I was able to enquire of the policemen whether in fact they would be seeking to arrest the culprits if they had in fact been young RN Midshipmen and not very young MN deck boys letting their hair down.

"Well, Sir, under the circumstances we would have a quiet word with the Duty Officer and leave it to him," was the fair and honest reply.

"Well, Sergeant, I assure you I will bring this matter to the attention of the Captain in the morning and he, I am sure, will discipline the culprits fairly as he thinks appropriate."

As the departing policemen disembarked, leaving the boys to sleep it off, it did cross my mind that my popularity on the mess deck might well have been enhanced – not a bad thing for a new young Third officer finding his feet early in a long voyage.

Medical Matters

In the 1950s the National Health Service was in full swing. Doctors were in full employment and in short supply ashore; a few of those going to sea appeared to me to be in the main eccentric or ex-service men who could not settle ashore. *Retainer* was sent a man who to my eyes was definitely one of the former. He looked a bit like Max Wall, the famous comedian, and in fact walked something like him. He had joined the ship in a hurry abandoning his car for some reason in Sloane Square, London and I believe leaving a private practice.

Once he discovered the ship was outward bound for at least a year with the Mediterranean Fleet based in Malta, a strict Catholic country, he began to order his medical supplies. Now I don't know whether he considered our crew to be composed of sexual athletes of Olympian ability or where he thought they would have the opportunity to make use of them or whether he imagined there might be financial benefit in having such a large stock in a Catholic country, where such items were forbidden, but the Doctor ordered thousands of condoms for the ship. These were stowed in the newly equipped hospital built on the poop in splendid isolation; in fact the hospital was packed with cardboard cartons stacked everywhere.

RFA Retainer off Gibraltar

Now the outward passage across the Bay of Biscay had been rough with a heavy south-westerly swell causing the ship to role heavily. On the Sunday morning Captain's Inspection somewhere off Lisbon, Captain Tommy Hill with the Chief Officer David Evans together with the Doctor in tow made their way aft to the hospital across a gently rolling deck. The first thing they noticed was water spilling out between the bottom of the beautifully varnished door and the very high storm sill which had been incorporated to prevent seawater getting into the hospital. Something was amiss. The door was unlocked and opened cautiously to reveal a disaster – the hospital was full of water into which the Doctor's precious cargo of cardboard boxes had fallen. The newly installed long-armed surgical taps on the hand-wash basin had swung on in the bad weather and remained on flooding the compartment up to the top of the storm sill with fresh water.

The packets of condoms escaping from the cardboard boxes had opened with the continual movement of the water to allow the condoms to swim free in their thousands. The water looked alive and full of strange white wriggling fish. The Doctor was in despair, the others fell about laughing to be joined quickly by a large crowd to see the spectacle.

The Doctor may have appeared eccentric, however he thought quickly on his feet and taking the Chief Officer quietly aside he asked if he might borrow a couple of the young deck boys to help him clear up the mess and to carefully bail out the hospital. I say carefully, for the outcome was that the Doctor diligently recovered the packets and had the deck boys put a half hitch of serving twine around the fighting end of each condom and had them suspended in long lines from the awning spars around the hospital to dry in the warm sunshine.

Retainer approached Gibraltar the next day with the poop dressed overall with Government Issue condoms individually stamped neatly with the message which I believe read; "Do not leave this in a park or public place it may cause offence."

Chapter 14

Life with the Mediterranean Fleet

Target Practice

In the 1950s there was no such expression as "risk assessment" and I wonder whether in fact anyone thought at that time that the exercise was somewhat lacking in caution. Had anyone even considered there was a risk element except me, as the officer of the watch of a Royal Fleet Auxiliary ammunition ship being used for target practice but as the quarry I certainly felt distinctly uncomfortable at the time.

In 1957 life on the Malta station as an officer with the Mediterranean fleet was idyllic. During the week we went to sea on exercise with the fleet or on courtesy visits to other NATO allies. At the weekends we might fill a 32-foot cutter with beer, wine victuals and young lady guests to run up the coast from Grand Harbour Valetta to the blue lagoon at Comino for a day of swimming and laughter. There were evening cinema shows on deck and a lot of hospitality between other ships of the fleet and the shore establishments.

This particular Monday morning RFA *Retainer* embarked the Fleet Gunnery Marking Team, a small group of Naval Ratings and a Gunnery Officer trained to record the fall of shot and accuracy from a moving target, which in this case was to be us, a ten thousand ton passenger and cargo ship packed with naval ordinance of all kinds.

Sailing south of Malta into the fleet exercise area on a beautiful sunny morning, with a sea like glass, we received our orders by Aldis signal light from the flagship HMS *Sheffield* to proceed independently zigzagging on a westerly course while the fleet retired over the horizon.

The fleet having disappeared into the developing heat haze, Captain T Hill left the bridge and the ship to me. As third officer I was tasked to proceed as I felt fit in a general westerly direction as instructed, ordering me to call him should anything untoward happen. And to avoid using any pre-planned zigzag patterns from the confidential books; on the grounds that the "enemy" would soon identify which pattern I was using and to adjust speed occasionally to confuse them.

Happily I threw the ship to both port and starboard at irregular times while on full speed of 15 knots on a calm blue empty sea, while on the forecastle the naval team set up their theodolite and ranging equipment.

All was going well; the radar was banned from use in order to prevent long-range detection by aircraft and with no visual sign of the fleet or indication of attack the morning watch ticked slowly past. The Maltese signal man was busily scrubbing the monkey island above my head as a cooling breeze generated by the ship's forward movement lifted and rustled the charts and papers through the open windows on the wheelhouse plotting table.

Suddenly the alarm on the Kidde Smoke detector in the wheelhouse burst into life shattering my idyllic morning. I rushed to the cabinet into which air and smoke was drawn through small individual pipes from each cargo hold, to pass in front of a photo-electric cell to indicate in which compartment fire had developed. Alarms of any kind on an ammunition ship have a remarkable effect and very rapidly the wheelhouse started to fill with people, while from the main deck anxious heads were turned upwards.

To my surprise instead of being able to inform the Captain exactly where in the ship we had a fire, I found the Kidde Cabinet to be full of bubbles. Puzzled for a moment I noticed the soapy water dripping down through the cabinet past the Photo-electric cell to hit the incoming air pumped from below where it was transformed into a mass of bubbles in the glass case. Obviously the deck head above the cabinet now leaked and the culprit was the poor innocent signal man who had been scrubbing the wooden deck of the monkey island above. Amid some laughter and some annoyance at the fear generated; I was able to quickly reassure the gathering throng that the alarm was false.

We had just returned to our duties when the RN fleet air arm arrived with the screaming of primitive jets to drop some bombs at what seemed to me to be a reasonable distance off the bow. I marvelled at their accuracy at the time and decided not to take evasive action in case that brought the bombs closer.

All went quiet for a while as we scanned the horizon for the warships; but we had seen nothing when, shells started to fall from HMS *Sheffield* firing from somewhere over the horizon. Again the fall of shot marked by large plumes of erupting water, seemed a reasonable distance off the bow but this time I contacted the Naval Officer marking the range for confirmation at the Master's request to be reassured that the fire was accurate and exactly where it should be.

RFA Retainer RAS in Mediterranean

I had begun to relax, confident that the Royal Navy had no intention of blowing up their main supply of ordinance, when over the horizon out of the heat haze and smoke appeared the cruiser HMS *Sheffield* accompanied by the destroyers *Cavendish, Cavalier, and Carysfort* turning to run parallel on a reciprocal course as they launched a torpedo attack.

Now nobody had thought to explain to me how any of these attacks might take place and, having watched with interest the previous fall of shot some distance off the bow and perhaps foolishly expecting some similar arrangement, I was horrified to see the tracks of at least four torpedoes in the crystal clear blue Mediterranean sea heading directly towards the ship. While I realised the torpedoes would not be armed, it did occur to me as I gazed mesmerized that at forty odd knots these projectiles might do some considerable damage if set at the wrong depth by mistake or if they were to porpoise through the water. What about the detonators we had stowed in number 2 hold? Despite my efforts to take evasive action we were straddled by all four torpedoes which, eventually, ran their course and finally surfaced to leeward like spent dead fish wallowing in the slight oily swell.

The exercise was deemed to be a success; we had been theoretically sunk by bombs, gunfire and torpedoes but had in practice survived and live to tell the tale. However I learnt early in my career to always question the detail in naval plans. I am still seeking the bright Royal Naval staff officer that thought that exercise up!

A Painful Souvenir

RFA *Retainer* was equipped with a 32-foot naval cutter fitted with a Kitchener rudder. This device consisted of two semi-circular buckets controlled by a small wheel and gearing to close around the propeller shaft ahead of the propeller, to drive the boat ahead or close behind the propeller, to drive the boat astern, the engine running full ahead at all times. It should have been easy to use but accidents did happen when the coxswain turned the handle the wrong way.

RFA's Fort Duquesne, Tiderace, Wave Victor and Retainer in Grand Harbour Valetta

One such incident happened late at night in Grand Harbour Valletta when after a great party in the wardroom two officers decided to return the lady guests, who were young VADs from Bighi Military Hospital, to their quarters using the 32-foot cutter. Coming into the berth at Bighi steps, the officer acting as coxswain had reduced speed by opening the buckets to a neutral position when the young ladies, seeing the berth coming up, rose unsteadily and excitedly to their feet; thus obscuring the view and disrupting the attention of our gallant volunteer coxswain. Anxious to stop the boat he rapidly turned the handle of the Kitchener gear but unfortunately the wrong way. The boat leapt ahead going up the Bighi steps with an almighty crash which caused the young ladies in their long flowing dresses to collapse in a giggling heap on the bottom boards of the cutter.

Once control of the boat was established and she was secured safely alongside, the young ladies were slowly extracted; that is all except one who lay awkwardly on the bottom boards accompanied by the giggles of her compatriots. Her problem soon became apparent when from under her skirt fell a large brass 4.5 shell case, previously used as a highly polished ash tray at the wardroom bar, she had taken it as a souvenir of her visit to the ship. She was, I recall, allowed to keep it but the officers despite their genuine concern were not allowed to examine the extent of her injuries and she was helped painfully up the steps to the hospital.

A Mystery Frogman in Grand Harbour

RFA *Retainer* was a very sociable ship and on the Mediterranean station we were to make many friends ashore and on other ships. One friend of mine, a Naval Lt-Commander, was a very keen yachtsman who we helped by lifting his yacht onto our deck; while he and friends cleaned and prepared the hull to give it some kind of miniscule speed advantage when racing.

Whether it worked or not I do not know but he felt indebted to me and shortly after I was to receive an invitation to dine with him when he was Duty Officer at Fort St. Angelo. It was an interesting evening, and my friend a kind and generous host. He had arranged to return me to my ship at the inward end of the creek while he carried out his duties of "rowing the guard" of Grand Harbour.

It was a beautiful still clear evening as we motored down through lines of ships until an alert member of the Maltese crew noticed a movement in the water and we diverted to investigate. As we came closer we realised it was a swimmer in a black frogman's suit and I suddenly recognised an officer from one of the RFA Wave Class tankers. Expecting trouble I ignored him as my friend went forward to question the adventurer. To this day I do not know what passed between them but the frogman was allowed to proceed on his way and we carried on to *Retainer*. Arriving alongside I politely invited my host aboard for a night cap in the wardroom, which was situated at the top of a grand curved staircase and stood on the after end of the boat deck. It was late and a quiet night aboard as we stood at the bar in our white mess undress uniforms exchanging pleasantries with a couple of the duty boys, when to my alarm I heard the unmistakable sound of flippers coming up the polished curved staircase...

Flip flop, flip flop.

Conversation died as the collection at the bar stood waiting expectantly the cause of this strange late night sound. Then at the top of the staircase a black diver's hat appeared surmounting the silly grinning features of the culprit. There emerged the dripping wet black neoprene clad figure of the mysterious frogman of our earlier acquaintance who had merely swum over for a night cap as well! Fortunately my naval friend had a great sense of humour but he did insist for his own peace of mind that the erstwhile frogman accompanied him back to his own ship in the duty boat.

EOKA Frogman Attack

At the time the people of Cyprus were seeking independence and were fronted by the terrorist organisation EOKA, the Royal Navy kept a considerable presence off the island, including an aircraft carrier, cruiser, destroyers and frigates all supported by a full contingent of RFAs.

A terrorist cache of limpet mines had been discovered ashore and RFA *Retainer* embarked the Fleet Diving Team to search the hulls of the anchored ships each morning or as and when required. We were also issued with a box of quarter pound explosive charges to scatter around the ship in the event of a suspected underwater attack and a set of coded instructions leading up to their delivery.

Now in the anchorage boredom was rife, beach bathing parties were not allowed and the weeks went by broken only by the occasional exercise at sea. It was fairly common practice for officers to send an RPC (request the pleasure of your company) to one's opposite number in another ship for drinks and a meal. So it was this particular day I invited the third officer (a future Hover-Craft pilot) aboard from one of the Wave Class Tankers on completion of our respective anchor watches at midday.

That evening once again we were on watch on our respective ships when a lookout on my friend's ship spotted an underwater swimmer wearing what looked like a bathing cap and performing a slow breast stroke. He immediately reported the sighting to my friend who called the Master, who promptly informed the cruiser, which was the Flag ship. The coded warnings started to flow and rapidly the aircraft carrier and sundry destroyers and frigates got underway and headed for deep water leaving the cruiser, the Wave Class Tanker and our ship full of ammunition to face the attack.

As the colour coded warnings accelerated to Red I kept the Master informed to be told in his usual confident manner;

"Carry on, Third Officer, follow the procedure."

Now it was nearly midnight when the procedure required that the quarter pound charges be dropped around the ship to stun any underwater swimmers. My problem was that I had never seen the charges before and certainly had never been instructed in their use. I decided, in view of the detonators stowed in number 2 hold, to avoid that area and advanced to the poop deck as far from them as possible. Now I do not know whether you have experience of similar devices but they let off one hell of a bang. The effect on those sleeping aboard RFA *Retainer* that night was dramatic, as alarmed people turned out of their bunks to come streaming up onto the deck from below.

The Cadet on watch with me asked if he might throw one and, being a sensible lad not much younger that myself, I stupidly in retrospect passed him one, showing him how to first pull out the pin and instructing him to throw it as far as he could. Out came the pin but for some unknown reason he seem to freeze and to my horror smoke began to emit from his clenched fist. I yelled a warning and hurriedly he let go, the charge dropping and detonating harmlessly close under the stern.

Having completed our pyrotechnical display, the Naval Fleet Diving Team took to the waters in search of the enemy and soon discovered a rather stunned turtle swimming in confused circles.

My young friend and his AB lookout were promptly summoned to report to the Flag Officer Second in Command Her Majesty's Mediterranean Fleet; something he did in great trepidation. He need not have worried for the Admiral was to commend the AB for his vigilance and my colleague for his subsequent action. The lookout's initial description was entirely accurate; he had indeed merely described a turtle.

A Series of Painful Experiences

I was to be admitted in September 1958 to Bighi Hospital myself and had to leave *Retainer* in order to have a large persistently in-growing toenail removed, a nail which had given me trouble ever since I had picked up an infection in it some years before on the beach in Guam. Following that time, the toenail had been removed about five times in different surgeries around the world but never had I been actually hospitalized. I imagine RN Hospital Bighi was short of patients at that time for usually the job was done quite quickly with a local anaesthetic. However that was not always the case for if infection had set in a local anaesthetic did not work.

The first time this happened was when RFA *Eaglesdale* put into Curacao for a day and I attended a spotless air-conditioned Dutch Clinic as cold as winter. The Doctor examined the foot, said he could do nothing but treat the infection and passed me over to an enormous male nurse who was to clean and dress the wound. Instead of merely cleaning up the infection this sadist firmly secured my foot between his knees and jammed a pair of scissors down under the nail cutting it in half and pulled the two halves off with surgical pliers. The pain was excruciating and my immediate reaction was to take a swing at the man but sitting on a cold metal swivel chair I missed as it rotated and I fell off. In fairness it was a case of being cruel to be kind and his unorthodox treatment after the initial pain had abated gave me great relief. Over the subsequent few years I had the nail removed several more times, including twice at the Naval Surgery in Singapore when the anaesthetic failed to be effective and the Doctor carried out surgery with a large glass of medicinal brandy each and two burley Sick Berth Attendants to hold me down; before finally I had an operation in the UK to remove the nail permanently.

Sally's Trip to Malta

Not only were the voyages long in the 1950s but communications were very poor and when before I left *Retainer,* Sally sadly miscarried our first baby; I was to receive the message visually via the Royal Navy at sea by Aldis Signal lamp from one of our escorting destroyers. As soon as she was able she flew out to Malta for a couple of weeks' recuperation, flying in an old BEA Elizabethan high-wing monoplane of the class which crashed at Munich with the Manchester Football team aboard when the wings iced up. Sally's BEA flight also iced up flying over the Alps and had to put down to make an emergency landing in Italy, an experience she did not enjoy. However she soon recovered and was to return to UK in a brand new BEA Vickers Viscount. Sadly that year another aircraft did crash outward bound for Luqa with heavy loss of life including one of the Nursing Sisters from RNH Bighi.

While in Malta Sally was allowed to come to sea with us where she was to witness her first RAS (replenishment at sea) with the aircraft carrier HMS *Ark Royal.* Standing at the rail watching with interest the loads going across between the two ships steaming at 14 knots through the Mediterranean, she no doubt cheered up the naval ratings on the aircraft carrier. Suddenly she remarked of one particular pallet and, in horror, realised our role in life:

"They look just like bombs."

Chapter 15

Continual RFA Service

It was to be a full eighteen months out from the UK before I was to get leave following my marriage to Sally in October 1957. Coming out of hospital I was fortunate to be temporarily appointed as Second Officer with only a 2nd Mate's Certificate of *RFA Wave King*, relieving another casualty before I was appointed as Third Officer of *RFA Tidesurge* bound east by way of the Persian Gulf to Hong Kong and Singapore. *RFA Tidesurge*, originally built as the *RFA Tiderange*, was one of four large fleet replenishment tankers of Admiralty design built by Swan Hunter & Wigham Richardson at Wallsend on Tyne.

I joined the ship in Famagusta, Cyprus, after travelling up in a BEA Vickers Viscount to Nicosia via Benghazi, on the day the terrorist organisation EOKA shot a British Sergeant's wife. Arriving at the Ledra Palace Hotel, Nicosia with a Royal Marine escort I received a telephone call from the local Senior Naval Officer asking me if I was armed and if not would I like a revolver? I declined his kind offer considering that I might be more of a menace with one than without. A Royal Marine escort arrived after breakfast the following morning armed to the teeth to drive me across the island to Famagusta. I had begun to wonder whether I, a very junior RFA officer had been marked down as a particular target of the EOKA as we set off in a large black car with a well-armed RM Commando sitting next to me and fully manned RM Land Rover leading the way. Proceeding down a long straight road to the east it occurred to me that if we were ambushed the commandos in front would deal with the threat but what if we were overtaken? I glanced over my shoulder to see we were being rapidly caught by another large speeding black car and quietly slid down in my seat keeping my thoughts to myself until, to my relief, a taxi swept harmlessly past.

Tidesurge was not a particularly happy ship that year. There was generally a shortage of seamen and many of the crew members had been virtually press-ganged, being given a £5 advance in Newcastle and a travel voucher they had been sent to join the ship in Portsmouth and promptly signed on for two year articles of agreement. There had been some minor trouble before I joined but to avoid future confrontation with crew members returning from a run ashore the worse for drink, I decided to establish a reputation as somebody to be avoided. In Singapore I bought an illustrated book on the subject of Karate. I then set my alarm clock in order to be up practising each morning, hitting a block of wood with the sides of my hands when the steward called me with a cup of tea. Word soon spread and it soon became obvious from the number of questions I began to receive that the Third Officer was being considered if not an expert then at least into martial arts. I was consequently treated warily and had few problems once I established with my pretended progress through my open book, a reputation entirely un-warranted.

I was not to escape entirely however for on our first night back into Plymouth after more than a year at sea replenishing the fleet, as the junior navigating officer I found myself alone on deck as duty boy, discharging three different grades of oil. The cargo capacity was 8,500 tons Furnace Fuel Oil, 4,600 tons marine diesel and 1,900 tons of Aviation Fuel.

The crew began to return during the night somewhat the worse for wear, but generally gave me no trouble as they headed through the night across the tank decks to their accommodation aft; that is all except one man. With a real chip on his shoulder this man not only decided against all the regulations to smoke on the tank deck but continually entered the amidships officer's accommodation shouting obscenities. I was too busy physically changing tanks and supervising the cargo to really deal with the miscreant, so I called the MOD Police for assistance and was told it was not their problem but mine and that I should deal with it myself. I was about to call the sleeping Chief Officer and tell him I intended to stop discharge unless I got assistance, when this clown became really aggressive and took a swing at me. Now I had disliked the attitude of this particular individual for at least the last nine months and in defending myself I hit him squarely on the chin probably harder than necessary. It was an action not to be recommended, no matter how macho a young officer you may be, for on impact my attacker flew backwards across the deck his head coming into contact with a steel watertight door; causing him to collapse in a heap. The old shore side night watchman suddenly and mysteriously appeared from nowhere and looking down at the comatose body said in a loud spine chilling voice:

"You've done 'im in sir, you've done 'im in!"

For a moment it was a real scare and momentarily I imagined I had put an end not just to this obnoxious character but to my whole career, despite the fact that I had been denied help when most I needed it.

Luckily the moment soon passed and the night watchman was to be proved wrong, as the recumbent figure shook his head with a crooked grin and put out his hand for me help him to his feet, something which I was only too happy to do. Having threatened to hit him even harder if he did not get off the deck and go aft to turn in, I was pleased to watch him meekly obey and make his way aft rubbing his bruises. When some days later I paid off the ship, I was surprised that it was this same individual who came forward and willingly offered, and in fact, carried my bags to my taxi. In retrospect, I suppose I had put down a challenge with my silly karate book, bringing the problem and subsequent fear upon myself.

Following leave I studied at Warsash and sat my First Mates Certificate at Southampton before joining a small tanker *RFA Teakol* based at Chatham while Sally produced Nicola our eldest child on Boxing Day 1959; it would have been Christmas Day but then there would have been nobody to supervise the cooking of the seasonal turkey. This was solved by the judicious use of a couple of codeine tablets to lessen the pain; Sally went off the boil and had to be restarted with a walk in the snow the following morning.

Returning to sea I was then sent to join the Naval Victualling Ship *RFA Fort Dunvegan* in a DAN Air Four–engine propeller driven Britannia Trooping Flight to Singapore via Teheran and Bombay. It was interesting that in those days the seats were all configured to face the tail of the aircraft in case of an accident. However I had a bit of luck on arrival for just as I joined *Fort Dunvegan,* the Chief Officer of a visiting tanker went sick and being senior to the Second Officer aboard that ship and the only navigating officer available at such short notice, I was appointed Chief Officer of *RFA Surf Patrol* with a hardly dry First Mates Certificate. I was now to sail for the second time in a superior position to normal RFA deck officer's expectations, something which undoubtedly helped my career.

RFA Surf Patrol (7742 grt originally built for the Polish Government but completed by Bartram & Sons at Sunderland under RFA manning and management) was a nice little Chinese crewed freighting tanker; at least I have always remembered her as such but for one particular recollection Captain Cox and I both considerably enjoyed the very hot crew curry on the ship which can hardly have been Chinese, so maybe they were Indian after all. It was a short voyage for me up to the Persian Gulf to load at Ras Tannura for Malta where I was to be relieved by a Chief Officer domiciled in Malta. I was nearly retained when he had a fall, putting him out of action but the powers that be found a more appropriate and senior officer on one of the other ships and I returned to Singapore to rejoin *RFA Fort Dunvegan*, by way of a few short days in the UK.

Fort Dunvegan was built at the Burrard Dry-dock Co Ltd, Vancouver in 1944 for the Canadian Government and assigned to the Admiralty while under construction. She was one of eight *'Fort'* class standard war construction design cargo ships with a speed of 11 knots and gross tonnage of 7,225 tons to serve the RFA service. She was engined by Canadian Allis-Chalmers, completed as a victualling stores issuing ship and initially had been managed by Ellerman Bucknall Line before being transferred to the Admiralty on the 31st December 1948.

With a Hong Kong Chinese crew she was an immaculate little ship in which we took great pride in showing off; for example, when we were replenishing at sea in daylight, whatever the weather, the quarter master would always place in position over the top of the navigating side light on the working side, to impress our RN friends, a highly polished copper emergency oil light to glint in the sun. The gangway with its ornate lifebuoy, bell and ship's crest was always manned by an immaculate quarter master in whites. Captain F A Shaw was a stickler for uniform, insisting the officers always wore long white socks and white shoes when in shorts and even the engineer officers were expected to wear a cap on deck if in his sight.

I remember one steaming hot day, storing the Australian destroyer *HMS Daring* in the Indian Ocean miles from anywhere, when as she approached our port side our Captain, stood chewing on the end of his handkerchief, the outward sign of his mark as a fully qualified RN Navigator. Immaculate in gleaming whites we stood contemplating on the cool wing of the bridge under the canvas awnings, the impressive dashing approach of the Australians, when the 'old man' peering through his binoculars observed that everyone on the Australian ship's open bridge were wearing baseball caps.

"Good Heavens Second 'Orfcer' don't they look ridiculous, they might just as well be wearing bowler hats," he exclaimed.

The fact that one of the objects of his derision was our own Admiral, the Flag Officer Second in Command of the Far East Fleet was of little consequence to Captain Shaw; to him they were out of uniform and in American style baseball caps; to his way of thinking looked ridiculous.

However he could be really amenable and one such time was on the occasion of a visit to Hong Kong, where it was customary at that time, for affiliation between the military shore establishments and visiting RN and RFA ships. Having a Chinese crew and only eleven officers, we found ourselves affiliated to the Royal Military Police in Kowloon who had even fewer officers, most MPs being NCOs. The MPs invited us first to their base for a superb party which included a dog handling display, Chinese acrobats, jugglers and great food and wine. It was going to be a difficult act to follow; the mess committee went into consultation. The first problem was how in fairness to our crew in their home port, we could staff the event? It was decided to seek the assistance of the Chief Steward, who with his connections might be able to help out with a few waitresses.

It was also decided to avoid uniforms and embarrassment, by having the party on the boat deck in barbecue rig, and I was chosen to break the news to our erstwhile Captain.

"Barbecue rig, Second Orfcer? What on earth is barbecue rig?"

When I explained that it meant a bright colourful shirt and casual trousers, he professed to not owning such a thing but on the night of the party, he turned out in the brightest red sports shirt imaginable, long white trousers and I seem to recall two tone shoes. The food and drink flowed and the party went well the Military Policemen seeming well satisfied with our efforts and the service we gave them. It had been interesting that most of the stewards stayed aboard to help, despite the young ladies swishing gracefully in cheongsams, about their business serving food and drink. At the debriefing afterwards when examining our mess bills, we began to think that the MPs had been very well served indeed. We paid for mess bills on a stripe basis and the Captain on being presented with his remarked:

"Well, Second 'Orfcer', a great party, well done but I think next time we will give the gals a miss."

Collision with a Whale

The weather was hot and humid as RFAs exercised in the Indian Ocean off Karachi with the British Far East fleet, American and Pakistani warships. There was no wind and without air-conditioning and with all the port holes closed to darken ship at night conditions aboard the ships were uncomfortable to say the least.

Sometime during the night, one of the fast fleet tankers ran into a large whale with such an impact, the body of the whale, which was probably killed instantly, became wedged on the bow. Despite engine movements astern, the carcass remained firmly stuck. The large tanker steamed slowly into the anchorage off Karachi, with what was by now in the blazing sun, a swollen and stinking mess of rotting flesh, around the bows; which attracted a number of large sharks and hundreds of screaming gulls. Regardless of the heat, portholes throughout the fleet remained firmly closed.

Collision with a whale

A small tug, energetically polluting the blue sky with black smoke, eventually appeared and was able to secure to the body of the poor unfortunate creature and tow it off towards the distant shoreline. No doubt during the following weeks, curried whale meat was on the menu at a number of local establishments.

Chapter 16

Trooping Flights

As a civilian RFA officer with no authority except that perhaps implied in the temporary appointment, I was somewhat surprised on two occasions to be appointed by somebody in the MOD as OC Troops on both a civilian aircraft chartered to the government and a genuine RAF transport aircraft. OC Troops being the representative of the MOD with whom the Captain of the aircraft is supposed to consult; should there be a proposed change of plan or a problem involving the intended delivery of the MOD personnel embarked at the time. Basically I suppose it is, or was in those days, a box-ticking exercise and one which did not normally involve or require any action by the appointee – but I was not so lucky.

Early in January 1961 I arrived at Changi Airport to join a four-engine propeller-driven Britannia Aircraft belonging to DAN (Davis & Newman) Air for the flight from Singapore to Stansted with fuelling stops at Bombay and Teheran. This was one of quite a large fleet of aeroplanes on charter to the MOD to cover service requirements all over the world; all the aircraft, if I remember correctly, having the seating facing the tail in order to reduce injury in case of a mishap.

I had just left RFA *Fort Dunvegan* where I had served the last year as Second Officer and was surprised by the appointment which I thought was without precedent and said so, but to no avail.

Half way across India in the middle of the night I was gently disturbed from my slumbers by the senior stewardess to be told the Captain needed to see me. I followed her apprehensively to the darkened cockpit which seemed to be a mass of twinkling lights, including a couple of lights ominously glowing red. From the darkness the Captain introduced himself and apologised for calling me.

"Sorry old chap but I have a slight problem; I have lost one of the starboard engines."

Horrified, I instinctively looked out the starboard cockpit windows imagining a large hole in the wing and some poor Indian peasant several thousand feet below having a rude surprise in the vast rural countryside;

how stupid of me, there were the engines looking normal. When he said he had "lost one of the starboard engines," it was some kind of aeronautical expression meaning the engine was broken, not that he had literally lost the thing.

The Captain ignored my initial shock and went on to say that the aircraft was perfectly safe to fly on the three engines but his problem was that he did not have a spare engine at Bombay and therefore he would like to fly onto Karachi, where he had all the facilities and another engine; to avoid a long delay in Bombay.

Naturally, having his reassurance that such a change was not only safe but in the best interest of the tax payer, I readily agreed but I have to say I did not go back to sleep and I was particularly apprehensive during the landing at Karachi. From Karachi, after repairs, we flew on without further problems.

I'm jumping a bit ahead of my story but my second trooping flight experience was in May 1965, when after some twenty-one months in the Far East as Senior Second Officer and then First Officer of the victualling store ship RFA *Fort Dunvegan,* I signed off in Hong Kong for the journey home. Having had my wife Sally and the children out to live in Singapore until the confrontation with Indonesia and subsequent security problems caused us to abandon our bungalow outside the more secure Naval Base and get the family home; I had accrued more than the usual amount of baggage and some items of furniture. This I had stored in Singapore while at sea.

Now at that time although it was usual practice to fly out to join and return from ships based in the Far East; there still remained the ability to use a sea passage. A privilege that I knew was about to be withdrawn. Now was the time to use it before it was lost, and in any case I thought it would be rather nice to travel by P&O in style and get paid for the privilege.

On the way up to Hong Kong we received a signal that my sea passage had been arranged from Singapore on a Blue Funnel cargo ship via all the liner ports en route to Liverpool. I was to fly to Singapore courtesy of the RAF and join Alfred Holt's *Dolius* shortly to leave for Port Swettenham and Penang. Not exactly what I had been expecting but at last I was homeward bound.

My first surprise came at Kai Tak the old Hong Kong airport built on the Kowloon side of the harbour when, reporting to the RAF Flight check-in, I was informed that I had been designated OC Troops for the flight.

RAF Hastings aircraft at Kai Tak Airport Hong Kong

Not a problem I thought until I discovered that to accompany me on this flight were a considerable number of service wives and children and a very loud number of odds and sods who had missed their ships, been picked up and confined prior to being returned to their establishments. Unfortunately their new found freedom had also given them the opportunity to indulge their thirst for beer and by the time I arrived the air was already blue with profanity. I sensed trouble for some of these characters were nearly legless.

I imagine I had only been asked to become OC troops because the majority of passengers apart from the families were Naval and RFA ratings. Realising that as this was a proper RAF flight being flown by commissioned RAF Officers I really had no problem, I sought out the Flight Sergeant and expressed my concern.

Flight with a twinkle in his eye listened patiently at my imagined possibilities and said;

"Don't worry, Sir, I'll put them all in the tail section, leave the door cracked open on take-off and I'm sure that will cool them down."

Happy that I had expressed my concern to the RAF, I settled into a forward window seat on the starboard side hoping to get a view of Vietnam as we headed south westwards to Changi.

It was raining as the elderly Handley Page Hastings trundled down Kai Tak runway between tall apartment blocks festooned with dripping wet washing on bamboo poles, gradually increasing speed as it bounced, generating clouds of spray through the surface water left over from the torrential tropical rain earlier in the day. The passengers were all seated facing the tail of the aircraft and the noisy crowd in the after seats did not see the spray of water coming through the slightly open doorway until they were soaked. Flight having achieved his aim by cooling the noisy crowd down, secured the door with an apology to his sodden passengers and a grin to the families and me. Wet and very cold, the miscreants soon sobered up as we gained altitude and remained quiet for the somewhat bumpy flight to Singapore.

Chapter 17

Freighting

The next couple of years I spent freighting oil between the Persian Gulf, and Aden and the Naval Ports of the UK, Gibraltar and Malta, Singapore and the oil hulk at Gan in the Maldives, serving as second officer and keeping the twelve-to-four watches. My extracurricular duties included the medical work, keeping a world folio of charts up to date and maintaining the gyro compass. Life was frustrating and boring; frustrating because too often our orders were changed and our mail the only contact we had with the outside world was sent to the wrong port and took literally months to catch up with us or simply disappeared. Boring because we were only ever in port briefly and rarely got ashore.

RFA *Pearleaf* 12,692 tons gross, built in 1960 by the Blythswood Shipbuilding Co. Ltd, Glasgow and engined with a six-cylinder Doxford engine giving an average speed of 15.65 knots was owned by J I Jacobs and Partners but was taken over on completion of her trials and bareboat chartered to the Admiralty for 20 years as an RFA.

She was a nice ship with particularly good accommodation and Chinese crew, but for us personally the first three months with a number of changes of orders and the consequent loss of mail was a disaster. Unbeknown to me the Purser had failed to post to the Admiralty my signed allotment authority payable to my wife which he had accidentally but carelessly managed to drop down behind his desk. Consequently the Admiralty, without instruction, did not pay into our joint bank account on my behalf and my poor wife was not receiving any money to live on and could not understand why I appeared to be ignoring her letters for help, letters which of course I had not received. The bills were rolling in and our bank manager, a proper little dictator who seemed to like to bully his female customers, was refusing even to help with the telephone account, suggesting that perhaps she was not receiving money because I had no wish to send it to her. What an unpleasant little man he was just because he had the power. His demise is today marked by a memorial public bench in the town to which I am tempted to give a swift kick when passing; that is of course if nobody is looking. Fortunately the late Captain John Fisher, an RFA Master living in the town, helped her personally over the crisis until I could eventually be contacted and the situation rectified. How lucky are seamen today with such incredible advances in communications in such a short few years, communications which most people now take for granted?

RFA Pearleaf at Suez 1961

Life in a freighting tanker was pretty much routine and one tends to remember the small things that brightened the day. One of the funniest being the day the new Captain arrived in Rosyth before we sailed for the Persian Gulf. We had a charming and always immaculate Second Engineer who was the very epitome of an English country gentleman, although born I believe elsewhere. With beautifully hand-made clothes and an account at the Naval Tailors Gieves and a regular rider down Rotten Row when in London; his final manifestation was the wearing of a monocle. A nice man, he looked the cat's whiskers as they say.

Standing with him in the officer's bar having an aperitif before lunch, the Second Engineer was resplendent in his number one uniform and monocle when our conversation was interrupted as the door to the boat deck swung open and in stepped the new Captain. He glared furiously at the Second Engineer through a monocle, his one magnified eye staring fiercely and accusingly at my immaculate companion. The Second Engineer in turn glared back in surprise through his, neither of them knowing which one was the joker. I started to laugh at this ridiculous confrontation and the assembled officers began grinning with amusement as two monocles both turned to glare at me. From that day I did not get on too well with the new Master but I could see that the joker was in the Admiralty Personnel Department, the person responsible for appointing these two somewhat eccentric people to the same ship; we had been sent a complete set.

I was to really fall out with him initially over the way he dealt with the problem of my missing allotment mandate when, having worked throughout the night discharging cargo into the tanks at Gibraltar, I waited until after breakfast to see him to state the problem my wife was having without my pay going through to our joint bank account. I needed to get it rectified before we sailed out of communication once again. He promptly told me he was too busy and yet he then spent the morning fishing unsuccessfully over the side; an uncaring attitude for which I could never forgive him. Possibly he had asked the Purser, unbeknown to me, and been assured that the document had been sent off to the Admiralty and certainly the monies were being deducted from my shipboard account. His indifference meant I had to resolve the situation by going over his head ashore to see the Senior Naval Stores Officer, Gibraltar; a caring civil servant who promptly and helpfully arranged for the situation to be rectified that very day.

The medical duties also caused us to disagree on another occasion when the Chinese Second Cook went sick; having what appeared to me after consultation with the Ship Master's Medical Guide, a severe case of appendicitis. I started to give the poor chap a course of penicillin injections in the rump, a particular hard piece of skin to penetrate resulting from the Chinese habit of years of squatting on little wooden stools. The ship was bound loaded for the Mediterranean from the Persian Gulf (as it was called in those days) and a day out before passing Aden; where in my opinion the patient needed to be landed to hospital. The Master was of a different view expressing what today would be considered a very racist opinion that the poor man only had a belly ache as a result of eating a lot of 'foreign garbage'.

I stood my ground but the Master, by now puce in the face, ordered me out of his cabin thundering that;

"We are not going to divert to Aden, Second Officer. Go away and give the man some digestive medicine."

I left and went up to the Chartroom to complete a medical entry in the Deck Log Book, when a solution occurred to me and, taking a black pen, I wrote of 'my diagnosis and recommendation to the Master to divert into the Port of Aden as a medical emergency' without mentioning his response and drew the entry to the Chief Officer's notice. On the way down to my cabin I knocked politely on the Master's door, put my head in and said quietly;

"Captain, just in case the second cook does die; you had better have a look at the entry I have made in the Medical Log."

The following morning RFA *Pearleaf* put into Aden and a Doctor boarded and took my patient off speedily to hospital for a serious operation; when peritonitis was diagnosed. I was later to receive a message from the military surgeon thanking me for my correct diagnosis and the treatment I had commenced. Happily the wiry little Chinaman survived and was to rejoin the ship later. On the other hand my hope of establishing a good relationship with that particular Master never did survive; I was pleased therefore that on return to the UK he was relieved.

I quite enjoyed the medical work but mostly it was routine cuts and bruises and the iniquitous results of the occasional seaman's unwise and unprotected liaison with a lady of doubtful virtue. I did however have to amputate the end of one engineer cadet's finger that the poor man had trapped and crushed working on the main engine. He sat up and watched the operation with interest after I shot some morphine into him; which is more than I can say for my volunteer assistant who, when I had to use a small medical saw, passed out cold.

Pearleaf had a somewhat chequered start to her service and as I recall had to change pistons on numerous occasions. The hard heavy work was usually carried out at anchor up in the Persian Gulf. Understandably it was noticeable that whenever the engineers were slaving away changing a piston, the air-conditioning (incidentally a new innovation on our ships at that time) for the rest of us was shut down. It was I believe on one of these essential repairs that the young engineer cadet trapped his finger. I met him on a train many years later and got chance to examine and admire the success of my handiwork.

The continual engine problems led to our return to the builders in Glasgow for repairs, where I was joined by Sally and our daughter Nicola.

During that time Sally started feeling sick and went to seek out a Doctor on the Dumbarton Road. He examined her and asked if she had been with a 'sailor'? When she indignantly replied that she had indeed and was married to him, he told her the happy news that she was again pregnant.

Some eight months later Neil Hamish Russell was born. Many years later he queried why, when we were all English, he had been given Gaelic names? I was able to reply with all honesty that like many a fine ship he had been conceived at a shipyard on the River Clyde and that it was therefore appropriate he should have Scottish names.

RFA *Pearleaf* sailed from the Clyde with sealed orders. Those aboard not knowing exactly when or if we would meet our loved ones again, for with the Cuban Crisis and Kennedy and Khrushchev going head to head over the Russian missiles in Cuba; a Third World War looked decidedly possible. Quietly and quickly behind the scenes, NATO Forces were going to sea.

The worst period of the crisis began on October 15, 1962, when United States reconnaissance photographs taken by an American U-2 spy plane; revealed missile bases being built in Cuba. It ended two weeks later on October 28, 1962, when President of the United States John F Kennedy reached an agreement with the Soviets to dismantle the missiles in Cuba, in exchange for a no invasion agreement and the secret removal of the US Thor and Jupiter missiles, which had already been sited in Turkey. The initial establishment of which the Russians felt threatened them and had been the cause and the subsequent response of the USSR to send weapons to Cuba; missiles which had not been requested by Fidel Castro.

The most fearful moment for me came when President Kennedy, in his first public speech on the crisis, given on October 22, 1962, gave the severe warning that;

"It shall be the policy of this nation to regard any nuclear missile launched from Cuba against any nation in the Western Hemisphere as an attack on the United States, requiring a full retaliatory response upon the Soviet Union."

Fortunately common sense prevailed, agreement was reached and the whole world breathed again and I went back to freighting until the problems with my large left toe once again needed treatment. I flew home from Gibraltar to have surgery at the Royal Victoria Hospital in Folkestone. This time the surgery was permanently successful and I was able to enjoy a long summer leave during which our son Neil Hamish was born at home.

Following leave I was to join RFA *Appleleaf* in Cardiff; just in time to view on the ship's hired television, the first transatlantic television broadcast press conference given by President J F Kennedy speaking between Andover in Maine USA and Goonhilly Downs in the UK via the newly launched satellite 'Telstar'. This particular satellite had a very short working life; although according to NASA it is still orbiting the earth today, even though it became a victim of the cold war.

The day before Telstar was launched, the United States tested a high-altitude nuclear device which super-energized the Earth's Van Allen Belt where Telstar was to orbit. The considerable increase in radiation, combined with further increases during subsequent high-altitude blasts, including a Soviet test in October, overwhelmed Telstra's fragile transistors, it went out of service in early December 1962. I wonder what those tests did to all of us on earth.

Viewing the picture below reminds me of an incident that took place in Port Said when RFA *Pearleaf* was also lying quietly on the same buoys; taking bunkers prior to transiting the Suez Canal southbound. It was a nice day, and Toby Groves the Chief Officer and I had decided on a run ashore swimming somewhere on a beach that Toby was familiar with from his WW2 service driving an MGB for HM Hydrographical Service to survey enemy held beaches.

RFA Appleleaf at Port Said 1962-63

I cannot recall the detail but vaguely remember the broad sea front boulevard, palm trees and beach loungers plus a few cold beers. Coming back we decided to travel in style and hailed a horse-drawn gharry and climbed in. Sitting back in comfort and complacency, full of self-satisfaction at having escaped from the boring routine of freighting we relaxed as the horse trotted, clip-clopping along the cool avenue in the dark shade of the trees. Suddenly there was a single shout soon echoed by numerous others;

"Viva Che, Viva Raúl, Viva Cuba."

We looked up in surprise as more and more people took up the chant and a multitude of running figures rapidly started to spill out towards the gharry from the crowded side streets; encouraged perhaps by our friendly waves. We had no comprehension as to exactly what they were saying or just why? The poor unfortunate horse slid to a frightened spark-generating, leg-splayed stop on the tarmac boulevard as the gharry driver applied the brakes and we became completely surrounded by cheering, dancing, happy excited people desperate to touch us but just who did they think we were?

The answer was that Raúl Castro and Che Guevara were visiting Cairo to established contacts with the African liberation movements stationed in and supported by Cairo, before both Cuban leaders were then to visit Gaza to express support for the Palestinian cause. Being bearded like the Cubans, and naturally suntanned from long exposure to the sun, we had been mistaken for the Cuban leaders.

There was great reluctance for the crowd to admit their mistake but those by now climbing on the gharry soon recognised our tropical very British shorts and long tropical socks, invisible from the road when sitting in the gharry. Encouraged by the cracking of the driver's whip the more enthusiastic members of our greeting party were soon driven disappointingly away and the poor traumatised horse was unsteadily but gently encouraged to continue our return from the cool boulevard to the searing heat of the Custom House Steps. It had been a good run ashore for all that.

The RFA *Appleleaf* was a nice comfortable ship, the ex *George Lyras* on a twenty-year bareboat charter and my home for eight months, where I cannot recall anything of great excitement happening except interminably long poker games each evening on the boat deck; as we plodded backwards and forwards between the Mediterranean, Aden and the Persian Gulf. I left to study for Master Foreign Going at Sir John Cass in London, travelling up to London each day on the steam train which took ten minutes less than our fine new electric trains today but were not quite so clean. On obtaining my Master's Certificate of Competency I was once again appointed to RFA *Fort Dunvegan* in the Far East this time to serve as Senior Second Officer and then First Officer.

First Officer RFA Fort Dunvegan

Peter & Sally Russell at Repulse Bay, Hong Kong

Chapter 18

Living in Singapore

RFA *Fort Dunvegan* was the Far East VSIS (Victualling Stores Issuing Ship) based in Singapore for which the officers received extra pay in the form of 'station allowance'. It was not a great deal of money and certainly did not compare with the Civil Service 'living allowance' and Government Housing to which the embarked Civil Service Naval Stores Officers were entitled; much to our envy. However as a Second Officer I thought that we could probably live frugally in rented accommodation if I was able to get an RFA indulgence passage for Sally and our two small children Nicola and Neil out to Singapore.

Indulgence Passage

Now it was my experience that when the fleet moved very often the accompanying RFA would carry a number of RN officers' wives as indulgence passengers, if there was available accommodation aboard. Such passengers were even, on occasion, carried in freighting tankers. This was my second tour in the *Fort Dunvegan* and I knew Singapore well, so following discussion with Sally and after I had established possible accommodation, I applied for an indulgence passage. The Marine Superintendent at the time was very supportive and soon found a freighting tanker outward bound for the Persian Gulf where it was to load for Singapore. The Master at first declined to carry my wife and children and another second officer's wife returning to her home in Singapore, although the owner's suite was available. When however he admitted that if asked he would carry RN Officers' wives, he was soon persuaded by the Marine Superintendent that in fairness to his own service on this occasion he would carry two RFA wives and our two children. It was to be a first and be a great experience for my young family. Nobody queried the idea or my arrangements and I opened a local bank account so as not to have to rely on our unpleasant bank manager in the UK.

RFA *Cherryleaf* had superb accommodation for Sally and the children and a Hong Kong Chinese crew who were to thoroughly spoil them with kindness.

J D Russell Peter

RFA Fort Dunvegan off Singapore Naval Base 1963

The passage out via the Suez Canal to the Persian Gulf to load for Singapore was, I believe, uneventful apart from bad weather in the Bay of Biscay and the children's subsequent delight at the movement of their bath water from end to end of the bath as Sally attempted, feeling none

Nicola & Neil on RFA Cherrvleaf

too well, to clean them up for dinner time. Taking the children ashore on a bitterly cold day in Abadan did prove something of an ordeal for Sally. Nicola was just four years old while Neil was only eighteen months old and in a pushchair, when they stepped ashore on their adventure to visit the bazaar. The problem Sally had was that the local Muslims became terribly excited at seeing a young boy with bright red hair; the true sign of a visit to Mecca! Shouting *"hǎdji"*, *"hǎdji"*, crowds of locals tried to touch his head and enough of them successfully so to make the poor child not only frightened but very dirty. Sally was pleased to return quickly to the safety of the ship.

110

The First Cobra

Our first accommodation in Singapore was sharing a big old pre-war colonial bungalow with large garden on the Thompson Road but it soon proved to be too far from the Naval Base and alive with tropical creatures. Quite frightening to Sally, the animals proved very interesting to two curious children.

The first were the monkeys in the trees, to which Nicola would feed the fresh bananas bought from the market. Then there were the scorpions which would hide in the babies' wet cotton nappies, only to appear angrily on the top as they were boiled on the stove. They would also walk around the rim of the bath as Sally relaxed after a hard day in the heat. Cockroaches were of course everywhere and then there were the bandicoots which were basically rats with long legs able to climb the curtains. Curiously we were not plagued with mosquitoes.

The worst experience my young family had was on the day Sally had put Neil, who at that stage had not learnt to walk and was therefore not very mobile but hotched along on his bottom; on the lawn with Nicola while she was briefly preoccupied with a family chore when Nicola called out in alarm;

> "Mummy, come quickly – Neil has got something in his mouth."

To Sally's absolute horror Neil had the tail of a fairly large writhing snake in his mouth. She shrieked loudly and ran towards him and he let go; allowing the snake to escape across the grass. I, as usual, was at sea but on return Sally identified the snake as being a cobra in the reptile museum; it being the one with a large flat head. It was a narrow escape, the fright causing a large patch of Sally's hair to temporarily fall out in the weeks shortly afterwards. We started immediately to look for something more modern and nearer to the Naval Base.

Pirate Taxis

In those days we did not own a car but travel to the Naval Base was fairly easy; for along the Thompson Road ran a constant stream of big Mercedes taxis acting like buses, usually driven by a large Sikh driver. These ran the length of this major road across Singapore Island and would stop and pick up or drop passengers, providing there was room in the vehicle; anywhere at the wave of an arm. The passengers sharing the cost and paying the driver according to the distance they travelled, subject to a minimum price which was hardly more than a bus fare.

Singapore is of course a wonderful multi-racial community where it seemed everyone in those days, despite their different cultures, got on reasonably well together; thus travelling in one of these shared taxis could be a really interesting adventure.

Sally tells of one experience when bound for the HM Dockyard swimming pool, on stopping a taxi on a small hill, she put Nicola and Neil in the back seat with the swimming and picnic bags. Already sitting there was a sleepy little Chinese man sitting alone, while crammed in the front there were two Malays with a couple of live chickens clucking in a rattan basket, and the large Sikh driver who sat passively waiting while Sally folded the pushchair to put in the boot of the Mercedes. Going around to the back she opened it up to find the space completely full of ripe pineapples; these promptly started to fall out and roll one after another down the hill into the monsoon storm drain. The little Chinese man came to life and yelling excitedly in Cantonese leapt out in pursuit. The driver, losing valuable time while he waited, glowered and the Malays smiled at the small China man's predicament; nobody spoke to the highly embarrassed memsahib.

Shortly afterwards we were able to move and rent a brand new semi-detached bungalow, 45 Jalan Malu-malu, immediately outside the Naval Base at Sembawang village. We employed a wonderful Chinese amah, Sah Wah, to help Sally look after the children and the house and a Tamil gardener, called Tan, to cut the grass and endeavour to make something of the bare piece of earth (inside a high wire mesh fence) we called the garden. Sally planted a banana tree which is there to this day visible on Google Earth. Next door lived Lieutenant Ted Lewis RN, wife Pat and daughter Christine who turned out to be wonderfully good neighbours during our sojourn in Singapore and who went on to live and settle in New Zealand, becoming lifelong friends.

Hong Kong

Sally and the children did one voyage up to Hong Kong for which the Second Engineer kindly lent us his larger cabin. It was to be an interesting voyage; for half way up the China Sea, in heavy north easterly weather, the old *Fort Dunvegan* had to climb her way through what appeared to be a tidal wave. The enormous sea, which I later learned was believed to have originated in Alaska, passed through the gap between Taiwan and the Philippines; eventually went ashore in Vietnam causing extensive damage. Maybe what I experienced was only a freak wave, for it has been said one cannot usually see a tsunami at sea; however this one I certainly saw coming a couple of miles away as I walked onto the starboard bridge wing at the beginning of my watch. This sea appeared to form a series of huge steps as the large waves gradually built up to this particular monster. I had sufficient time to reduce speed, put out a warning to 'hold on' through the internal broadcast system and start to turn to starboard to meet the brute head on. The quartermaster at the wheel was thrown off with the impact as the old girl, not quite fully round at the crest of the wave, lurched heavily to port before falling off the top and heading downhill to the trough. Everything not soundly secured in the twenty-year-old ship came loose, as straining and creaking she protested the harsh treatment being given her. There were a number of minor injuries aboard but fortunately most people had gone to bed; none were serious injuries and there was no serious damage. Young Neil had been wedged in the space under the 2nd Engineer's desk and did not wake up, while Nicola was like many people thrown out of bed. We reported our experience to Hong Kong by radio, and on arrival I visited the naval base to examine some other plotted hydrographical reports and was told that our experience had almost certainly coincided with a tsunami that went ashore in Vietnam drowning many coastal people; so maybe one can observe such phenomena after all.

Another Cobra

While at anchor in Johore Strait off the Singapore Naval Dockyard I took revenge on cobras in general for earlier frightening my family. It happened one afternoon when as duty officer I heard a commotion at the gangway and went to investigate. I found the Chinese Coxswain of the ship's 25-foot cutter alongside the gangway pontoon fending off a poor unfortunate cobra with a boathook. Desperately trying to climb aboard the ship via the gangway pontoon, the snake had obviously fallen into the Johore Strait from a tree in the adjoining jungle.

The irritated and frightened cobra did not appreciate the Coxswain's attempts to prevent this course of action and, with its flat head poised to strike, had gone into attack mode. Sally's earlier experience and my consequential dislike for this particular venomous reptile species drove me to feel I needed to take action. I called the cutter and ordered the coxswain to stand clear of the ship and sent a Cadet to bring me a 303 rifle and some ammunition. Opening the brand new box I took out one cartridge, loaded and resting the rifle on the guard rail took careful aim at the poor creature swimming innocently for the jungle. Now by this time the main deck had filled up with interested spectators curious to see just what I was up to;

some in awe that I had the temerity to actually open a box of live ammunition. I had been quite a good shot as a young sea cadet, although somewhat hampered when competing in rapid fire shoots due to my natural left-handedness. I fired and to my and everyone else's surprise blew the wretched snake in two pieces, the halves being quickly recovered by the coxswain who promptly presented them to the cook.

In retrospect perhaps I should have let the poor innocent creature escape; his compatriot had, after all, despite our small son's efforts to eat it, done him no harm.

Weapons Officer

The Captain on hearing of my adroitness with the rifle and on the strength of one shot, promptly made me the ship's weapons officer; with the task of teaching the other officers to use the weapons we had just received as Confrontation with Indonesia turned into a small shooting war. We took a few rifles and a Lanchester Sub-Machine Gun, a gun which was built in the 1940s for the Royal Navy and a copy of the German MP28 and very heavy for a sub-machine gun; up into a quarry somewhere in Johore and fired at targets. It was supposed to fire 600 rounds per minute, but I recall we only had a box of fifty and these we fired as single rounds with a range of 150 yards. My shot at the cobra remained, however, the only shot fired in anger.

The 'Confrontation' was one of Britain's forgotten wars, yet it was a major commitment involving over 50,000 British servicemen and very nearly escalation into full-scale war with Indonesia. I imagine the cause of the dispute was probably about the oil in Borneo and Malaysia, but I remember the argument was about territorial limits and in particular the claims by Britain on land between two headlands where there just happened to be oil.

In an attempt to destroy Britain's plans for Malaysia, President Sukarno of Indonesia began guerrilla warfare including air and sea landings, and Britain responded with a secret war by supporting rebel groups, propaganda and clandestine cross-border raids using Royal Marines and other special forces.

Mislaid Midshipman

Actually on one of these patrols I carelessly lost a young RN Midshipman who was supposed to be studying practical stellar navigation at sea under my instruction. This followed a request from the First Lieutenant of the aircraft carrier he was serving in, which was dry-docked in Singapore. During our progress issuing victualling stores around the area, RFA *Fort Dunvegan* was to be in Kuching, Borneo for a week and the young officer asked if he might be released from his tuition in order to join a patrol of Royal Marines in the jungle rather than hang around the ship. Thinking the exercise would probably do him good and being unable to continue practical navigation in port, I wished him well and he disappeared in a RM Land Rover. Unfortunately the patrol did not go at all well for the young Midshipman who somehow managed to get himself shot in the posterior and had to be evacuated by helicopter to hospital; where I am told he was to spend some time recovering from quite serious injuries. Now I never did find out whether he was shot by the Indonesians or accidentally by the Royal Marines or tripped over his own weapon. On meeting this particular First Lieutenant on our return to Singapore, considerable displeasure was expressed at my carelessness in losing this young man; who it appears was an Admiral's son.

President Sukarno of Indonesia, who was literally in bed with the Soviets, was finally overthrown by a pro-Western military government which renounced the Confrontation and accepted the expansion of the Malaysian Federation. It was however some time before that, and prior to there being any real trouble, that Sally with our small children, Nicola and Neil were to arrive in Singapore.

Opportunist Burglars

Initially we had few problems but eventually the unrest built up in Singapore and the police were withdrawn from the suburbs into the city at night to deal with demonstrations and as extra security; meaning that the opportunist burglars arrived in Jalan Malu-malu. One clear moonlit night in the days before air-conditioning I awoke to see a man's silhouette outlined against the narrow decorative bars of our open window and a long bamboo pole extending across the bedroom towards Sally's handbag, which was on a camphor wood chest at the foot of our bed. I lay still and tense, figuring that if the burglar managed to hook the bag he would then have to withdraw the pole hand-over-hand and eventually reach inside the bars to take it before it fell on the floor. Right at that point I would leap up and tie his arms in a knot inside the bars and trap him – but what if Sally awoke in the meantime? I put my hand reassuringly on her back as she slept peacefully beside me; at which she awoke and, startled, let out a piercing scream clearing the bed by about a foot before coming down on top of me to knock my breath away. The long bamboo pole, which turned out be our washing line pole and handbag remained abandoned in position, the pole sticking out the window while the wire mesh gate at the end of the short drive gently vibrated in the still night air; the only sign of the escaping miscreant. I called out to my naval neighbour to tell him what had happened and his response was somewhat unsympathetic.

"Yes I know, the whole neighbourhood knows and with all that noise you must have frightened all the burglars back to Singapore; go back to sleep," he said.

When I was at sea Sally slept battened down after that; while the dear amah Sah Wah would shout out in Cantonese on, hearing prowlers, that they should go away for we were 'only a poor family' but little did she know just how poor we were.

After Sally had been hospitalized with pneumonia in the Military Hospital, which meant that we had to call upon friends and the Singapore-based RFA Marine Superintendent for help with the children when I was away at sea, the Confrontation began to escalate and we began to think of a way to get home to the UK. Luckily I was the ship's operations officer and privy to confidential information not generally known and one day I learnt of the imminent arrival of six Britannia aircraft out from the UK with several hundred troop reinforcements.

I immediately telephoned the appropriate RAF staff at Changi and put my wife and children down for an Indulgence flight back to the UK. It was to eventually cost in total about £2.50. I was told that they had been added to a list and might possibly get a flight in a couple of months. Stressing to the Flight Sergeant in charge that they would be ready to go at 24 hours' notice; I thanked him for his help. Happily Sally and the children were flown home 36 hours later, courtesy of the RAF via Gan in the Maldives, Aden, El Adem in Benghazi and Lynham.

Rum Barrels

Sometime during the subsequent months when the Navy still issued a regular tot of rum I found myself as the senior watch-keeper on the bridge with Captain Colin Barker as we stored HMS *Bulwark*. Everything had been going well as we steamed south-easterly alongside the carrier on a lovely hot sunny day in the Indian Ocean. The sea was calm with a long gentle swell when, meeting a somewhat larger swell, the two ships diverged slightly and the jackstay carrying the sling of stores between the two ships, being manually controlled by our Cantonese winch-man, came bar tight before he could slack away with the steam-driven winch. The result was that a cargo net full of rum barrels being returned to us from HMS *Bulwark* shot upwards out of the net and dropped neatly into the sea between the two ships, steaming at ten knots side by side and rapidly started to drop astern.

Now a couple of miles astern we had the destroyer HMS *Carysfort* acting as a plane guard, following patiently behind us just in case somebody fell overboard during an operation not entirely without some risk. The Captain called out to the Royal Naval Yeoman of Signals who was on hand to communicate by semaphore or the ten inch Signal light. Yeoman make to *Carysfort*;

"Rum Barrels Coming Your Way"

The signal light clattered away and we watched through our binoculars with interest the excitement as HMS *Carysfort* smartly reduced speed and launched a motorized whaler which headed rapidly for the barrels floating scattered towards them. Just before they were about to reach them the Captain called the RN Yeoman again. Yeoman he ordered make to Carysfort;

"To my last add EMPTY."

Chapter 19

Homeward Bound by Sea

Having got the family home, it eventually became my turn to follow them on completion of my tour of Duty. This time however I had accrued more than the usual amount of baggage and even items of furniture; all of which I had crated and stored in Singapore Naval Base awaiting my return from sea.

RFA personnel normally flew out or back to join their ships in the Far East and in the 1960s this was done using four-engined propeller-driven Britannia trooping flights operated by the RAF and DAN Air. I had done a number of these flights when I learnt that the option to travel by sea on a passenger ship was to be withdrawn. Now was the time to use it before it was lost, and thinking it would be rather nice to travel by P&O in style and get paid for the privilege – I applied.

On the way up to Hong Kong we received a signal that my sea passage had been arranged from Singapore on a Blue Funnel cargo ship via all the liner ports en route to Liverpool. I was to fly to Singapore courtesy of the RAF and join Alfred Holt's Dolius shortly to leave for Port Swettenham and Penang. Not exactly what I had been expecting, but at last I was homeward bound.

Once back in Singapore I picked up my stored extra baggage and joined the *MV Dolius,* a 12-passenger cargo liner belonging to Alfred Holt & Company of Liverpool, on her way home from a voyage east as far as Japan. There were only five passengers as I recall, a Cornish Daffodil farmer, a retired Scottish boiler maker, a publisher and his wife, and me for the voyage to the UK; but we did have the company for one day of a very ancient retired tin miner who, with no more baggage than a plastic bag and a bottle of gin, joined us to take passage up the Malay coast to Port Sweetenham. Brief contact with this old man left me with the feeling that he would have been a fascinating raconteur with stories of tin mining before the war. All I can remember however was his warning that the mosquitoes at Port Swettenham were as big as bats and if I was to go ashore I needed to be sure to wear 'mosquito boots', whatever they were.

Alfred Holt's Dolius in Suez Canal

The ship was carrying a Doctor although this was not a manning requirement on ships with 12 passengers or less, hence the reason cargo ships restricted the number of passengers. The Doctor, a young Canadian on a holiday job, had been specially employed because the owner had taken passage to Japan. I cannot remember his name but he was fascinated with the Far East and desired to know everything he could possibly learn of the countries he visited. With little to employ him, the Doctor spent much of his time with the passengers and in fact with only a uniform cap supplied by Alfred Holt he looked like a passenger most of the time.

As we approached Port Sweetenham the Doctor picked on me as being an old Malaysian hand, after all he had discovered I had just spent more than a year on the coast based at Singapore. Did I know if he could visit a rubber plantation? I did not, but interested in a run ashore to a place I had never visited I suggested we should go ashore and try.

Having landed at Port Sweetenham first thing after breakfast, we took the train up to Klang in the heart of rubber country. Klang turned out to be much like a cowboy town in the American mid-west with just one large wide main street and I desperately wondered how I was going to satisfy the Doctor's wishes. Fortunately the young man was an inveterate postcard writer with many relatives and, with a large bag of cards to post, he set off to find the post office while I looked around desperately for something to do with rubber plantations.

Now you need a bit of luck in life and I have certainly had more than my fair share. This was to turn out to be a really lucky day, for my eyes suddenly focused on a shop front proclaiming the owner to run a "Planters' Agency". I headed for the porch and entered the cool dark interior where I met a tall friendly gentleman, of Tamil or Malay lineage, with the name of Lionel Proctor. My eyes were immediately drawn to a black and white framed photograph of a man being presented with the MBE by King George VI; the man in the picture was Noel Proctor, Lionel's father. I had by chance come across the son of one of Malaysia's most interesting characters. Apparently, despite the considerable danger to his own life, this man had helped British troops who were trapped and living behind the Japanese lines during the Second World War. I would guess that he had been rewarded for his efforts and set up the Planters Agency but he may well have been in that business in any case.

Once again the Proctors came to the aid of a young Englishman as I told him of my situation and the Doctor's hopes. I could not have found a better man, for by the time the Doctor found me I was sitting in the shade on the porch of the agency with a nice cool Tiger beer, while drawn up outside was a large black Mercedes with a Sikh driver sitting patiently waiting. It had been arranged for us to visit the Bukit Raja Rubber Plantation, one of the largest and oldest established plantations in Malaysia.

The car delivered us to a large imposing bungalow built on the top of a small hill, amid beautifully manicured gardens with wide sweeping lawns. There was no ground cover on the approaches to the house, a reminder of the days of the troubles with the communists when an Emergency had been declared in Malaysia and the house had been turned into a small fortress against attacks. There was no sign of life as the car swept off down the drive leaving us at the porch in which stood a solitary pair of wet Wellington boots. The door was open and, putting my head inside, I called to see if anyone was at home.

A deep voice answered from somewhere far off in the cool depths of the large house, telling us to "come on through". Inside we found an elderly gentleman swathed in a white terry towelling bathrobe, a large glass in his hand. He introduced himself and we had found a second famous Malay character, an expatriate by the name of McGee, the original planter manager of the estate who had managed the Bukit Raja before the war with eleven under managers, and who had been brought back out of retirement post war to put things in order. He was now running the estate with just one young Australian under manager. Our charming and generous host had arranged a light lunch at which we were to be joined by the young Australian who was to take us on a tour of the estate before the car returned to pick us up.

It had not been a good day for Mr McGee as he explained that, despite his many years of experience, that morning he had completely miscalculated and ordered his foreman to tap; that is cut into the bark of a section of rubber trees allowing the milky white sap of the tree to bleed into tin containers, attached to the tree for collection. The operation required a dry day to allow the pure latex to collect in the tin containers attached to each tree below the tap, but unfortunately he had been caught that morning by heavy unexpected rain. The rain had filled the containers to overflowing a great deal of the latex onto the ground. The latex was still collectable but of second grade material, and I seem to remember Mr McGee telling us the difference that day was something in the region of $24,000 Malaysian dollars.

It had been an annoying day for him but was a truly memorable day for us, as we toured the vast estate and viewed rubber and palm oil in all its growing sequences with our enthusiastic new friend before returning to the ship at Port Sweetenham. Whether or not the Doctor ever realised just how lucky I had been or whether he was convinced I had real connections in Malaysia, I do not know but certainly it did my standing in his eyes a lot of good and had made me a firm friend for the passage home.

Aboard the *Dolius* I was also to become fairly popular that voyage for resolving a small problem involving two of my fellow passengers. These men had taken to appearing for dinner in loud Hawaiian unwashed sports shirts; in the days when aboard those ships the officers were expected to dress for dinner when eating with the passengers. The two elderly passengers, who had a rather un-seamanlike relationship with washing in general, were causing real ill feeling among the officers who were fearful of speaking their minds in case a complaint was made about them to the company. Having discussed the problem with the publisher in the next stateroom, we decided we would dress for dinner each evening and shame our fellow passengers into making an effort. It worked after the culprits enquired just why we were getting all 'toffed up' and I explained that it was in fairness to the ship's officers who had no choice in the matter. From then onwards they made an effort, although they failed perhaps to match the sartorial elegance of my white dinner jacket tailored by 'Toothy Wong of Singapore'.

One of the passengers, a Glaswegian boiler maker, turned out in fact to be a lovely natural man who claimed he was being sent home in disgrace after visiting his daughter, who had become what we called a GI bride. This girl had however done rather well for herself, marrying a young submariner who as a naval officer had risen to the very top of the United State Navy and was at that time serving as Commander-in-Chief of the United States Pacific Fleet. We could see just why perhaps father had not fitted in with his daughter's new world but he was a funny and amusing man for all that with tales of his most embarrassing foibles.

The leisurely voyage home in good company, visiting all the liner ports was a real privilege and an opportunity to witness the activities of one of Britain's finest shipping companies in its prime. Sadly those days and those magnificently designed and strongly built ships with the skilled seamen to man them were soon to become just memories, disappearing forever to be replaced by the large ugly box boats of the world today.

Fishing for shrimp at Dymchurch on leave

Chapter 20

Final Days in the RFA

For some time it had been obvious to me that there were two branches of the RFA. There were the frontline fast tankers and supply ships directly supporting and replenishing the fleet at sea and then there were the freighting tankers, Landing Ships, station store ships and odds and sods that supported the former. It was also clearly apparent that the fast track to promotion was through the former and although I was to be promoted to First Officer in situ, a somewhat unusual occurrence at that time, I realised I was playing too often for the wrong team and needed to get into the first eleven. The term 'Front Line Support Ships' first appeared in the Statement on Defence Estimates dated 1962; it had therefore been official for a couple of years before I awoke to the dangers of being left behind. At that time in my career I had no thoughts of eventually being a Trinity House London Pilot; my horizons were firmly set on a career in the RFA to Command and nothing else.

How to ensure that move then to the other team? Enquires soon led me to discover that for just a couple of years, 2 RFA Second Officers had already been assigned to join 48 RN Lieutenants on each of the three monthly Lieutenants General Courses (LGC) held at the RN Staff College Greenwich. The College was established in the wonderful old baroque masterpiece of English architecture designed by Sir Christopher Wren in 1694 and built alongside the River Thames at Greenwich. On the Greenwich meridian at 0° longitude, the very centre of the earth and certainly of all things maritime, I applied to join immediately and was provisionally accepted subject to my return to the UK.

The only problem was that by the time I returned I had been promoted to First Officer and the course was really for Second Officers; I argued my case and was allowed to go to Greenwich. Luckily it seems I must have made some influential friends, although I was unaware who they were but naturally enough my appointment did cause some resentment among those not selected or given the same opportunity. Life is, of course, not fair and sometimes one has to recognise and take advantage of the chances given and this was a real chance to put my head above the parapet.

The LGC was a junior staff course designed to take officers who had specialised throughout the fleet in their own particular fields and give them some basic staff work and generally broaden their education. There were therefore navigators, aviators, submariners, engineers, pursers, weapons specialists, Royal Marines, communicators and boffins, you name it they were probably present. The teaching staffs were from the Royal Navy, Army and RAF as well as a number of civilian academics. It was an opportunity for the Admiralty to see exactly what they had produced after a number of years' service and a real chance for the individual to demonstrate his or her ability. Although that statement may be politically correct, there was a stunning absence of women on my course in the autumn of 1965.

I started by bringing myself to the attention of everyone in the first three days, but definitely not by design. Being the third senior officer on the course, according to a list that was published for our benefit only but which indicated curiously two Lieutenants had more points than me, I found I had been designated to read the daily morning lesson in the RN College Chapel on the third morning of the course being the Wednesday. It was a beautiful Chapel and one where as a young Sea Cadet I had first attended a service some eighteen years beforehand. My reading was from the Book of John Chapter 5:1-9

Now I was not used to reading publicly and so I quickly practised and took someone down to the Chapel prior to the service for him to check my voice could be heard at the back. On the morning the reading seemed to go well.

It was the parable where Jesus cured a long-term lame man at Bethesda saying:

'Rise, take up thy bed, and walk.'

Now Wednesday was the day we were all expected to participate in some kind of sporting activity and here a little pre-knowledge was useful. Those in the know would spend a leisurely afternoon exercising one of a string of horses belonging to the Military tutor, who just happened to be a Major in the Hussars. Not having had the benefit of such pre-knowledge or much opportunity for sport since leaving school some sixteen years previously, I opted for hockey and was asked to play in goal.

The first and only game I played for the RN College Greenwich was against a team from King's College, London School of Medicine. It was to be a very brief appearance for me for unfortunately when going for the ball to prevent a shot in the first fifteen minutes, a large forward stood firmly on my left foot as I swung my right leg to kick the ball clear. I went down with a crash and both my fibula and tibia on my left leg broke above the ankle strap for the shin pad. Lying there on the damp grass with the lower part of my leg now at right angles to the rest, I was soon being encouraged to get up by some of the students of one of the country's largest and oldest medical schools with a history that can be traced back several centuries. Fortunately the referee recognised a serious sporting injury, even if they did not, and an ambulance carried me off to a small Cottage Hospital nearby before the more enthusiastic could attempt any kind of treatment.

The leg was set in plaster and I came to from the anaesthetic to find myself in a small ward full of men of diverse age, coughing, spluttering and breaking wind. This was the first time I was to come across the Rotary wheel logo, and words 'Rotary International', which was later to play such a significant role in my later life for there was a telephone on a small mobile plug-in unit donated by the local Rotary Club which allowed patients to make contact with the outside world.

Quickly I called the RN Medical Officer at Greenwich and asked for help, although strictly speaking I was a civilian and it could be argued not entitled to the use of the medical services of Her Majesty's Armed Forces. The Army turned up trumps and a military ambulance collected me and transferred me to an officers' private room at the Royal Military Hospital, Woolwich. The Surgeon Colonel came to see me clutching an X-ray he had ordered and informed me just how lucky I was that I had been transferred to a Military Hospital and to him personally, for the X-ray indicated that the bones had not been set properly by the NHS and that unless the leg was reset, I would spend the rest of my life with one leg shorter than the other. Now I have to say I did not feel exactly lucky at the thought of having my leg re-broken and was slightly suspicious that perhaps they just needed the practice? However shortly afterwards there was a knock at the door and a smartly dressed military steward appeared to see if I required an aperitif before luncheon and my doubts were to dissipate.

My left leg plastered from groin to toe and on crutches, I obtained approval with some difficulty to continue with the LGC and shortly afterwards returned to the course in the back of a canvas-covered military Land Rover driven by a young lady who I am sure shot through the imposing gates of the Royal Naval College Greenwich on only two wheels.

Having been struck down immediately after reading John Chapter 5, I sought out the Naval Padre on my return to see if he thought I had been punished personally for a particular misdemeanour; only to discover that he lacked a sense of humour about such matters.

Although not by design I had therefore brought myself to the attention of a number of people and it served me well and particularly so when on crutches at the wardroom bar, where even the College Commandant would address me by name and offer me sustenance. We worked hard and had an excellent social life.

Water Rats

After entertaining the Grand Order of Water Rats (a charitable organisation of comedians founded in 1889 with a membership limited to 200) to a Mess Dinner, I remember the plaster on my broken leg was signed by Alfred Marks (the King Rat at the time) and a number of eminent comedians – among them being Ted Ray, Norman Wisdom, Tommy Trinder, Cyril Fletcher and several others. The plaster, an appendage adorned with signatures probably worth some money today, soon became grubby and somewhat smelly and naturally I was delighted eventually to discard it after three months of confinement.

Dining in the Painted Hall, probably the finest dining hall in the Western world, decorated with stunning paintings by James Thornhill and designed and built by Sir Christopher Wren, as we did for all meals was a real privilege and one which filled me and most visitors with awe. The allegorical theme of the huge and exuberant Lower Hall ceiling painting depicts the triumph of Peace and Liberty over Tyranny, and pays due tribute to William and Mary and British maritime power. Within the oval frame are the four seasons – the model for Winter was said to be one of the inmates, John Worley, an energetic Greenwich pensioner still being punished for drunkenness and swearing at the age of 96. In the Upper Hall Queen Anne surveys the continents of the world (America reputedly represented by an image of Pocahontas), while on the west wall her Hanoverian successors, King George I and his family, and are shown in sober glory. Hobbling around in these grand surroundings on my crutches I was to imbibe a great sense of history.

The two long tables in the main Lower Hall led to the top table which was set at right angles on a dais in the Upper Hall. On the occasion of the Water Rats' Dinner, Ted Ray (who was seated as I was, at the lower end of the Lower Hall) had been chosen to reply on behalf of the guests. He rose to his feet and paused, standing looking thoughtfully up the long hall towards the top table on the dais and we all turned to look and immediately got the same impression as the one he was about to mention; we waited in anticipation.

Now of all the gentlemen present that night Ted Ray had come across, certainly to me anyway, as the most knowledgeable and thoughtful of men. We had been studying a variety of problems which raised questions in our minds. There was for example Rhodesia with Ian Smith about to declare UDI. There were the racially motivated Watts Riots in Los Angeles when 34 people died and 1,032 people were injured while thousands were arrested. There was a noticeable lack of coloured policemen in our own metropolitan police force. On the scientific side there had just begun the hunt for oil in the North Sea and the Americans seemed about to reach the moon. We discovered in conversation that this man was interested in our opinions and not scared to express his own views. He had certainly done his homework, for his speech mentioned Lord Nelson lying in state in that very room and his awe at the magnificence of the whole place; making reference to the original use of Greenwich as a seamen's hospital, he made a sly dig at me bearded and on crutches as being perhaps one of the original patients. His speech naturally being one of considerable humour he built up our expectations as he said that while he recognised the Royal Navy as being the senior service, he had not realized before that night just how well connected we were and, with that, he finally drew our attention to the top table where the Commandant, Alfred Marx and other senior guests sat, many bearded. In the lighting of the hall the small elevated group resembled a certain famous painting. After toasting his hosts Ted Ray closed with words giving us the benefit of his perception; that the top table reminded him of;

> *'Leonardo de Vinci's painting in Milan of the Last Supper.'*

The North Sea Oil Hunt

Part of the course involved groups of five officers giving a presentation on a number of preordained subjects chosen as being of current interest by the directing staff. While others got their teams together first and pondered over which subject to choose, I noticed that one subject was 'The North Sea Oil Hunt' and on the hypothesis that the team choosing that subject might be able to obtain help from the giant oil companies; I quickly put my name against it and started to recruit a team, looking in particular for an officer with connections in the industry. Now here was my second bit of luck for one Royal Marine Officer just happened to be the son of a Director of Shell International and we were home and dry.

After the LGC acronym we called ourselves the 'Licentious Gasoline Company' and managed to recruit a number of the young ladies on the Wrens OCTU based at Greenwich to sing and record a saucy little advertising ditty which we had playing to welcome our audience. Rather sexy, it was based on a piece of fun now lost somewhere in the wealth of irreverent music of the Swinging Sixties. This had been fun to record but I have to say that Sally was not too impressed that on the few times she needed to telephone me at the college; the calls had to be transferred to the wrens' quarters and my protests of innocence and reminders of my disability were greeted with considerable scepticism.

We divided the team up into Technical, Geological, Research and Marketing and on the day wondered at the influence of our young Royal Marine, when a large black pantechnicon van rolled up outside the conference hall and a team of men carried in a large diamond-headed drilling bit for an oil rig, a large model of an oil rig plus maps and charts. The help saved us a great deal of work and incidentally made the whole presentation very professional. As the team leader I chose to be the expert on the actual different types of oil rig in use around the world and learnt a lot in my research. As a team we obviously scored well with our presentation but the 'sugar on the cake' was that we had stated that we confidently expected that a gas or oil strike was imminent and the staff and audience returned to the wardroom for afternoon tea to find the headlines of London evening papers stating; *GAS STRIKE – NORTH SEA KLONDIKE*

As well as working hard we had a very good social life as one can imagine. On one occasion attending the Black and White Minstrel show at the Victoria Palace Theatre to dine out our retiring commander, we took the entire front row of the circle and the adjoining box, (my disability meant I could not sit in an ordinary theatre seat) dressing alternately in black and white dinner jackets.

There were also tremendous physical advantages being on crutches; for example, visiting the RAF Vulcan base at Grantham I was pushed around and entertained to tea in the mess by a pretty little WAAF while the rest of the course clambered into and out of aeroplanes and other places considered to be of interest. Going home was usually no problem by train, except one busy Friday I struggled on with my crutches at Charing Cross Station to find the First Class Compartment full; nobody offered me a seat and I was forced to stand in the corridor as the train moved out. A little man quickly dived into the toilet compartment and was still there as we passed Chislehurst. Annoyed that with my disability nobody had offered me a seat and that I was forced to stand in the corridor, I banged on the door with my crutches and said in a loud voice;

'You can't sit in there all the way to Folkestone you know!'

The door opened and this rather sheepish little red-faced man appeared, apologising profusely as I towered bearded over him and fiercely glared down at him in his embarrassment. I quickly took over the compartment and 'sat all the way to Folkestone'! Life is not always fair and you have to make the most of opportunities.

Law Enforcement

Among the various subjects we studied at the Royal Naval College, Greenwich to broaden our education was a brief look at the operation of the law enforcement in the United Kingdom. This included a visit to the 'Old Bailey' where special visitors or observers were allowed access in one court room, through a narrow door into a small compartment, seating two people and resembling a minute theatre box. The trial was in progress on the day two of us were shown into the box, a process that did not prove easy for me being hampered by my crutches; my efforts to clamber in and sit down proved to be noisy. Once settled, I looked across the famous court room scene to the ashen-faced lady defendant staring directly back at me in fear from the opposite side. It was a spooky moment.

It was only when the trial developed that I realised the poor woman must have suffered a terrible shock when first my crutches appeared through the small door to be followed by my bearded figure, for she was on trial for murder, reduced to manslaughter, of her drunken crippled husband who had gone to strike her with his crutches in the kitchen of their home. It would appear that in a drunken state he had over the years regularly abused his wife but this time she picked up a kitchen knife in her defence and struck out with what proved to be a fatal blow. Whether the Judge or Jury noticed as I had, her obvious reaction to my innocent arrival, I cannot say but I can remember being relieved that she was treated with sympathy by the court and for those less tolerant times; she was given a very light sentence.

On another occasion we had a comprehensive lecture from a Deputy Commissioner of the Metropolitan Police Force who welcomed questions afterwards, but who had generally come across to me as being very self-satisfied with the standard of policing in the capital and perhaps just a little too complacent. We however had been studying many general subjects and the large scale Watts race riots in Los Angeles, California had only taken place in August of that year, lasted for six days and before the riot had subsided, 34 people had been killed, 1,032 injured, and 3,952 arrested. In our discussions about the likely cause and effect, some of us had come to the conclusion that the fact that the Watts neighbourhood of Los Angeles was basically an Afro-American community, which appeared at that time to have been policed somewhat heavy-handedly by only white policemen, may been one of the core problems.

Probably the senior police officer thought it impertinent of me to ask, but I was curious in the light of the growing number of coloured immigrants populating certain areas of London and the problems in Watts, as to whether the Metropolitan Police had a policy to recruit any coloured police officers to prevent such problems and to retain a balance. The answer I received indicated that they had not done so because some areas were basically West Indian communities, while others were Nigerian and Ghanaian etc., and the mere sight of a coloured face would not necessarily be beneficial.

I was not convinced, but looking back now it seems extraordinary that we had such a situation just a few short years ago. Even more so that it was not until 1967 that a young black police constable was appointed by the Metropolitan Police and, perhaps cynically but certainly inappropriately, photographed guarding South Africa House at the time of apartheid in that country. I believe his name was Norwell Roberts and that he served for 30 years, retiring with the rank of Detective Sergeant and received the Queen's Police Medal in 1996.

Helicopter Flight Deck Officer

Undoubtedly the Lieutenants General Course put me in line for the first eleven. I returned home on leave to finally have the plaster taken off my leg and to begin a course of physiotherapy at the military hospital at Shorncliffe Army Camp in Folkestone before going down to Portland to begin a Helicopter Flight Deck Officer Course.

The leg had healed well despite the social challenges endured at Greenwich but I was still walking with a stick and limp when time came to start the course at Portland.

I drove down and joined a number of other officers as the snow set in over Somerset. The Naval Air Squadron CO took one look at me with my walking stick and declined to accept me on the course. I protested that even if I was expected to go up in his flying machines; surely I was only going to sit beside the driver? And in any case the MOD was paying a lot of money to train me. We compromised and agreed that the squadron medical officer would be the final arbitrator. He examined me carefully and remarking that I did not have to fly the helicopter but merely sit in the observer's seat, he passed me fit. Getting into the dry suit was a bit difficult but once

Helicopter Flight Deck

in I was able to drive down to the helicopter pad, pass my walking stick and car keys to a waiting member of the flight and pull myself up into the Wessex or Lynx helicopters. Now it was snowing and very cold but I noticed we always flew with my door missing, I imagine this was for my personal safety in the event of an accident I could abandon the aircraft quickly but I suspect it was to teach that cheeky bugger a lesson!

To me it was a wonderful exhilarating experience which I thoroughly enjoyed as we climbed vertically and then always seemed to fall off the top of a roll with my side underneath and nothing between me and the snow below. The pilot's with great humour did their best to put this RFA officer firmly in his place; in between dummy runs to the training flight deck to learn the real problems such aircraft experienced approaching a rolling and moving flight deck at sea.

On completion of the course I had a few more days at home in our new bungalow at Dymchurch, did some more physiotherapy and as it happens caught chickenpox from our young daughter Nicola although I was yet to realise it.

My appointment came through to RFA *Olynthus* as First Officer to join at Portland and it seemed I had made it to that first eleven for the ship was brand new and the latest edition to the fleet.

Completed on the 21st June 1965 at Hawthorn Leslie at Hebburn on Tyne, she was the first of a class of Admiralty-Designed Large Fleet Replenishment tankers. 648 feet long she was of 18,582 gross register tons, with a displacement of 32,027 tons fully loaded. Powered by two Pametrada steam turbines giving 26,500 shaft horsepower, she had a single screw and a speed of 21 knots. At the time she had a complement of 99 RFA personnel and for her helicopters a 32 RN flight support team. Carried two Wessex helicopters and had seven abeam fuelling rigs with automatic tensioning winches and two astern rigs managed from a central control room. She also had a hold for refrigerated, dry cargo and munitions.

All was to go wrong fairly quickly. At Portland *Olynthus* was working up and I spent considerable time day and night feeling gradually quite ill on the flight deck as we exercised our helicopters. The ship's doctor diagnosed influenza despite my hint that I had been in close contact with chickenpox and I was ordered to bed. The following morning the Doctor visited me having already given his diagnosis to the Captain and was horrified to find me covered with the unmistakeable red spots of chickenpox. It was decided to quickly get me off the ship before the disease spread but the Admiral had developed appendicitis and he was using the duty ambulance to get to the RN Hospital at Haslar. I was given a railway voucher and told to take the germs back to whence they came.

Unplanned Change of Career

Home slowly recovering from what turned out to be a very unpleasant illness, I was very disappointed to receive a letter from RFA Headquarters stating that I had been blamed for some damage to one of the new RAS (Replenishment at Sea) derricks on *Olynthus* and that I was not to be re-appointed to the ship but to be sent for retraining on the small training tanker RFA *Black Ranger* based at Portland. Despite my protests that I had not in fact used one of the ship's own RAS derricks, but had exercised using the derricks of RFA *Black Ranger* during my short stay aboard. Therefore the blame was either genuinely misplaced or perhaps somebody else on the ship was 'clearing their own yardarm'; there was no doubt I was not to go back.

Fortunately the Marine Superintendent of the day was not taken in by what he suspected to be the convenient mendacity of my accuser, for a similar thing had happened to him earlier in his career. Therefore after a slow recovery from chickenpox and a few days on *Black Ranger,* I was subsequently re-appointed as First Officer and travelled down to Plymouth and joined an even newer addition to the class RFA *Oleander.* This was to be my last ship before I left the RFA service to become a Cinque Ports Trinity House pilot working the next 32 years into and out of the Port of London.

The re-appointment had however come too late; the damage to my aspirations was complete and already I had started to look elsewhere outside the RFA Service, being bitterly disappointed at what at that time I considered unfair treatment. It probably would just have been a small blip in my career but it turned out to be a major and unplanned change in the direction of my subsequent career, for I had never even considered being a marine pilot prior to this particular episode. Actually the event and a certain amount of luck did me a great favour in the long run which completely changed my entire life and subsequently brought me considerable opportunities for which I am most grateful, complete job satisfaction, an almost normal family life, an opportunity to serve others and led to honourable recognition by my peers.

A Lucky Break

Lying recovering in bed from my illness while Sally went shopping in Folkestone with our new neighbour, and being somewhat dissatisfied with my treatment at that particular time, I had virtually run out of reading material. I was reduced to reading the advertisements in the *Daily Telegraph* newspaper when I came across the one legal requirement of The Corporation of Trinity House, the country's major Pilotage Authority, to advertise the opening of the London Sea List to prospective pilotage candidates. I was immediately tempted to enquire further and suddenly remembered my mean little bank manager belittling my sea-going career some years before, telling me that the only mariners who actually made real money were the local Trinity House Pilots – maybe it was worth enquiring. However, not working for a commercial company, I had rarely come across these gentlemen and knew nothing of their work or required qualifications and so I telephoned the Superintendent of Pilots in Dover an ex-RN officer who encouraged me to apply. When Sally came home with her new friend I told her of my enquiry; she made me a cup of tea and said our new neighbour had invited her in for a coffee, but she would not too be long.

Telling this friend of her conversation with me the reply was:

"Well if he is really interested he had better meet my father – he is the Senior Pilot."

Well after a few days serious thought and some research I became really interested, met the Senior Pilot and before going back to sea had applied to Trinity House to be considered for the Pilotage Service. Despite my new contact my expectations were not high, there were just so many applicants for the few vacancies and at 32 years old I was well aware that the closing top age was 35 years and most successful applicants were closer to that age; but first back to sea on contract to the RFA.

RFA *Oleander* sailed from Plymouth, exercising in the Channel and Bay of Biscay before proceeding to Gibraltar and then out to the Caribbean and back to Rosyth; after protracted exercising in the North Atlantic with submarines and helicopters. During our stay in Rosyth I was able to get a long weekend home leave and arrange on the Friday, unbeknown to anyone, my official interview as a candidate Trinity House Pilot. The sea list was open for candidates for the four pilot stations covering the Thames Estuary; those being The Cinque Ports based at Dover and shipping at Dungeness and North East Spit off Margate inwards to London and the Medway. The North Channel Pilots based at Harwich and shipping inwards to London, Harwich and Felixstowe. The Medway Pilots working inwards from Garrison Point up the River Medway and outwards to the seaward limits of the Compulsory London Pilotage District and The Channel Pilots based at Gravesend working outwards again to the limits of the District.

Now in my defence I have to say I was not particularly well-briefed as to how to present my case, there just had not been time; for instance I had not been informed that I only had two choices and needed to accept the second offer if I declined the first. I was unaware that candidates by tradition were not usually appointed to the district of their birth because they would have grown up with the local boatmen and perhaps have advantage in the race to offer pilotage services to approaching ships. I had not planned my career with a view to eventually becoming a pilot, I knew little about the service and was not sure how with a mortgage and children at school I was going to be able to fund six months' travel, training and living entirely at my own expense. The other candidates in the waiting room depressed me with their knowledge and experience of command and more than one interview. One had flown in from a ship in Japan and several from pilot districts in Africa and beyond at their own expense.

Entering a large room with a superb large, wooden, highly-polished table reflecting the bright sunlight from the south facing window, I found myself facing a line of very serious elderly and important looking gentlemen sitting on the other side with the light and the Tower of London behind them knowing that one (but not realizing which one) was the Elected Representative of the Cinque Ports Pilots on the Trinity House Pilotage Committee. If it had not been for this particular man I am sure I would never have been given the opportunity for I did just about everything wrong. I had been warned that the CPP would never take a bearded candidate and that prior to the interview I should shave; I had declined. When offered The Medway I declined, not wishing to live there; and again I declined Harwich, remarking that it was far too cold up there and that in any case I was born in Folkestone and owned a house in nearby Dymchurch and could not afford to move. I only wished to be a Trinity House Cinque Ports Pilot and if that was not possible I was very happy with my position in the RFA, my promotion I had just been told was going through to Chief Officer and I would stay at sea.

There was a stunned silence; nobody it seems had ever, having been offered an appointment, refused both the choices. I left the room hoping that I had impressed the Senior Pilot sufficiently while crewing for him in a small sailing dinghy in Dover Harbour, even if I had not impressed the interview board, but happily I learnt soon afterwards that I had been accepted as a candidate Cinque Ports Pilot subject to checks on my documentation. I would accompany working pilots for six months' training at my own expense and then having memorised all the regulations, the navigational marks, depths of water and courses between the buoys throughout the London District and been examined as to my competence to pilot the smallest ships subjected to compulsory pilotage; I would be let loose on the unsuspecting shipmaster.

My last voyage with the RFA was to be something special, for the Prime Minister Harold Wilson had decided to send Great Britain's very latest missile carrying destroyer, HMS *Devonshire* and our latest Fast Fleet Replenishment Tanker RFA *Oleander* to Leningrad on the first Royal Naval visit to the Soviet Union since the Second World War. We were also expecting to take with us that new British invention the hovercraft and had actually built the chocks for it on our fore deck. It was however not part of the MOD establishment and was being flown for some unknown reason at that time by the company chief test pilot who had a Norwegian passport and was not allowed – perhaps a little short-sightedly – a visa by the Soviet authorities. At the time the visit seemed very strange, but who were we to question authority.

HMS *Devonshire* was having some minor mechanical problems and started to drop astern as we proceeded up the English Channel independently, the Royal Marine Home Fleet Band exercising on our flight deck. Considering it prudent to allow the Admiral and the Royal Navy the opportunity to arrive first at the Kiel Canal, we reduced speed and picked up a German Brunsbüttel pilot while HMS *Devonshire* slid past into the fog; exercising her right to navigate independently without a pilot. Unfortunately lying at anchor in the fog on her track was a British tanker waiting on the tide to go up the River Elbe to the oil refinery; the German pilot having local knowledge knew of this and watched the radar in alarm as the missile cruiser headed directly for the innocent tanker where all were probably having a leisurely breakfast.

Due to the warship's automatic fog signal coinciding with a warning report from their own manned radar plot, over the ship's internal communications system of the imminent risk of collision being missed, the two ships were nearly involved in a serious collision; only narrowly averted by the quick last-minute action of the bridge team. As it was the warship just clipped the tanker with her port quarter damaging the guard rails and the Admiral's pristine barge. It was immediately decided that if we could get our forward ten ton crane and dry cargo hold close enough in the Canal Locks at Brunsbüttel to HMS *Devonshire,* we would lift the Admiral's damaged barge off and hide it in our hold. After some careful manoeuvring by the German sea pilot this was achieved and carried out while the two ships were locked into the Kiel Canal.

The Kiel Canal (until 1948 known as the Kaiser-Wilhelm-Kanal) is a 61 miles long canal linking the North Sea at Brunsbüttel to the Baltic Sea at Kiel-Holtenau. By using the Kiel Canal instead of going around the Jutland Peninsula the two ships saved 280 nautical miles on the passage to first of all Gdynia in Poland and then the Soviet Union. Busy in 1966, it is claimed today to be the most heavily used artificial seaway in the world; over 43,000 ships passed through in 2007, excluding small craft.

The two ships not only had Russian speaking Naval interpreters, ours being a well-known BBC parliamentary reporter from the Royal Naval Reserve but we naturally had intelligence lectures prior to visiting two Eastern Bloc countries at the height of the cold war and most amusing they were; one quoting the visit of the President of a Far Eastern country to Russia who, as an elderly statesman, was compromised and filmed with two athletic young ladies in his hotel bedroom. On returning to his own country he and his wife were supposedly invited to a film show at the Soviet Embassy where we were told the expectation was one of blackmail, but alas the Soviets obviously knew little of the Far Eastern male mentality. The surprised President, conscious of his great age and delighted with the photographic evidence of his own performance, is reputed to have promptly ordered sufficient copies of the film to distribute to every one of his country's provinces where his countrymen would be left in no doubt as to his current state of vigorous good health.

We were warned that the Soviet intelligence, in order to keep a data base on all the NATO officers, at some stage in our visit we would individually be photographed. A year later a copy of the picture would be sent to our ship with some excuse for the delay and because you had probably left the ship by then, it would be forwarded to your next appointment or home address and being a polite English gentleman you would write back to thank the sender; don't!

The first port of call was Gdynia where we were opened to the general public, carefully shepherding the people up one gangway aft and through the ship on a roped-off route and off the gangway forward. During the visit some 27,000 people are reputed to have visited. On one of the days the Captain and Chief Officer having gone off to Warsaw to the tomb of the unknown warrior with the Admiral, left us to entertain a Polish Admiral and his staff to lunch. It seemed to go well although telling a joke with a Polish interpreter was, I found, a little long-winded. After we poured our happy guests over the side, I went up on the bridge to see how the junior officers were managing with the general public. I sat down importantly in the absent Captain's bridge chair and almost immediately a beautiful young blonde lady appeared through the throng of people to stand demurely before me, her hands behind her back. She curtsied and said loudly and clearly in English:

"Captain, I give you my flower."

I was not sure exactly what I believed I had heard and asked her to repeat her question?

"Captain, I give you my flower."

She said it again, smiling sweetly, and from behind her back she produced a beautiful bunch of roses. I smiled with relief and the cameras flashed. Exactly a year later a nice little packet marked in several languages 'do not bend' arrived at my home address via BFPO Ships, it was of course the picture of me on the bridge of RFA *Oleander,* to be re-named RFA *Olmeda;* although by then a licensed Trinity House Pilot, I did not reply.

HMS *Devonshire* was given a berth in the centre of the city of Leningrad on the River Neva and just around the corner from the moorings of the Old Russian warship *Aurora* representing the battleship *Potemkin;* where the original revolution is said to have begun. Because RFA *Oleander* was too large for the river berths she was moored to a buoy at the Soviet Naval Base at Kronstadt and had the use of Admiral Bykov's barge, a luxurious fast motor yacht, to ferry us up and down the river between the two ships.

First we had to secure to the buoy, and that proved to be a problem for the Soviet Navy had supplied moorings that were far too light and feeble for us to moor safely. I reported this to the bridge from the forecastle and was asked to explain my problem to the Russian Sea Pilot, who was like most international pilots from a mercantile marine background and spoke excellent English. Having been appointed a prospective Trinity House Pilot myself, I watched with particular interest the reaction of the Russian Sea pilot responsible for mooring our ship when confronted with the problem. I quickly understood that as with a few of our own countrymen in the merchant service who hold a certain unfounded feeling of derision for the practical seamanship abilities of the senior service, even in the Soviet Union the Russian Pilot was no exception and obviously not being polite when he tore into the Soviet Naval Captain acting as our liaison officer asking him – we understood – just how the Soviet Navy was going to resolve the problem? However without further help we solved it by hanging off the port anchor and using our own anchor cable to secure to the buoy. I felt comforted by the impression that if there were ever to be a revolution in the UK the job of the pilot looked fairly secure.

We were given VIP treatment during our visit and although we had to wear uniform all the time, we did get to see all the tourist attractions that visitors now pay a fortune to enjoy. One interesting fact was that our Royal Marines were asked not to wear their pith helmets when ashore for it was claimed the Soviet people would immediately as a result of Bolshevik cartoons take a dislike to them, relating them to colonial troops.

The most stirring occasion for the whole of that Baltic Cruise took place at the close of the official cocktail party on HMS *Devonshire,* when with thousands of Russian people lining the banks of the River Neva, the Royal Marine Home Fleet Band beat 'Retreat' on the *Devonshire's* flight deck. The sunset ceremony on a still summer evening was magical and followed by considerable applause from both banks of the river despite the cold war. It was a proud moment for all aboard.

Helsinki and Copenhagen proved to be a mad social whirl with cocktail parties aboard and ashore but without doubt the finest was aboard RFA *Oleander* at Langeline, Copenhagen just seaward of the Little Mermaid. We had somewhere picked up a frigate and a destroyer and having the largest space on the monkey-island, the deck above the bridge was decorated with bunting and manned by smart naval stewards for a joint cocktail party. What made it so special were the clear blue sky and the view from the monkey island over the two warships up the harbour into the sunset where all the tall ships were moored on completion or perhaps the start of the Tall Ships Race 1966. To complete the party, the Royal Marine Home Fleet Band marched and counter marched on the quay alongside as they beat Retreat once more and the Sunset Ceremony was completed. What a final cruise, I realised I could not have been luckier. On return to the UK I was released reluctantly from my contract to join the Cinque Ports Pilots and started training immediately. Leaving the ship in Newcastle I was sent off in some style following lunch with Captain Ditchburn and a large number of the ship's officers. Poured into a First Class compartment on a London train, I was left entirely in peace with the blinds drawn until arrival at King's Cross where I emerged sleepily to find stuck to the compartment door window a printed notice on official crested A4 which read;

"Do Not Enter, Prisoner Under Escort from Durham Jail."

Well my colleagues had a great sense of humour but indeed I had escaped; arriving home that weekend I began my training that Monday and so began an entirely new unplanned career.

Chapter 21

Joining the Cinque Ports Pilots

'Downies' Landing at Dungeness with Mick Bates

Before I was first licensed as a Cinque Ports' Trinity House Pilot I did six months' unpaid training at my own expense, accompanying Licensed Pilots working on ships between Dungeness and Gravesend and all the ports in between. At the time I lived at Dymchurch on the Romney Marsh. I used to start early in the week by getting the pilot tender out from Dover to the Pilot Cutter stationed off Dungeness, my wife having driven me to Dover. I would then spend the whole week going backwards and forwards between Dungeness and Gravesend, usually ending up at Dungeness which was of course closest to my home. During training we grabbed what sleep we could between ships, either on the pilot cutter or in the stuffy smoke-filled little pilot office on the Royal Pier at Gravesend. Sally and I had one car at the time, a large Humber Hawk. A car was something that a good number of pilots had yet to find a use for because most of them lived within close proximity to Dover. When called for work to make up another watch at Dungeness, these men were collected by the Pilots' Messenger, Billie Munn who drove them to the pilot tender at the dump head in the

Granville Docks. Having shipped inwards from the cutter they would on the completion of their act of pilotage get a train back to Dover and either walk a short distance home, get a taxi or perhaps take the bus.

The Trinity House Channel Pilots based at Gravesend working outwards to the Sunk off Harwich or south to Dungeness, ended up on the cruising pilot cutters to await the next run of the pilot tender coming out from Dover or Harwich to top up the cutters with more inward pilots. This could mean a frustrating delay in getting home but at Dungeness there was a choice. Here a local fisherman who lived in a little house with a watch tower on the shingle beach; would, on seeing the signal from the cutter *Pathfinder* requiring his services, launch his open clinker built wooden boat off the steep shingle of the Dungeness beach to land the 'Downies' as they were known by the 'Gentlemen of the Cinque Ports', for the princely sum of ten shillings (50 pence) each.

Mick Bates was an independent character and a fine boat handler who was a joy to watch picking the right wave and driving his small boat up the shingle on a large swell, while the 'Downies' stood together puffing on their pipes, their white cap covers contrasting with their dark navy blue Burberry rain coats as they huddled together telling stories of their adventures outward bound during the night. Once on the shingle Mick would leap out and attach a long wire to the stem of the boat, walk up to his power-driven winch which would roar into life, the wire would tighten and slowly the boat would be pulled clear of the water. Then and only then would the 'Downies' stop talking and begin to climb wearily down onto the shingle using the portable wooden steps Mick neatly placed for them alongside the beached boat. Usually they had Mick arrange a taxi to run them to the nearest railway station. I was the lucky one, for Mick knowing I was unpaid as a 'tripper' and lived on the Romney Marsh always refused my money and on occasion even drove me home to save my wife coming out to fetch me at some unearthly hour.

Some years later I was asked to say a few words at the dedication of a new pub sign at the '*The Pilot*' public house built close by on the beach; a sign showing Mick in his boat heading for the beach just as I remember him. I was delighted to be invited for I will always remember his kindness and his skill. It was interesting to find many years later that one of Sally's ancestors from Lydd had been a Landlord of '*The Pilot*' in the previous century in an earlier building.

Mick Bates landing in good weather

The six months training was hard without pay but we soon learnt to survive. It always aggravated me on the Pilot Cutter that like the working pilots, the trainees were expected to buy meal tickets at three shillings and sixpence each, money I could ill afford. I refused and instead would (despite the aromas of well-cooked food wafting about the Pilot Cutter) hungrily scan the horizon for an inward ship and hope that whatever the time of day the master might offer the pilot and his trainee a sandwich. My first lesson therefore was to appreciate that if offered food I should always accept because one never knew when the next meal might be forthcoming.

I soon learnt that some pilots did not like taking a candidate, perhaps because they always eat the sandwiches but I imagine often because they did not appreciate the questions as to why a certain course of action had been taken, it becoming apparent that some of the best pilots seemed to have a natural reactive ability to handle ships but could not explain their actions in a theoretical manner because they had not been trained to be proactive in the first place. There is no doubt in my mind that the ship-handling aspect of our training was in those days generally poor or ignored, the candidate being expected from his earlier sea-going experience to be totally familiar with the subject, but of course few were so accomplished because of the nature of our careers.

During our training we witnessed the very good and the not so good without the benefit of an explanation of the theory but at the end of the day we did learn the pilotage district thoroughly, the characteristics of the navigational aids, the courses and distances, the depths of water and the effects of the tides. No longer left to personal experience good or bad, today the need for training in and a thorough knowledge of ship handling is recognised and that aspect of pilotage training is good and improving all the time around the world. This is thanks to the use of manned models, simulators, better equipment and assessment and a far better understanding of the theory; something which I like to imagine that perhaps in some very small way somewhere I have contributed to that improvement – but more of that later.

At the end of the six months 'tripping', as the training was called, I presented myself to Trinity House at Tower Hill London for examination, feeling very nervous and a mere boy once again despite my previous years of experience. I stood before a large table on which my examiner an Elder Brother of Trinity House had spread before him Admiralty navigational charts of the entire London District. Putting me in an imaginary ship of the maximum draught and tonnage I might be expected to pilot and telling me the state of the tide, he instructed me to take the ship from one end of the district to the other, reciting the characteristics of the buoys, lighthouses, the courses and depths of water. He asked questions about the regulations and procedures at the various ports en route inward to Gravesend, and I sweated in my warm Gieves naval doeskin uniform with the black pilot trainee's uniform buttons; as the spring sunshine of 1967 streamed through the window.

Much to my relief I passed, and on 27th May 1967 I was licensed as a Fourth Class Cinque Ports Trinity House Pilot.

The first day I walked into the Dover Pilot Office to start work I was greeted by a first class pilot who, having ensured that I knew it was my place to make the tea, told me his father had been a Gravesend pilot and his grandfather a pilot at another London pilot station before him; presumably to establish his own superiority in the pilotage hierarchy. He then fiercely demanded to know from whence I had come?

Now it just so happened that while waiting in the corridor outside to present my documents to the Superintendent of Pilots (the same man who had advised me to apply the year before), I had been examining with interest a number of framed pilot lists from the previous century called

'Progressions' which adorned the walls. They depicted not just the names of the pilots at Dover and Deal in the 1800s but also had painted on them each individual pilot's personal pennant or burgee. These flags being flown on the port side of the piloted ships so as to be visible to lookouts around the Kent coast as the ships passed inward and from which the number of remaining pilots on the cutter could be calculated. Taking my colleague out into the corridor I pointed to a *Stanley Russell* and *Charles Russell* listed about 1842 with Deal addresses and told him my father's name was *Stanley Charles Russell* and being born in Folkestone remarked truthfully;

'I am bit of a local lad myself.'

The gentleman was completely taken in by my auto-suggestion and, from the odd remark over the years, I imagine he must have passed his belief to others in the service, doing my reputation no harm at all.

Sadly he went to an early grave firmly believing that like him, I too was of genuine old pilotage stock but the truth of the matter is that I have never checked to verify it being unlikely and in any case, my great grandfather was originally from Bridport and a publican with two pubs in Sandgate that exist today, *The Ship and The Providence.* Sally however, while tracing her family history did find that one of her ancestors was a Trinity House Pilot about that time.

Chapter 22

Early Piloting Days

In the following written account of my experience of pilotage incidents, dilemmas and near disasters, the reader might be forgiven for thinking that my life has been one of continual drama and adventure but one should realise that I have over the years piloted more than seven thousand ships of different tonnages, from the 299 gross ton Schuyt to the Very Large Crude Oil Carrier with a displacement in excess of 300,000 tons; the vast majority without recordable incident except for those words inscribed in that particular ship's deck log stating;

'Courses and engine orders TPA.'

I have written of the amusing, frightening and I hope the more interesting of my recollections, though all but a few of my ships have been entirely without incident except for the opportunity to meet with and daily work alongside mariners of all different nationalities. Establishing initially a good working and trusting relationship between the Master and me, the complete stranger charged in a compulsory pilotage district with the safe navigation of *his* precious command. I have been privileged to meet many interesting and highly competent people and alarmed by just a few less competent souls. I have been privileged and paid for the joy of handling many wonderful and a few not so well found ships. I have had many frustrating moments, and a few more of sheer terror. I have experienced the most wonderful sunsets and far too many beautiful sunrises. I have experienced the best of days with clear fresh air and the sea like glass and I have fought through the worst of adverse weather, howling Gale Force winds and giant seas, violent rolling and pitching ships with shifting deck cargo and lively pilot boats and, in my earlier piloting days, prolonged dense fog before the Clean Air Act improved the Thames Estuary. I have on more than one occasion doubted my own abilities and having run out of ideas been forced to turn to 'higher authority' for guidance but in the main the job has given me nothing but considerable satisfaction and sheer joy and particularly so the berthing of large tankers at Shellhaven and Coryton; but that is in the future.

Off Dungeness

Here let my adventure begin, the daily thrill of not knowing in advance what challenges the day will hold, who one will meet or what the weather man has in store.

First Pilotage Experiences

One of the very first ships I piloted was a small Dutch coaster or as we knew them, a 'Schuyt'. She was of 499 gross tons and draft of 9 feet 6 inches called the *Labrador*. I was to pilot her on the 18th May 1967 from the North East Spit buoy off Margate to Gravesend where I was to hand over to a River Pilot for somewhere up the River Thames. It was a beautiful spring day with the sea like glass when I boarded about lunchtime. The friendly Dutch Master who was alone on the bridge greeted me with a brief instruction as to how the magnetic compass autopilot worked, gratefully accepted the daily newspaper I gave him together with my Trinity House A Form which was my bill and contract and therefore proof as a sign of my officialdom; before telling me he had his family on board and that he was going down to lunch – and with that he disappeared below.

Having put the ship on course for the Princes Channel, I went out on the port bridge wing to get some fresh air (away from the wheelhouse which smelt strongly of old Dutch cigar smoke and animals) to enjoy the sunshine as the little Schuyt chugged along contentedly at a full six knots.

I leant on the rail and contemplated my first few days as a pilot, not rating it very high on a scale of one to ten and felt disappointed after the considerable expense of six months' training without pay to be restricted, although of course it made sense, to piloting such small ships for the first two years of service. Small ships, which more often than not had a Master who was also the Owner and therefore someone who bitterly resented the fact that he had to pay for the services of compulsory pilotage. It was even more annoying to know at the end of the day as a Fourth Class Pilot I was only going to receive 45% of the agreed 'Sharing Turn' calculated from the total fees charged by Trinity House for our pilotage services.

I was standing there feeling sorry for myself when I heard the pad of feet and a large friendly but smelly black Labrador waging its tail stood up on its hind leg and leant on the rail beside me on the wing of the bridge, presumably to keep lookout. My new friend was shortly to be followed by a second dog that joined her companion, black tail wagging vigorously on my other side.

The humour of the situation of our three black-coated figures standing in line together brightened my day and especially when I imagined how amused my posh friends in the Royal Fleet Auxiliary and Royal Navy would see the situation. The day brightened further when the Captain's wife arrived on the bridge with lunch of pea and ham soup together with a large fresh hunk of homemade bread. My fee for the day was £14.19s.5p and I had the expense of the train back from Gravesend to Margate.

At Margate I remember walking bearded in the late afternoon sunlight down from the railway station to the pier to collect my car while being badgered by a column of small excited children who shouted '*Captain Birdseye,*' behind me after the cartoon character on the TV commercials, encouraging me to turn suddenly and frequently to shout '*Shiver my timbers*' or something of a similar nature. We all had a lot of fun, it being the end to a memorable day.

Car Carrier 'Castor' for Granville Dock Dover

Dogs on Board

Dogs were not uncommon on ships in those days and occasionally made one feel distinctly unwelcome when ascending the pilot ladder to climb aboard. One particular animal I remember was aboard another little Schuyt, this time bound from off Folkestone to Whitstable. Having been restrained from having a piece of me on boarding, I saw nothing of it until we were safety moored up in Whitstable. It was normal practice on completion of an act of pilotage to go down to the Master's cabin for a tot of something warm to keep the cold out while the Captain signed the Pilotage Order for the services rendered. We went down below to be followed by the Master's large scruffy long-haired German Shepherd dog which promptly sat next to me on the L-shaped stuffed hair and leather-covered settee built around his desk; eyeing me in a distinctly unfriendly manner.

"Don't touch the dog he is a one man animal,"

Warned the master, pouring out a small whisky for me into a grubby looking tumbler before signing the paperwork. With that there was a knock at the door and a Customs officer appeared to seal the ship's bonded stores and the Captain stood up to show him the way, warning me again as he started to leave.

I glanced at the brute and the German Shepherd grinned back, showing his long white teeth as a deep rumble came wafting up to me with the odour of something unpleasant. I quickly looked away and decided to avoid eye contact and ignore the animal. I sat cautiously for a few minutes before attempting to casually pick up the glass in front of me to have a sip of Dutch courage, when the dog erupted fiercely going for my hand which I withdrew quickly. Satisfied, the scruffy animal relaxed and sat watching me alertly; daring me to make my next move.

I sat still but certainly not relaxed until the Master and Customs Officer returned from the alleyway outside the door shaking with laughter.

"There Mister Pilot I told you he was a one-man dog."

A few years later when I had moved on to First Class Pilotage and was handling large ships, the port regulations had tightened up considerably and the pilot was tasked to enquire of the Master of a ship 'if he had any animals to declare to Port Health'; in order that they could be restricted from going ashore at the berth and possibly spreading rabies.

One day having piloted a large bulk carrier, inward bound for the Tilbury Grain Terminal, I anchored off Southend to await the tide before proceeding up river. I had enquired on embarking off Folkestone if there were any animals aboard to be told there were none. I was walking out to the bridge wing while in the process of anchoring the ship, when on the beautifully polished brass door sill I noticed a perfect paw print of a small animal. Waiting until I had finished anchoring I then asked the Master;

"Where is the dog?"
"What dog?" he replied innocently.
"This dog," I said pointing to the paw mark.

"Oh my God, that stupid Chief Engineer; I told him to keep the wretched animal in his cabin and now you, the first person on board, already realise we have a dog onboard."

Although as a Master from a totalitarian state he imagined he was already in real trouble, I was able to reassure him that there was still time to inform the Port Health and correct my original statement but he would be expected to ensure the animal was secure and not allowed the free run of the ship.

Paddle Steamer *Ryde*

On a warm sunny but misty September morning in 1968 I was called to the Folkestone Pilot station where the duty pilot informed me that had 'just the job' for a pilot of my ability, a nice little paddle steamer to take to Gravesend on her way to the Upper Pool somewhere for a catering exhibition. I was not exactly enthralled by his cheery sarcasm but at least she was a British ship and probably fairly fast. I quickly walked around the harbour and bought the Captain a newspaper deciding that the *Daily Mail* would probably be appropriate but one could never tell; some Masters claimed to prefer the *Daily Telegraph* but secretly would probably have preferred the delights of the *Sun* tabloid.

I looked her up in the pilot station copy of Lloyd's Register of Shipping and immediately recognised her as the old Southern Railway side-wheel paddle ferry that used to run between Portsmouth and Ryde on the Isle of Wight. Built by William Denny & Brothers at Dumbarton she was of 603 Gross tons and was driven by steam-powered triple expansion engines with a maximum speed of 12 knots. With tide about to turn in our favour, it looked like being a fairly fast run and with a draught of only 7 feet we should be able to cut some corners by going across the flats past Herne Bay and the Spaniard Buoy if the Master was in agreement. The task ahead did appear 'just the job' and I was grateful as I walked down to join the pilot boat and set off to meet the little ship puffing inwards from Dungeness.

Shortly out of the mist the *Ryde* appeared into the breaking sunshine with her funnel painted like a Gilbey's Gin bottle and her two big wheels churning away. Getting aboard was not really a problem as we landed alongside abaft the paddle box sponson. The Captain pointing at the funnel greeted me with the words:

'Sorry we haven't got any Pilot.'

Well it was not just gin they were short of but stokers; in fact I recall they only had the one to shovel the bags of coal which were even stacked in the passenger saloon for the comparatively long run up the English Channel. The few hands they had were helping, and when I went aboard the indicator in the wheelhouse showed a full head of steam and off we leapt. Past Dover and up through the Downs we cut across to the Broadstairs Knoll and rounded North Foreland a mile off; to run past Margate through by the Hook Spit. It was an hour before high water and at the current speed of 14 knots cutting across the flats past the Spaniard buoy off Herne Bay was going to be no problem.

Eastern Entrance Dover on a summer's day

There was little traffic and the Master decided to get some rest but unfortunately no sooner had he disappeared when the needle in the steam gauge started to creep slowly back and it became apparent that as the hour approached high water we were losing speed. I was reluctant to disturb him and hoped that the pressure would soon build up with a fresh hand on the shovel but, as the tide peaked and started to fall, the speed dropped very rapidly and was down to 6 knots passing the Spaniard buoy. I called the Master and explained that unless we got more steam pressure we would not get off the flats into deep water in time and might even be *using his paddle wheels for a purpose for which they were not designed*. The response from the Master was dynamic and very rapidly help was given to the weary stoker, but it seemed to take considerable time for the needle on the gauge to start building up again and even longer for the speed to rise above 8 knots. It was with a great sense of relief that we tumbled off the flats into the deep water at the Nore.

Unbeknown to me there had been an aircraft searching for us in the mist in order to take some PR pictures for the charterers; without success. He had over flown the Princes Channel and main Yantlet Channel while we had taken the more exciting route across the mudflats.

The NATO Standing Force

It was black and unfriendly on the morning of the 21st February 1969 when I was called from my warm bed at the Folkestone Pilot station, to join a fast plastic pilot launch for the run out to board HM Norwegian Frigate *Narvik,* 18 feet draught, displacement 1740 tons, one of the NATO Standing Force's six warships on passage inwards to London. It was bitterly cold with a full easterly gale blowing and driving snow; weather that cut right through the warm clothing I had taken the precaution to wear. Warm leather boots and heavy socks and thermal underwear was the order of the day as, bent against the wind, I trudged through the snow to the boat moored snugly in the lee alongside the west side of Folkestone Pier; her engine running and the steam from the cooling water being whipped away in swirls to seaward. We slipped our moorings and quickly cleared the shelter of the huge harbour breakwater, gradually encountering larger breaking waves from the port quarter as we surfed downwind to the Norwegian frigate, punching her way through the heavy seas from the direction of Dungeness. As we approached down her port side she turned to starboard to make a lee for my boarding and we ran around the stern into the relatively smoother water on the lee side. The pilot ladder had been rigged correctly on the starboard side but right aft on the quarter deck, not the ideal position and particularly so when as she pitched into that extra large wave; her propellers were exposed menacingly close to the short ladder.

I wish I could remember who the Trinity House Coxswain was that night but they were all equally competent and it could have been any of them who laid the pilot cutter neatly alongside. Together with the deckhand I made my way up the outside of the cabin to the foredeck and, as the launch rose and fell violently alongside, clung to the centre guard rail. As we rose the deck hand passed my bag across through the driving snow to waiting hands. The climb was to have been only about six feet but as the ship ran into some particularly large swells I waited for that quiet spell that always occurs amid the most violent seas. The burly Norwegian sailors on the cold windswept deck however had different ideas. As the pilot boat rose to the top of the highest wave they leant over and physically wrenched me off the foredeck and, with the upward momentum of the boat, lifted me easily over the rails to land unceremoniously on my backside in the sea water sloshing around the scuppers. My fairly new uniform cap which had been secured with the chinstrap (a part of the cap I had always considered to be merely ornamental and never used until joining the pilot service) blew or was knocked off and disappeared astern as the ship started to move ahead. I trudged wet, cold and not in the best of humour to the enclosed wheelhouse where the overpowering heat immediately struck me and the steam soon started to rise from my person. While I was dressed for the elements and possibly even an open bridge, the officers were in their shirt sleeves and totally immune to the weather outside.

However I was made very welcome and soon discovered that HMNS *Narvik* in company with the remainder of the NATO Standing Force was required at Gravesend at a particular time to proceed up the river in a certain order. She was the only ship to take a pilot, the others having gone ahead with the Flotilla Leader in line ahead. Identifying them on the radar it was obvious that they planned to go outside the Goodwin Sands into the teeth of the gale; which, while a simpler course of action, was a longer passage and one which would be very uncomfortable. I suggested to the Commanding Officer that we take advantage of the shelter in the lee of the Goodwin Sands and pass up through the Downs. It would by then be breakfast time and we could eat in comfort. His orders were to proceed independently but to be at Gravesend at the appointed hour, which I assured him this was in fact my planned ETA but we had so much time we could do the job in reasonable comfort. The CO readily accepted my advice and was delighted to eventually get into the relatively sheltered waters off Deal. However, our absence had been noted and we were to be questioned continually by the Flotilla Leader over the VHF radio as to our intentions and whereabouts. The rest of the NATO Standing Force entered by the North Edinburgh Channel while we popped out from the relatively sheltered waters of the Downs, across the short bumpy waters off the NE Spit and in through the Princes Channel; finally dropping into our assigned position and time in Gravesend Reach. The Flotilla Leader's Plan was an early case of an inflexible Passage Plan which did not have the local knowledge familiar to that of a district pilot.

At the end of the day I was out of pocket driving to the then Deal Branch of Messrs Gieves Ltd, The Naval Tailor, to buy a new uniform cap and Trinity House badge.

Egyptian Potatoes for Ramsgate

The sea was like glass but the fog was as thick as a hedge as we slowly motored out from Folkestone Pier early one November morning to meet a little Dutch Schuyt inwards from Egypt with a full cargo of potatoes for the port of Ramsgate. I sat waiting patiently in the cabin as the coxswain, head in the radar cowl, negotiated his way to the ship at reduced speed. Suddenly a shape loomed up out of the murk and the engine sound alternated as the coxswain manoeuvred the pilot boat alongside. I climbed the few short steps of the pilot ladder with some trepidation; she was very old and appeared to be in a poor condition, with the paint peeling off the hull and considerable corrosion adorning her buckled riveted rusty plates. I guessed she had an owner Master and my heart sank; but immediately it occurred to me that rather than begrudge paying for the compulsory pilotage, today in this fog he might be relieved to have one aboard.

French Train Ferry 'St Eloi' on a misty morning

The young man who greeted me undoubtedly was relieved after a tiring night plodding up channel through the traffic. He did not need to tell me but he obviously felt it necessary to inform me that the owner Master was on leave and that he was Mate acting Master. I quickly took over the only radar for it was obviously going to be a blind passage, and finding nothing between Folkestone and Dover set off on an easterly course. The radar was a good one for 1968 and although pleasantly surprised, I still had ahead of me the last outward shipping from London on the tide as well as the port of Dover to pass with its constant stream of ferries to avoid as I steamed inward for the Downs.

We passed Dover without incident and rounded close off South Foreland following the coast. Passing close east of the Deal Bank buoy I crept through the fog looking for the three black conical buoys that marked the Ramsgate Channel and was pleased to find three small targets exactly where they should be marking the west side of the Brake Sand. It was not a channel I had much experience of before or since, but I remembered the story of a loaded Liberty ship in World War 2 successfully negotiating the channel at the top of a spring tide to show up unexpectedly at Ramsgate looking for a pilot; if he could manage it then most certainly I could. Keeping to the westward of the B2 and B3, in order to avoid the Cross Ledge, I suddenly came out of the fog with Ramsgate clearly in view. The young Acting Master who had previously stood morosely staring worriedly into the fog suddenly came to life and started to fire questions at me.

Detached Mole Dover on a beautiful day

It was one and half hours before high water and a good time to enter the harbour as the tide had only just started to run north-eastwards outside the pier heads. As we approached, the RNLI Lifeboat put to sea which was not very helpful because although there was a diamond mark on the East Pier Landing Platform, the lifeboat at her mooring was usually more visible and a better mark to keep in view until within the entrance. The importance of steering directly for the West Pier head as the ship set to the north east, proved difficult to communicate to the young Master on the wheel; who seeing before him a 200-foot wide entrance naturally but dangerously wanted to steer for the middle. We shot into the harbour having to kick her ahead to get round the corner and there he saw the entrance to the enclosed dock waiting enticingly before him and, ignoring my helm orders for a second time, he chose to steer directly for the middle of the open gate. The problem was that within the harbour the tidal current ran anti-clockwise and to make the inner harbour one needed to steer for the east side of the entrance. Despite my desperate efforts to correct the approach and reverse the swing to port, the little Schuyt set down tide at the entrance and cannoned shuddering off the port side granite knuckle with a load bang and a cloud of rust particles.

Reviewing what went wrong, when safely moored up in the inner closed dock without further incident, the young man was most apologetic and I think more afraid of his employer but quite oblivious to the fact that there was a possibility of sheering a couple of rivets at the opposite end of the ship to the point of contact. Forward it was difficult to see any damage at all among the many bent and buckled plates; he was happy and unconcerned. I had a nasty feeling that the impact had been hard and possibly consequential and my last words on leaving were;

> *'Captain be very sure to take soundings aft and in the engine room,*
> *in case you have sprung any rivets.'*

Driving down to the harbour the following morning I sensed the inevitable. The beautiful red coloured sandstone Georgian balustrade sweeping down past the Royal Temple Yacht Club was lined with people, shoulder to shoulder, gazing down with considerable interest at some particularly exciting event; not that Ramsgate was without its fair share of maritime incidents. I turned along the harbour road at the bottom of the hill and parked outside the agents and walked back to see what was causing the great interest and yes, you have guessed it; obviously the little Schuyt had sheered at least a couple of rivets and quietly settled on the dock floor in the night, partly filling the hold with sea water. The stevedores, much to the amusement of their friends, relations and passers-by, were wading about in the hold trying to salvage the bags of wet potatoes.

I walked into the Agent's office and presented my bill for Pilotage Services rendered and was received with some scorn.

> *'You not only sink the ship but you actually want paying as well?'*

I protested my innocence but to no avail; the ship had a pilot, I was that pilot and the ship had collided with the harbour wall and subsequently sunk alongside. I was paid in cash and left the office realising that life was not always fair for just as the Master, in law, is ultimately responsible for the actions of his pilot, a fact which in itself is of course blatantly unfair, so to is the reputation of the pilot for situations sometimes beyond his control.

I now had to go home and write out a collision report which would go on my file and, if my explanation was not accepted, present myself before higher authority at Trinity House to elucidate and face possible suspension of my pilotage licence and ability to earn a living. Fortunately my report was accepted by the authorities and I heard no more, but my colleagues who always seemed to take a great delight in recounting the misfortunes of their brethren had a field day and no doubt my exploits caused considerable mirth as the story became enhanced with exaggeration. At least the Egyptian potatoes got a deservedly thorough washing.

Seacon

Listening to a presentation about cruise liners using the Port of Dover I was very interested to learn that because of the current size and length of these very large ships the planned passage inwards to the berths is always to use the Eastern entrance and swing to port by rounding the wreck buoy at the Western entrance, until almost parallel to the Admiralty Pier and then manoeuvre stern first towards the berth. The limitations on this manoeuvre, which has been practised by the pilots on a simulator somewhere in Scandinavia fed with all the necessary tidal information and proved in practice are, I understand, from approximately one hour and a half hours before high water to half an hour after high water at the Eastern entrance, with a further restriction to avoid the inrush of water at the Western entrance on a spring tide in particular.

It is a critical, highly professional manoeuvre which relies on the use of the Eastern entrance only. With over 120 Cruise liners due this year my thoughts turned to a time when the Eastern entrance became blocked for some considerable time, not hours or days but for many weeks.

The 7th October 1970 was an incredibly clear night when I was called at approximately 01:00 by Port Control from the Pilot Office in Marine Court, Dover to attend the MV *Seacon*, a small British Coaster with a cargo of fertilizer in plastic bags for the Granville Dock. I looked out from the office balcony and could see all the bright lights from Dunkirk right along the French coast to Calais. They were so bright it was difficult to make out the many ships in transit through the Dover Straits.

Eastern Entrance Dover in bad weather

The weather was cold that night but the sea was calm with a moderate smooth swell. I dressed warmly and quickly and drove down to the submarine pens in the Eastern docks where the pilot boat supplied by Walkers was moored. As I climbed down the ancient metal ladder to the boat the engine roared into life. I joined the coxswain and seaman in the small open cabin aft as we prepared to leave the old World War 1 pens to rendezvous with the MV *Seacon*, in a position one mile or so to the east of the Eastern entrance. As we started to move there was a loud explosion overhead as the maroon exploded to summon the crew for the RNLI Dover Lifeboat.

I turned to the coxswain and jokingly said, "I hope that's not my ship!"

It was! We proceeded as fast as our old heavy wooden boat would go, which I recall was not much over ten knots, and arrived on the scene to see in our searchlight the upturned hull of the *Seacon* slowly and gracefully slide stern first beneath the swell. We quickly found the Master with his three-man crew in an inflatable and pulled them aboard the pilot boat, wet and somewhat shaken but glad to have survived a collision with the Belgian Ostend ferry *Arteveld*. The ferry which had left the Eastern entrance at some speed had just not seen the navigation lights of the small coaster approaching from the east against the glare of the background lights on the French coast and had for some reason not detected on radar the echo of the *Seacon* approaching for her pilot.

Fortunately the *Seacon's* small crew were up and dressed for entering port when the ferry sliced into her and they were able to abandon ship without injury or loss of life. Hammonds the local agents were called and we landed the survivors into the small boatmen's' office below the old signal station on the Eastern Arm, where we were able to warm them up in front of a single-bar electric fire. As soon as the Master had some feeling in his hands, I asked him to sign my Pilotage Bill for attendance! There was of course no charge but I needed to establish for the record that we had indeed made an effort to give service. His response at the time was predictable, understandable and unrepeatable.

Container Ship – New Zealand Pacific
southbound off the Goodwin Sands

The outcome was somewhat less predictable, for the Seacon with fertilizer in plastic bags initially had a little reserve buoyancy which allowed her to bounce along the sea bed until she quite neatly blocked the Eastern entrance to the port for some considerable time. There were a few cruise liners in those days using the Eastern Arm in the summer months but none really to be inconvenienced during that time. However the ferries and other ships forced to make do with the Western entrance, for that long period until the wreck could be moved, were subjected to some alarming experiences and particularly so during periods of strong wind and a spring tide. There was great relief when the wreck of the MV *Seacon* was subsequently removed. With the much larger ships using the port today, such an accident would have really heavy financial implications on the operation of the port.

A Raw Experience

On the 2nd May 1970, following two years as a fourth class pilot, (restricted to vessels of 2000 gross registered tons and one year's experience of piloting small coasters not exceeding 4,500 gross registered tons, but in actual fact few ships that had been over 500 grt throughout) I was once again examined as to my competence as a pilot and promoted to Second Class; but not authorised or empowered to take charge as a pilot of any ship or vessel exceeding 12,000 gross registered tons for a further year.

On the 16th July 1970, just over two months later, I had through the luck of the alphabetical roster piloted just five second class ships of about six thousand tons, while the remaining twenty ships had been small coasters. Life had settled into an easy routine and I had yet to be challenged when along to Folkestone came the Finnish tanker *Ragny* – 11,029 gross registered tonnage with a draught of 30 feet –bound for Cliffe Oil Jetty, on the south side of the Lower Hope Reach with a full cargo of petrol; to do just that.

Now we had a system at that time which limited the pilotage of tankers over 11,500 grt to First Class pilots in what we called the Middle Cut; the intentions to presumably ensure such vessels were piloted by men of experience. What the system did however was to deny the younger men the very experience they were expected to have achieved by the time of their elevation. There was no doubt that I was still raw; I had yet to pilot a ship using tugs or one of that draft. I had only ever been to Cliffe Jetty a couple of times during my training more than three years before but the Master was not to know that and besides I was bearded, had a couple of strange campaign medal ribbons on my uniform and hopefully looked older and more experienced for all that.

There was little wind and excellent visibility on a glassy calm night as we progressed inwards via the North Edinburgh Channel to meet our two conventional single-screw tugs at the Mucking buoys, planning to berth at the top of high water, head to the first of the ebb tide. It was sometime in the middle of the night when with the Sun tugs secured each on a single tow line, one forward and the other on the starboard quarter we approached the upper end of the Lower Hope Reach and needed to cross the traffic to the south shore. Now Cliffe oil Jetty is on the starboard hand around the corner as ships come down the Gravesend Reach to turn to port through eighty degrees around the 'Ovens Buoy' at Higham Bight; and unless one is on a ship's bridge very high above sea level, it is not always possible to see other ships approaching from either side of the bend. I needed to take the water on the south bank to approach the berth for an ebb tide berthing, and therefore called the Thames Navigation Service to clarify my intentions which hopefully would be heard by any outward ship. I had carefully ensured that my ship was showing the three vertical lights indicating her deep draft and, there being nothing in sight outward, started to move across the river.

Making my final approach at very slow speed, probably too slow due to my inexperience, I suddenly became aware of an outward ship in the lower end of Gravesend Reach showing me a red sidelight and coming out fast. Nothing untoward yet, but I listened with interest to hear the unknown ship report her name when passing the 'Higham Bight Outwards'. Nothing was forthcoming on the radio but the approaching ship was turning to port and I was relieved to see both her sidelights and masthead lights in line as she headed straight for me. I waited anxiously for her red side light to disappear and for her to come down my starboard side showing a green light, but lo and behold she steadied up and then started to turn back again to starboard; red only. She was going to attempt a passage between me and the approaching jetty – there surely wasn't room; I felt a rush of adrenalin and mounting panic.

I ordered my forward tug, who had already called me in alarm, to tow the bow off into the middle of the river and went astern on the engines to help the swing. Ragny, with her more than 12,000 tons of petrol, came around sluggishly in the shallow water, steam and fumes drifting to leeward as collision was narrowly averted and the large long black shape of an outward exempt ship slid perilously close down our port side to briefly take the bottom further downstream.

My berthing approach had now been completely ruined and it took me a considerable time to berth the ship as the ebb tide came away strongly, forcing the bow off the upper end of the jetty causing the headlines to part and much frustration from all concerned as time ticked away and I moved tugs and eventually re-moored well into a long night.

The near miss raised probably more questions than answers, for although I wrote a report raising questions as to just why the outward ship was apparently unaware of my intentions and there was undoubtedly a company inquiry and perhaps a PLA inquiry. Further action was not taken for very sadly the friendly, patient hospitable Captain and his six deck officers were drowned in the North Atlantic when *Ragny* broke her back and the bow section sank on her very next voyage. Thirty-one other members of the crew were rescued from the stern section by the US Coastguard cutter *Escanada*.

Nemesis

26 December 1970 was our daughter Nicola's eleventh birthday and I was on call but I had managed Christmas Day at home with the family and I hoped to avoid working on this special day as well. It was snowing hard with a strong easterly wind when after breakfast the telephone suddenly and unexpectedly rang and the Duty Pilot offered me a continental job; the Nedlloyd fast cargo liner *Zuiderk* from Rotterdam to Gravesend. This work was rare for a Second Class Pilot, it being only the third opportunity I had been given in nearly a year; it paid extra money and was a decent ship. Christmas was an expensive time and we were still endeavouring to pay off the overdraft run up at the bank during my six months' unpaid training. Obviously my less hungry senior colleagues when called had looked out of the window at the snow and turned back to their tables laden with Christmas fare with satisfaction and little interest.

Amidst a few tears from a disappointed small daughter and a few caustic comments from my normally delightful mother-in-law Dorothy questioning the real need for my expedition, I set out into the snow to make the midday Belgian ferry to Ostend from Dover. The weather was worse than I imagined with very icy snow-covered roads and at Nickolls Quarry on the A259 I spun off the road; fortunately into a snow drift without damage. Recovering the car I drove on to Sandgate where it proved impossible to get up any of the hills into Folkestone. I abandoned the car and set off up Sandgate Hill walking through the snow to Folkestone Central Railway Station, only to find the trains were not running due to the ice and snow. I found some coins and a working telephone box and called the Duty Pilot at Folkestone Harbour and asked him if the pilot boat was not busy, could it possibly run me along the coast to Dover and take me to the Ostend Ferry.

He was more than pleased to help and I set off on foot through the snow to the Pilot Station.

The fast 40-foot pilot boat *Vedette* lay quietly in the lee of Folkestone pier when I joined; the crew, pleased to be relieved of the boredom of sitting in the boat with nothing to do, were less pleased when we rounded the end of the breakwater and turned east into the teeth of a howling gale and driving snow. We pounded our way to Dover, the surfeit of seasonal over-indulgence uncomfortably reminding us of better occupations. We reached Dover to find the Belgian Commandant had held the sailing for me and rigged a pilot ladder which I quickly scrambled up gratefully. The ferry arrived in Ostend on time and the Belgian and Dutch trains ran on time despite the continual snow. I arrived aboard the ship in Rotterdam at the same time as the Dutch officers and crew to find the ship without any form of heating; everything had been shut down over Christmas. I was to spend one of the coldest nights of my life before we got underway for London; serve me right for leaving our young daughter on her birthday.

The English Like W'abbits?

It was late at night on a clear New Year's Eve 1970 when I climbed aboard a small Japanese fast refrigerated ship the MV *Asakaze Maru,* 16 feet 6 inch draft, 2816 gross registered tons, one mile off Folkestone Pilot Station. The elegant little ship was inward from Communist China with a full cargo of frozen rabbits for Tilbury but the aromas rapidly reminded me of my many years in Japanese waters. I greeted the Captain in my limited Japanese, remarking on the fine weather.

> *"Kómban-wa Captain-san, Li o-tènki desŭ, ne?"*

The result was astonishing but I suppose to be expected; the Master, clearly surprised to have an English pilot speaking Japanese, replied in a torrent of Japanese far beyond my limited comprehension. I backed off quickly reverting to English realising that my further limited knowledge of the Japanese language (while it may have been useful on a run ashore in Yokahama) would be useless here, for the Captain obviously would not wish to dance with me or be pleased to hear how attractive he looked!

I asked what the cargo was to be told – *"Chinese w'abbits"* – to be followed by a question from the Master delivered with obviously some degree of disapproval as to whether –

> *"English people like Chinese w'abbits to eat?"*

Not wishing to lose face, I quickly explained that we did not actually eat the rabbits ourselves but undoubtedly his cargo was destined for an animal feed factory where the rabbit would end up in cans of dog and cat food. Making the point that while we in the UK were not at the height of the industrial boom engulfing Japan in those years, we had not resorted to living on rabbit from China.

At that moment we were distracted by a Mayday call from a motor cruiser which called on the emergency VHF Radio Channel sixteen to say he had run aground on the Goodwin Sands and needed assistance. The coastguard informed the casualty, who was unsure of his position, that the Walmer Lifeboat would be launched to come to his assistance. In view of the New Year and timing I was concerned that the call maybe a hoax, for it was in the days when the position of the instigator of a malicious telephone call could not be easily identified; unlike today. Certainly it was a strange time of year to be taking a small cabin cruiser to sea, but as I tuned into the conversation between Coastguard and casualty it was obvious that the yacht operator was a real amateur.

He gave the time he had left Ramsgate and how since he had run ashore "all the water had run away"; asking the coastguard "if it would come back?" From the information he gave I reckoned he was on the Brake Sands having had insufficient time to reach the Goodwin Sands. I called the Coastguard to report my position and intentions to use the Gull Stream Channel between the two sandbanks inwards for London and passed on my thoughts about the Brake Sands.

With a Spring tide still running to the north east through the Dover Straits we soon picked up speed and shot past Dover Harbour in the darkness, inward bound for The Downs at just over twenty knots, keeping a lookout for the casualty.

Approaching the entrance to the narrow Gull Stream Channel the Coxswain of the Walmer Lifeboat and I had a brief conversation when approaching one another at high speed on a collision course and the lifeboat being on my port beam altered course to pass astern of me. I mentioned my thoughts to the Coxswain of the lifeboat about the Brake Sands said that I would look there as I went past while he had been tasked to search the Goodwin Sands. Not more than a few minutes later we picked up a small radar target on the Brake Sands, reported our findings to the Coastguard at Dover and while we speeded on towards Tilbury and into the New Year, the RNLI took care of the casualty.

Home for Christmas

In 1973 most ships only had the one radar which in daylight was fitted with a rubber cowl in order for the operator to see the screen while at the same time avoid light penetration, but the disadvantage was of course that only one person could view the screen at a time. At night it was easy; one just removed the cowl and several people could see the approaching targets at once. The cowl had a second disadvantage in that the old ones tended to leave a dirty black ring around the pilot's face after prolonged use, causing some sniggers and much delight among the small children one might meet on the train going home.

Radar Cowl

The real problem was of course when in compulsory pilotage waters, the pilot responsible for the safe navigation of the ship engaged in collision avoidance, plotting approaching ships and navigational aids was competing with the Master and his bridge team who had ultimate responsibility for the safety of the ship and a need to keep a check on the actions of their pilot. Usually all went well, and on this particular day they certainly went well from my point of view but it must have been a particularly harrowing time for the Master of a ship I took into London one Christmas Eve and I had to admire his patience and trust.

The MV *Roybank* arrived inward from, I recall, Fiji in dense fog at Folkestone Pilot station with a draught of 26'6 and 13,924 gross tons, fully loaded with a cargo of bulk sugar for the Thames Sugar Refinery. I was delighted to get her for she had orders to berth immediately that day providing we could negotiate the thick fog by a certain time at Gravesend. Failure to do so would mean a delay at anchor off Southend for several days because the tugs annually stood down over the Christmas holiday and with them the Thames Watermen. I would not get home and the officers' family members waiting in London would have difficulty getting off to the ship if she had to anchor.

We set off with my head firmly stuck in the radar cowl at Full manoeuvring speed when clear of ships, reducing right down when passing the Port of Dover and outward ships kicked out of the port by charterers and owners before they became subject to the Christmas shutdown. The air in the wheelhouse was tense as the automatic fog signal sounded mournfully on the ship's siren a prolonged blast once every two minutes. We would listen intently for other shipping and quickly tune in to the sound of other ships approaching, the sounds getting louder until with relief they passed the beam and began to fade away. Occasionally a ship outwards, perhaps with poor radar, would stop and blow two prolonged blasts as we felt our way past.

There were so many ships in the Downs that morning we chose the outside route and passing east of the Goodwin Sands made good time to the NE Spit buoy and slipped in through a clear North Edinburgh Channel. Then listening to the half-hourly broadcast from Gravesend Navigation Service I realised that between me and Gravesend was a very large American 'Seabee' type barge carrying vessel, the *Doctor Lykes* bound inward for the moorings specially laid for her at the top of Gravesend Reach. She was a big brute, some 876 feet long with a 21,700 gross tonnage and not due at Gravesend until just on High Water where she would flood her dock and float out the cargo. Somewhere I had to get past her to achieve my ETA, but I was now too far behind to pass before she entered the Sea Reach Channel although closing fast. Approaching Sea Reach No 3 it became apparent that I would not be able to use the south side of the channel and pass up her port side because of outward traffic. I did a quick tidal calculation and realised we could cut the corner and pass her at the west end of the West Leigh anchorage. Consulting the Master, the TNS and the pilot on the *Doctor Lykes,* all was agreed and I hauled off to starboard. It was very tense and the adrenalin flowed in the *Roybank's* wheelhouse as we passed the giant bulk of the other ship increasing speed to get past quickly and back into the Seareach Channel. At no more than a cable off, we just did not see sign of her but we certainly heard the boom of her big fog siren which reached a crescendo as we passed ahead of her and back into the channel.

Back on course we were able to reduce and adjust our speed to achieve our ETA, pass our thanks and compliments of the season to all those concerned and have a well-earned cup of tea brought up to the bridge by an immaculate Indian steward in a starched white jacket. There were no other ships between us and Gravesend where, arriving on time, I handed over the ship to the River Pilot for the last leg up the River Thames; noticing that at last the fog was beginning to break up.

I paid my compliments of the season and said my farewells to the Captain, a nice man who had stood beside me stoically, patiently trusting and virtually blind throughout the pilotage because of the limitations on the use of the radar. Fortunately today equipment has been duplicated and designed for both daylight and night time viewing which has solved such dilemmas, and the whole bridge team usually has access to one of a number radar displays.

Storm Force 12

It was blowing freshly from the south west on the 11th February 1974 when the small roll-on roll-off ferry *Stena Sailor,* 14-foot draught, 2573 gross tons, left Dover for Zeebrugge subject to Compulsory Pilotage and on charter to Townsend Car Ferries. I was the pilot as she rolled easily in the strengthening swell, but by the time we returned to Dover in the early hours of the next morning a full gale was blowing. Being unable to enter port we sought shelter in the Downs anchoring off Deal, where the ship lay comfortably for several hours until the shifting wind made our position untenable. We decided, as the wind veered more southerly, to seek shelter in the Margate Roads and found a reasonably sheltered position 1.6 miles NNW from the old Margate Pleasure Pier head; where we laid out two anchors in the early afternoon. Unfortunately as it got dark in the middle of the afternoon the small German Schuyt *Crail,* one of the forty-five odd ships I counted sheltering in the Margate Roads; dragged her anchor as the winds gusted to Force 12 south-south-westerly and the sea became white-streaked and turned to foam, really angry even in the lee of the town. The *Stena Sailor* had been riding reasonably comfortably to two anchors despite the wind and now the ebb tide, as slowly and inexorably the German dragged down towards our two anchors, eventually bringing up to a second anchor approximately 400 feet ahead of the *Stena Sailor.*

Despite requests to move, the *Crail* remained put and a decision was made reluctantly for the *Stena Sailor* to weigh anchor and move before her anchors became fouled by those of the other ship. After slacking away to 7 shackles on the port cable the starboard anchor was recovered without incident. However the *Stena Sailor,* built with a solid block of accommodation forward under the bridge which presented a slab side to the wind and with nothing aft to counter balance the wind effect, immediately began to sail up wind like a paravane. Following skilful operation by the Master of the bow-thruster and twin screws, the port cable was slowly and painfully shortened to 3 shackles before the wind and tide proved too much for the windlass and bow-thruster. With a crashing and violent banging the port cable began to jump the windlass brake and was only temporarily held by the mechanical stopper before eventually parting at the 5th shackle.

Shipping from THPV Pathfinder

Fortunately, despite the real danger on the forecastle head and the violent rolling of the ship, the anchor party managed to avoid injury. The ship paid off downwind rapidly to starboard and peeled out of the anchorage just as I noticed and immediately recognised the dark silhouette of the Trinity House Vessel *Patricia* close astern coming into the anchorage for shelter. I called her on the VHF radio, explained the situation and asked if she might possibly try to recover the 2.3 ton anchor and 5 shackles of cable we had lost and perhaps drop them off in Dover for us to collect. Without hesitation the reply was in the affirmative.

We now had only the one anchor and because the shape of the ship precluded anchoring successfully for long, we left the anchorage and spent the rest of the night steaming very successfully 'half astern' on the engines in order to maintain a static position. As the wind went down and the back log of traffic at Dover was sorted out, we finally returned on the 13th February to the vessel's normal berth to find neatly stacked on the quay a 2.3 ton anchor and 5 shackles of cable. Well done THV *Patricia;* not just a pretty face for leading the Royal Yacht during the Queen's Review of the Fleet at Spithead or for cruising the navigational aids with the Elder Brethren, but a real work horse.

Chapter 23

Increasing Responsibility

The 2nd November 1972 I very nearly grounded with a deep draughted tanker but for the saving grace of the 'cushion' effect. The *British Dragoon* had a draft of 36-feet and was of 31,143 gross registered tons bound for the Isle of Grain. There had been some fog patches but the Medway Pilots had moderate to good visibility in the river and asked me to bring the ship into the port, despite the fact that approaching the Medway Channel I had run into dense fog. I was quite happy to do so, the ship having two radars considered good for those times and I was also being assisted on the second radar by the ship's very competent second officer who quickly verified everything I asked of him. This was at a time when Bridge Team Management was just a dream and pilots were not used to getting much help. As we came down the approach channel one radar or the other would lose the target of a particular buoy in the sea-clutter, only to have its position verified on the other radar.

Just past the wreck of the ammunition ship *Richard Montgomery* I ordered a last small alteration of course to port and identified the pilot boat coming out to meet us, but could not see the last starboard hand buoy. I asked the second officer if he could identify it and there was no reply; the Master then told me he had quite correctly sent the second officer down to meet the Medway river pilot. Unfortunately nobody else had taken over the task he was doing so well; backing me up. I looked in alarm at the helm indicator and saw it was still hard to port. Neither the helmsman nor anyone else had thought to tell me the ship was not answering the helm, or perhaps even noticed or maybe the message had been drowned out by the monotonous booming sound of the fog siren. I should in any case have noticed it myself, the speed was obviously too slow. I kicked the engines ahead just as a shout came from the Chief Officer on the forecastle head;

'We have a starboard hand buoy under the port bow.'

I reported to the Master that we were just running out of the channel. Fortunately the water was still deep close north of the buoy and the ship was now beginning to turn away from the danger, but would she go clear?

The pilot boat had arrived alongside the port side as the buoy came crashing and banging down the ship's side through the fog towards it. The very concerned Medway Pilot jumped nimbly aboard and arrived excitedly on the bridge shouting orders for actions which were already in hand and giving us information of which we were only too well aware.

'Ulabella' & Car Carrier off Dover

Turning slowly to port with the increased speed and helped by the cushion effect from the shoal water the ship regained her planned track around Garrison Point out of danger, and calm was restored, but it had been a very close thing. I was never in my subsequent thirty-two years of pilotage to ground a vessel or to come so close to a real disaster. The forces acting in our favour can best be described in the following manner: As the bow pushes water away in opening space for the passage of the hull, shallow water on one side will restrict the flow of that water. The result is a 'cushion' effect between the bow and the shoal or bank. The bow wave becomes higher on the side toward the shoal and the increase in pressure forces the bow away from the shoal.

September 1974 was a particularly interesting month for me starting with the arrival on the 9th of the month at Folkestone Pilot Station of the Ben Line ship *Bencruachan,* 28 feet 6 inch draft, 12,092 gross tons, inwards from Durban, South Africa after extensive repairs following an incident off the South Africa where she had hit a giant freak wave and broken her back and been escorted by tugs into Durban for repairs. She eventually arrived at Folkestone Pilot Station still looking to me somewhat bent but we had a clear run up to Gravesend without further incident.

On the 23rd of the month I was called to pilot the French BP VLCC 'Blois' Draft 38', 118,415 gross tons from the NE Spit Pilot Station to Garrison Point where the Medway Berthing Pilot was to take over. The Blois had come from the Arabian Gulf around the Cape of Good Hope at greatly reduced speed, this being the aftermath of the first major oil crisis when consumption was drastically reduced and much oil seems to have been stored in slow moving tankers. It was also the time that the pride of the French Mercantile Marine, the passenger ship France was sold to Norwegian owners to be converted and to be renamed the Norway. The action caused the French Trade Unions to block her in the port of Le Havre and deny entrance to the VLCC Blois.

The 'Blois' was subsequently lightened into another tanker I think at Lyme Bay, to a draft acceptable for the Medway and turned up with a French Deep Sea Pilot at the NE Spit instead of Folkestone. I can remember thinking it would be a good opportunity to give my wife's newly purchased car, a second-hand Ford Anglia, a test run to Margate and off I set. No trouble with the car which I parked in the Margate Council Car Park at the landward end of the Margate pleasure Pier from which the Cinque Ports Pilots operated at that time. Out of interest the CPPs left the pier to move to Ramsgate Harbour just one year before bad weather destroyed the vulnerable old Victorian Pier at Margate.

The ship was at 1026 feet LOA and with a displacement of 239,708 tons, at that time the largest I had the privilege to pilot but with a draft of only 38 feet and a favourable tide for immediate berthing, I entered the North Edinburgh Channel finding little difficulty in manoeuvring this powerful single-screw three-year-old ship once the Commandant had agreed to allow the engines to be un-restricted and on Full Manoeuvring speed if necessary. Unfortunately what should have been a nice quick job soon turned into a long drawn out but pleasant interlude; for half way inwards in the North Edinburgh Channel I received a message that the wind was now too strong for the Medway Pilots to berth the ship. This meant at least a twenty-four hour delay because at that time night berthing was not allowed on the River Medway.

Clearing the North Edinburgh Channel inwards I reduced speed to arrive at the Shivering Sand Towers and the Knob Anchorage at the first of the ebb tide; thus avoiding the necessity to turn the ship around. The Knob anchorage was seldom used and I certainly had never used it before, but all went well and we sat there for three days awaiting suitable wind conditions for berthing, swinging around on a single 25-ton anchor.

I know it was three days because we had three superb French dinners despite the fact that after a particularly long passage and the subsequent denial of access to her provisions at Le Havre; the *Blois* was now running out of stores. Fresh provisions were I believe sitting in French refrigerated trucks at the Isle of Grain refinery awaiting the tankers arrival; but in the meantime the Commandant, a charming hospitable French gentleman, greeted me over an aperitif each evening before dinner with an apology.

> *'I am sorry, Monsieur Pilote, we 'ave no flour*
> *the cook cannot make fresh bread rolls.'*

And the second day:

> *'I am sorry, Monsieur Pilote, we 'ave run out of butter*
> *to use for the cooking.'*

And finally on the third day disaster:

> *'I am very sorry, Monsieur Pilote, we 'ave run out of the Johnny Walker*
> *Black Label, we will just 'ave to drink ze Red Label.'*

Well that was a long time ago when certainly all French ships and most ships from the Mediterranean countries always accompanied a meal with wine and the one aperitif was usual; it was a privilege seldom abused but never understood or allowed in American or Scandinavian ships. Today alcohol is taboo and a hindrance to 'elf and safety', but these were happier times that I write about as we waited for berthing orders.

After the first couple of days I began to worry about Sally's little car sitting in the sea spray and wind-swept council car park at Margate, being concerned that Council officials might decide it had been abandoned and remove it. I called the NE Spit Pilot Station on the VHF radio to ask them to explain my predicament by telephone only to hear the north east coast accent of one of my close colleagues come up on the radio to say;

> *'If you sit on that ship much longer with the meter running,*
> *you'll be able to buy her a new car.'*

We were of course paid hourly detention rates and indeed I had done quite well staying aboard, but I really had no choice for the only way off would have been to charter a tug to land me, a far more expensive exercise and in any case it probably would have been considered imprudent of the Commandant to discharge his pilot from a such a very restricted anchorage.

West Oaze in heavy rain

September 1974 was also interesting from a financial point of view for it was the first time but by no means the last when my fee for one single ship was actually considerably more than I was actually to receive for a full month's work; the cause I think of my bank manager's earlier misapprehension that Trinity House pilots were particularly well paid. He had obviously noted the large payments being received from the pilots' agents into individual accounts without enquiring as to where such monies were eventually destined. In order to eliminate luck appertaining to a strictly regulated alphabetical roster where the size of ship and subsequent fee could vary dramatically, as self-employed men we operated a central Common Purse into which all pilot fees were paid monthly and from which each pilot received an equal sharing turn per ship piloted with the surplus being shared out each quarter. The Sharing turn for September was £75 and my total for the month a mere £654.88 but the fee for the *Blois* was £1206.77 plus Detention of £54.88 and my payments to the Common Purse for that month in excess of £2500. It was a fair system but did cause some envy among Masters who were only aware of the vast payments their owners seemed to be paying to the individual standing beside them giving orders on their own bridge.

Mail Order

A sister ship to the *British Dragoon* anchored some time in the mid-1970s in the Spile anchorage to await her berth at the Isle of Grain refinery. She was loaded with Nigerian crude oil but had been away for some time from the United Kingdom. The agent very efficiently arranged for the crew's mail to be delivered to the ship in the pilot boat sent out to land the sea pilot.

Garrison Point from Zulu 7 ⊾ age.

It was a quiet still night as she lay at anchor but very cold when a lookout on a large passing ship inward bound on the tide up the Seareach Channel reported seeing the body of a young woman floating on the surface. The Sheerness RNLI lifeboat was launched and sped to the position of the sighting and worked up and down the river as the crew spent a very cold night searching for the distressed female. Come daylight the story goes they recovered a scantily clad inflatable doll and were not amused. The strong suspicion, and of course it was only a suspicion, was that the mail delivered to the large British Tanker (which had included at least one large brown paper package) had brought a new lady into the sad life of one lonely sailor, a poor man who in his excitement had not considered the consequences of divorcing his perishing older model and promptly launched it through the porthole into the dark unforgiving sea.

The First Young Ladies

Not long after I became a First Class Pilot I was stood off for a British cargo ship to join her in Antwerp for the inward passage to Gravesend, from where she was bound up the River Thames to the Royal Docks. The ship which was owned by a well-known British consortium had several young lady cadets who dressed in jeans, working shirts, heavy safety boots and gloves were working the mooring ropes as the ship passed out through the locks at Antwerp. There was some merriment and considerable leg-pulling from the seamen but the girls worked competently and I was impressed. To see women in this role on a British ship was something of a new experience, although I had many years before met while I was serving out in the Far East, a famous British lady Chief Engineer who I believe had been awarded the MBE for bravery during the Second World War.

It was probably not as strange for the seamen of that era, as it was to us older salts having women aboard but I did not give it much thought and turned in to get a couple of hours' rest. Certainly it was quite pleasant being woken from a deep sleep by a soft voice offering a cup of tea and telling me that the Belgian Pilot would shortly be disembarking at the A1 Buoy off Flushing; instead of the usual bellow from a hairy-arsed AB banging the cabin door open. The rest of the passage passed uneventfully and we rounded the Tilbury Buoy some twelve hours later on programme for the Royal Docks. However coming up the Gravesend Reach, one of these shapely young ladies was part of the bridge team making a record of all the engine movements and the times of passing buoys etc. When I mentioned that the tug leaving the moorings to meet us was to accompany the ship upriver, she naturally asked me for the tug's name to note in her book. Being a typical British-owned ship of the '60s, she was equipped with only one pair of binoculars in the wheelhouse; binoculars which as pilot I had kept a firm hand on.

I raised the glasses to my eyes and read to my horror the name *Moorcock* and pondered exactly how I was going to tell her. This could be embarrassing, should I say "Moorcock as in bird" or what? I was fearful of misinterpretation and chickened out, quickly passing her the binoculars without comment in order that she might read the name for herself. I am sure to this day she must have wondered how I piloted ships around successfully with such poor eyesight!

Heavy lift specialist vessel at W Dunkirk 1983

More Haste Less Speed

Just a few days before Christmas 1974 the telephone went in the morning and Billie Munn the Pilot's messenger came on the line to ask me how quickly I could get to Rotterdam by air for a rush job. Apparently the large New Zealand Shipping Company container ship *Remuera,* at that time in Wilton's shipyard Rotterdam, had completed her engine repairs ahead of schedule and ordered a pilot at very short notice. The only way to get to her before she sailed was by air from Southend Airport and that meant driving to Southend immediately and leaving my car there for collection after the ship berthed at Tilbury. My colleagues ahead of me on the alphabetical roster had all declined the job, not considering there was sufficient time to get across to the continent, but the ship was only one year old and at 20 knots plus, 42,000 Gross Tonnage and 827 feet long she was a 'lovely job' in my view. The fact that she was from outside the Pilotage District and therefore meant I would earn more and have my expenses reimbursed was naturally quite an incentive for me to quickly telephone Southend and try and book the first and, I think, only flight left that day to Rotterdam. I was lucky the airline told me they just had the one seat available, I took it. The timing meant I only had half an hour to get from Rotterdam Airport to Wilton's Shipyard, but if the Rotterdam agent had a taxi waiting for me I could just make the sailing or head the ship off at the Hook of Holland as she came down the river.

All was arranged and I set off; arriving at Southend with half an hour to spare, I felt pleased with myself. The aircraft was a Bristol Freighter which carried both passengers and, behind a canvas screen, cars. My seat was in the back row where one could usually and particularly in bad weather hear some kind of vehicle straining at its lashing behind the screen. The passengers boarded on time and the aircraft bumpily taxied out to the end of the runway where looking at my watch I was delighted to see that everything had turned out well, we were running to time.

Suddenly there was then a loud alarming bang and the aircraft tipped forward as the small front wheel collapsed. Not to worry, the Captain's calm reassuring voice came over the loudspeaker, it was only a minor incident, the airline had another aircraft available and we would be transferred to that. He was right and within half an hour we took off again in another aircraft, but that was my timing gone and now my only chance was to head the ship off at the Hook.

It was a dark cold winter's night and bitterly cold at Rotterdam as the Customs and Immigration officers recognising my Trinity House Pilot's uniform waved me hurriedly through as I made a dash for my taxi – but alas no taxi! I managed to contact the agent only to find the sailing had been postponed and the ship was still at the shipyard; I took a taxi from the airport rank and set off for Wilton's Shipyard on the River Maas.

The Captain was playing darts in the officers' smoke-room as they were called in those days, when I joined the Remuera. She lay at the shipyard in an adjacent berth to the *Queen Elizabeth 2* who had also been having teething trouble with her own steam super-blowers; I believe a newly developed innovation at that time. I was too late for a meal and had no time in my rush to eat during the day but after hearing of my adventures and endeavours to get to the ship on time, NZSC hospitality soon produced sustenance. The ship was in fact to sail sometime in the middle of the night and the Captain told me that my services would not be required until we had crossed the southern part of the North Sea and entered the compulsory London Pilotage District. Grateful, I was shown to a comfortable cabin and turned in for the night; a somewhat disturbed night as things started to go wrong once out in the River Maas and the air filled with the sound of engine-room alarm bells. When all went completely silent I sensed a real problem and got myself dressed and made my way to the bridge.

The ship had lost all power and was about to lose steerage way as the Dutch Pilot spoke anxiously on the VHF Radio to a number of tugs. These were rushing seaward the other side of the long groyne separating the Europort Refineries from the river to round the seaward end and come back up river to our assistance. I kept well out of the way as the situation developed and on hearing the engine room report the ability to proceed at reduced speed, I left the bitterly cold bridge to return to the warmth of my bunk.

I had just gone back to sleep when about an hour later a Cadet knocked on my door to inform me that my presence was required on the bridge and how would I like my tea? I returned to the wheelhouse to find the ship just approaching the Maas Buoy at 4 knots on one engine. The Captain was most apologetic but told me he really had experienced a dreadful night and feeling exhausted he asked if I might take over the conduct of the vessel from the Dutch Pilot, in order that he the Master might get some rest before the ship reached the Thames Estuary and he needed to resume another long vigil on the bridge.

I was only too pleased to be of some use as the Dutch Pilot indicated the position of the Maas Buoy on the radar to me and the plotted tracks of other approaching shipping in the vicinity, but less pleased when asking him where the Maas Buoy was visually. It soon became apparent that we could not see any of the buoys due to Frost Smoke. I had rarely come across these fog-like clouds at sea which are formed by the contact of cold air and relatively warm water but that particular night while one could see clearly the mast head lights of other ships, their sidelights and the navigational buoys were invisible.

Fortunately with *Remuera* in ballast my height of eye on the bridge was well above this low-lying fog allowing me to see the masts of the many ships in the area, while the majority of smaller ships had low bridges well into the fog and were restricted to navigation by radar only. I set off at four knots but gradually the speed increased on one engine towards twenty knots and then the Chief Engineer brought on line the second engine and we were romping along clear of the coastal fog. Having calculated our ETA with a draft of only twenty-five feet at Gravesend, the gangs for loading were ordered together with the tugs for berthing. All was going well when once again the air was filled with alarm bells, we lost one engine immediately and had to reduce speed on the second; arriving late we incurred considerable extra charges.

Remuera subsequently was re-engined and changed her name to the *Remuera Bay* in 1977 but it was a long time before I saw her again.

The Sinclair Executive Pocket Calculator

I have always been attracted by gizmos, and I could write at length about them but I am conscious that the reader may not share my enthusiasm. Here therefore is just one of my earlier amusing gizmo experiences. It occurred, with one of the first pocket calculators, aboard a Greek cargo ship I had brought over from Antwerp for the Royal Docks. Clive Sinclair had stunned the world in the summer of 1972 by producing his first electronic calculator, the Executive, which was smaller and much thinner than any other on the market and for people in the United Kingdom Clive Sinclair, was known as the inventor of the pocket calculator. I immediately bought one because I thought it might be very useful calculating speed between navigational buoys and ETAs etcetera but principally because it was black and very smart looking and at 2.2" x 5.4" x 0.35" it would fit into the top pocket of my Trinity House uniform reefer jacket, a smart gizmo, expensive but one I thought well worth having.

I used it continually on passage across the Southern North Sea and the Greek Master was duly impressed, it was the first pocket calculator he had seen and he wanted one, in fact I think he wanted mine.

Off Southend we had to anchor for a couple of hours to await the vessel's berthing programme and it being lunchtime the Captain invited me down to his private dining room to eat. He lived well in his private little world and I could not help but wonder just how the rest of the crew faired. Following luncheon he carefully wrote down the name Sinclair Executive and the address of the London Company from where my purchase had been made and told me of his intention to ask his agent to buy one.

We sat back enjoying strong Greek coffee with a glass of unhealthy looking water when from my top pocket there came a small explosion and a wisp of blue grey smoke curled slowly upward. I quickly pulled out the warm pocket calculator smoking gently and was tempted to dip it into the glass of water but realised it was probably the battery and refrained, placing it on the glass top of the dining table where it quickly cooled down.

Asking if this had happened before I could see the Master was rapidly losing his enthusiasm for the cutting edge of technology and I guess he did not buy the Sinclair Executive. I wrote to Clive Sinclair and returned my calculator explaining the embarrassing circumstances of my experience and received by return of post another model which served me without fault for a good few years until I replaced it with a mathematical calculator which could calculate all kinds of calculations the vast majority of which I had never heard of or would ever need but gizmos are fun.

Chapter 24

The Home Front

Evening on the sea wall at Dymchurch, Kent

My obvious love of the sea and the amusing and more interesting memories I have recorded, have I imagine so far left the reader with little idea of my home life, which is remiss of me; and perhaps here is the right place to take a pause in matters maritime and turn to those domestic.

Behind every successful person and I think my career at sea and my life generally could be considered reasonably successful, there stands a loyal supportive partner. For more than fifty-three years now my rock has been my lovely wife Sally, without whom very little of my career would have progressed and to whom I literally owe my life for it was her insistence and hers alone, that finally achieved lifesaving medical treatment for me in 1996.

It takes a special kind of woman to live the lonely life of the wife of a mariner, to bring up children on your own, to manage the finances when your husband is virtually out of touch the other side of the world. While I was still at sea with the RFA Sally used to pack the two children in our old Morris Cowley, swing the starting handle, no mean feat in itself, and set off from Folkestone or Dymchurch to meet my ship wherever in the country it berthed from Plymouth to Rosyth. She realised it was imperative that she learnt to drive even when she really did not like driving.

When later I was a serving pilot I would often be away on the continent for days at a time. While at home and on call, those loud telephone calls too often came in the middle of the night waking Sally as well as me. The hours were quite irregular and quite unpredictable as we worked on an endless alphabetical roster. Expecting a night's sleep, one could often be called to work within half an hour of going to bed as in those days many ships turned up unexpectedly. Should I set off in the middle of a cold night and a howling gale, it was unlikely that Sally would return to sleep as she worried about me not just trying to climb aboard a ship using a rope pilot ladder, as it rolled and crashed about in heavy seas but driving across country on the wet and windy motorways or country lanes to get to my point of departure or return. Come the morning the day had to go on and the children would require feeding and possibly transport for their activities. There would be the Brownies to run or later some Girl Guiding activities and duties as a Parent Governor at Southlands Comprehensive School and of course the demands of swimming. I would return after a night out to crash into bed tired and invariably bad tempered and particularly so if kept awake and unable to sleep as the day progressed.

Nicola and Neil, having learnt to swim at a very early age in Singapore, had become very good competitive swimmers and trained daily. Because there were very few swimming pools in the area that meant leaving Dymchurch at about six thirty in the morning to swim from seven to eight am, non-stop at the new Folkestone Sports Centre before returning to Sally's mother Dorothy in Julian Road; for a large cooked breakfast with hot nutty bread and then on to school. At the weekends they had to get up even earlier in order to make use of the training facilities at Nonnington Teacher Training College, Eastry. They worked hard and did well; the Folkestone Swimming Club and East Kent Invicta engraved swimming cups bearing evidence of their success. Neil breaking a number of records and for a while winning everything in his age group until a much taller boy (who eventually went off to play basketball in the USA) came along and outreached him. Nicola went on to make county standard and still swims competitively today in Canada where she is currently the local coach and a lifeguard in Steinbach Manitoba. Swimming in the Welsh Masters just before she emigrated in 2006 she won five of her six races and came second in the sixth.

Sally, an only child, is the daughter of the late Jack and Dorothy Cooper who, at the outbreak of World War 2, also lived in the village of Postling up on the hill at the Farthing with wonderful views across Kent to the Sussex borders where Jack had been brought up in Rye. Jack Cooper was the third partner in Snape, Leslie, and Cooper Corn Merchants a major commercial enterprise in East Kent. The partnership owned local mills and before the war were importing cargoes of grain from Canada. Sadly when Sally was only four years old her father was admitted to hospital with appendicitis and caught a virulent form of tuberculosis from which he died within a year at home at The Farthing, Postling, in 1940; leaving Dorothy at the beginning of the bombing with a young child to bring up alone. Dorothy, who was born in Belfast where her father had worked, had come over to Folkestone when her father Frank Jordan took over as landlord from his father Harry Jordan, the 'South Foreland' public house and hotel at Folkestone Harbour. For a while after their sad loss, mother and daughter returned to the family home, "South Foreland" to be with Dorothy's parents and her sister Patricia. Folkestone Harbour was at that time a prime target and sixth sense or common sense saved Sally and her mother when Dorothy insisted on moving at short notice away from the area to Peasmarsh; just days before the "South Foreland" was totally destroyed by an aerial mine, striking early on a Sunday morning and taking the life of a young man who had rented their room. The rest of the family were dug out of the rubble and together with Sally and her mother moved to Hertfordshire. The pub safe without the Saturday night's takings or anything of value was found empty half way up the Road of Remembrance, probably not the work of the Luftwaffe.

Sally and her mother returned to Folkestone in 1955 and I was fortunate to be introduced to her and immediately smitten outside Bobby's Department Store, one Saturday morning in 1956. My mother however was difficult from that first day and when I brought Sally home for the first time to meet my parents for tea, as we did in those days, we walked in to find that she had invited along two other girls who were quite unknown to me. Despite her obvious disapproval we married after a short engagement at Holy Trinity Church in Folkestone on the 5th October 1957 and rented a flat in Clifton Crescent on the Leas within sight of the church. We had very little money but a lot of hope; I was just starting out on my career proper having obtained my Second Mate's Certificate of Competency after studying at King Edward Vll Nautical College in London, while Sally worked as a secretary for the giant American Pharmaceutical Company Pfizer earning more than me. I originally thought she worked for Tizer the soft drinks manufacturer having never heard of the other company but that was hardly surprising for at that time Pfizer consisted of a mere handful of staff working out of offices above a car showrooms in Sandgate Road, Folkestone, marketing antibiotics manufactured in the USA. It is amazing to see just how that company has developed into a vast industrial complex at Sandwich after moving from Folkestone when their plans for expansion were denied.

Money was not plentiful, interest rates were high and banks were reluctant to give loans in the 1950s. Sally and I spent all our income on renting property, living and being together for the first eight years of our marriage before we managed to buy our first property – a bungalow on Shipfield, an award winning estate by the sea wall at Dymchurch on the Romney Marsh. Meanwhile the family was growing; we had Nicola and Neil early in our marriage and they, as I have written earlier, had some adventures in the Far East but we had planned to have more children, both of us being well aware of the disadvantages of being an only child. Sally, earlier in our marriage, had lost our first baby and was to lose another not long after we moved to Dymchurch. On advice and after talking it over and gauging the reaction of our natural children we decided to look at adoption.

It was to be a long journey; our finances, health and existing childcare provision together with our religious attitudes were all carefully examined over months before we were invited to visit a large children's home. The beautiful home on the east cliff at Ramsgate was full of small people, some of whom looking expectantly at us asked if we had come to take them to their new home. It was a moving and heart-breaking experience which convinced us that we should help some of these children, but we had been invited to meet a specific little boy that the representatives of the society thought would fit into our family. Poor little lad, his expectations must have been high when Matron had prepared him to meet us; but nice as he appeared he was a little older than our own expectations and he neither took to us or we to him. On the way out Sally and I both noticed with immediate interest a much younger fair-haired boy, sitting quietly by himself on the staircase; he had been watching us intently and seriously and once outside we asked about him. We were told his name was

Matthew but he was not available for adoption due to health problems which he was hopefully expected to grow out of in the coming year, when his situation would be reviewed. We asked if we might be considered as potential parents and after several meetings and much correspondence it was agreed that we should visit the home regularly to take him out for the day and establish a relationship with him before fostering him with a view to adoption, once he was considered medically fit. It was several weekends before he said a single word but gradually he responded to us and we were allowed to foster him and take him home to Dymchurch on the 14th September 1969 after he had passed his medical. He was two years and two months old when he came to live with us and it was to be a further eighteen months before we were allowed to adopt him at the Court in Ashford; eighteen months of not knowing if his natural mother would sign the papers releasing him to our permanent care and eighteen months when he could have been taken away from us. A quiet sensitive and very intelligent boy he was over the years to give us all a great deal of pleasure, pride and laughter but after the ordeal of his adoption we decided to settle for our family of three children, content and very proud of the best of all their achievements.

Matthew did not take to competitive swimming although he became a good swimmer; he turned out to be very musical, having a wonderful clear voice as a choir boy and going on to become a very competent musician playing the piano and clarinet. He might have stood a better chance of a musical scholarship and career had I not decided that he should take up the clarinet because it was easier to transport and reasonable in price without considering the possibility that too many parents might make the same decision and therefore the competition for clarinet places was extreme.

Not long after Matthew arrived on the scene we sold our bungalow and moved diagonally across the estate to a house adjoining the sea wall and just below sea level. We bought for £7,000 and were to live in the new house for some seventeen years until after building an extra wing on it for our growing family we sold it later for £75,000. The children by the time of the sale had all flown the nest.

During those intervening years as a family we had become heavily involved in the many village activities – the School PTA, Girl Guiding, Brownies, and Army Cadets, the Day of Syn festivities, the Parochial Church Council and choir, the local riding stables, and I had become a Founder Member of the Rotary Club of Romney Marsh. We made many lifelong friends and lived in a village with a real sense of community. The two boys both boarded at schools for a period of their schooling. Neil because I thought it would give him a better chance in life, and the sort of discipline which had done me no harm and I thought he needed. Sadly the decision was badly timed, the teaching was poor and boarding perhaps made him feel rejected; consequently I was to bitterly regret it. Matthew, who was a quiet sensitive academic boy, was subject to severe bullying at school and was moved on the advice of staff to board at Sir Roger Manwoods in Sandwich. Boarding was the last thing we wanted to do with him considering his start in life and today I cannot recall how exactly that sad choice was made.

Playa Blanca holiday destination

From Don Davis, a pilot colleague, we acquired a bloodhound by the name of 'Felderland Placid' who, being of a lovely but slobbery nature and too large and boisterous to live indoors, was billeted with us for eight years outside in her own kennel. She was inclined to bay at the new moon and was sometimes mistaken for the fog siren at Dungeness, but she was hopeless with burglars. When in the process of licking him affectionately, she had to be pulled off one burglar which she had pinned against the wall at the bottom of the garden; the burglar promptly escaped but may have been the local man later apprehended with a list of houses with large dogs; ours at the top.

Nicola went to school in Folkestone on the bus, became a Queen's Guide carrying the County Colour at St Paul's Cathedral and developed a very keen interest in horses and one day asked me to buy her a large horse. It was indeed a beautiful horse but having seen the mothers of other girls in the village grooming, feeding and fetching for their daughters; I was determined that Sally was not going to be so burdened. I told Nicola that I would buy the horse and annually insure it but I was not going to feed it, stable it or exercise it, she would be entirely responsible for the horse and its welfare.

Postling Village Charity Ride

I imagined that I was setting impossible conditions but they were conditions which she readily accepted and strictly adhered to and "Rustler" the horse she had for 21 years; never cost me a penny more than my original outlay and for the insurance which I paid until Nicola started work. It must have been very hard for her as she set out in all weathers early in the morning before school across the cold windy Romney Marsh on her bicycle to clean Bellinzona Stables to earn her horse's daily feed and go back again in the evening to bed the horses down. She had on occasions to arrange to put her horse out to livery and watch other girls ride and compete on him to pay for his keep. She worked teaching younger children to ride to buy the necessary tack and she competed, making me as proud as punch of this smart young lady, on her immaculately turned-out horse. I regret now how hard I was at the time but Nicola learnt all there was to know about horses and became a proficient and knowledgeable horsewoman, riding judge and riding club chairman.

Neil went to school in Folkestone to Westbrook House Preparatory School and then to Southlands Comprehensive at New Romney. Undoubtedly bright and the only one to actually attend University eventually as a mature student, Neil never did well at school probably because instead of encouraging him to work harder, I made the fatal mistake of trying to drive him to achieve better results, concentrating on the negative aspects of his work instead of being positive.

I must have been a very hard father and regret many of my decisions and much that was said when tired and angry as our independent teenage children stood up to me and fought their corners; but they have all made me proud and both Nicola and Neil are today bringing up their own children with a patience and wisdom which I can only envy. Maybe I taught them what not to do, what to avoid and to think before you speak by my own poor example.

Matthew told me the other day that I came into his room one night to say goodnight when he was seven, looked at his feet and muttered something about him having "ancient old feet"; which he now claims scarred him for life. While on another occasion he called me up from the USA late at night to find I was in Scotland and had just gone to sleep after being the guest speaker at a Nautical Institute Dinner; the conversation going something like this;

"Hello who IS THAT?"
"It's Matthew here"
"Matthew? MATTHEW you say? MATTHEW WHO?"

Well I guess Matthew had not been in the United States for long at that juncture and had not realised quite how late it was in the UK. I, a trifle confused from the effects of dinning rather too well, certainly did not recognise his voice and thought I was being called by a member of staff. Matthew understandably was not amused at the time but now dines out on the story.

So where are the children as I record my life today? Nicola went on to join the Police Force in the Thames Valley after buying her first house in Hythe when in her early twenties and working a number of years for a building society. She subsequently married one of her colleagues, Tony Trimble at Postling on the 6th May 1989 when they were both stationed at Wantage.

Tony, a tall lovely friendly man, was a police dog-handler who loved the countryside and is an ideal partner for Nicola. They blessed us with two lovely grandchildren – Adrian and Ella – who, like their cousins, have given us immense pleasure and reasons to be proud.

Following her specialisation and considerable experience in the policing of domestic violence and abuse cases Nicola was appointed the Domestic Violence Response Coordinator for Pembrokeshire not long after she and Tony moved to West Wales; following a major change in their lifestyle. Not wishing to bring up their two children Adrian and Ella in the rat race of urban Berkshire, they had used the soaring house prices in the Thames Valley selling their house at Cold Ash to buy a smallholding in rural Ceredigion stocking it with cows, sheep, and pigs and of course horses. Nicola resigned from the police service and the family began to live the simple country life. Adrian and our only grand-daughter Ella took to the Welsh language and singing with consummate ease both choosing to go on to Welsh speaking Secondary school when the time came. Tony continued at Thames Valley commuting between the farm and work in Berkshire with his two working police dogs. Another smallholding followed the first, yet despite the requirements of her animals and family Nicola settled into the new job she had taken on, being able to hold down her work load as technology allowed her to fulfil much of her work from home without travelling to Haverford West.

Tony, who had started life as a Police Cadet, retired as soon as he was able and joined the rural leafy but very wet tranquillity of Ceredigion just three miles from wonderful beaches, working on the property and preparing family meals thus lightening the heavy work load Nicola had managed to absorb. After a year however he had been unable to find the kind of work he wanted and following an HGV course, which he thought might prove useful for the farm work; he took a job long-distance lorry driving for the experience, a decision which was to lead to another major change in their family prospects. One day he was approached by a Canadian who having watched him park up a heavy load at a motorway truck stop; offered him a job driving in Canada. Tony went out to Steinbach, Manitoba, liked what he saw and the farm was put up for sale. Immigration papers went through, the sale of the farm gave them some concern following their purchase of a lovely property in Canada but all went well and the family said a sad farewell to their many friends and set out for the New World in 2006 taking with them the two German Shepherds in the aircraft.

Bettwes Ifan in Ceredigion Wales

Today Tony has a new adventure each day driving the length and breadth of North America from the Ice Roads in Northern Canada and Alaska to the deserts of Arizona and Nevada to the busy eastern seaboard and Confederate south, some loads actually spanning the entire width of Canada and the USA. In Canada Nicola returned to her swimming interests becoming a swimming coach in the small town of Steinbach before recently returning to her earlier specialisation in the world of child protection, becoming a franchise holder for Kidproof Canada and taking on a whole new business and lecturing career.

Adrian, having graduated from High School in Steinbach is currently financing a long distance learning degree in Bachelor of Science Computing and Information Systems with the University of Athabasca in Alberta. In this programme he is studying numerous aspects of information technology. He is able to pay for his university education from work obtained after winning first in the Graphic Design Gold Medal for Manitoba and then the Gold Medal for the whole of Canada; in the Skills of Canada competition. Learning to fly in Canada he first flew solo the week of his seventeenth birthday some five months before he passed his driving test. At eighteen he became the holder of a private pilot's licence.

Ella who has inherited her mother's strong competitive swimming ability is developing into a tall willowy blonde and is settled in well at High School, has made many friends, and following her Welsh outset has developed a wonderful singing voice and a position in the local choral society. Like most young people in Canada, Ella works in her spare time, at the time of writing with jobs in retail and at the local municipal swimming pool. Despite the lack of hills in Manitoba, both children have developed a passion for skiing kindled in the European Alps and developed in Ontario.

Steinbach a small German Mennonite dominated town is situated literally on the longitudinal central divide of Canada suffering from a fierce continental climate, bitterly cold in winter and roasting hot in the summer. With agitated wild turkeys racing loudly at great speed across the lawn and cautious deer stepping silently through among the silvery birch trees around the perimeter of the garden, a garden capped with an almost perpetual blue sky filled with skeins of geese honking noisily on their migratory journeys overhead; it is a good place to live. Of course the dogs, having adapted to pulling sledges, have to wear shoes in the winter and the mosquitoes take some satisfying before they finally disappear in the late summer. The land is so flat in Manitoba it is said that if you set your dog off down the road and stand on a chair you will be able to see it for two whole days! Such flat land however is a phenomenon which, as a painter, I found gave inspiring light and cloud effects. Following our visit last year we look forward to going back.

Neil, since leaving school has never been unemployed. Initially he spent a couple of years following his interest and infatuation with the internal combustion engine, undertaking a diesel fitter's apprenticeship with a local haulage and quarry owner but a couple of winters in a cold concrete servicing bay looking up into the interiors of the same old heavy plant, rather dampened his ardour. With something like three million people unemployed he came to me one Friday and said he had had enough of the grease and dirt of the internal combustion engine; he was going off to London to work in the construction industry and with that he was gone. He had arranged accommodation with an old school friend living in Peckham and telling me that there was always work for those who were willing to graft he dispelled my concerns about the unemployment situation and left for London, starting work on the Monday morning at Heathrow Airport digging holes with a gang of Irish navvies. Life was hard but his earlier experience moving and servicing heavy plant soon meant that he was inside a cab, while his less qualified new friends worked outside in the cold and wet that winter. After a couple of years, encouraged by his employers to better his position, he came back home in order to take a bricklaying course at Hastings College of Technology. Work locally soon followed and he built up a reputation for speed and technical ability sufficient to become established as a reliable and successful builder in his own right.

Today Neil is a teacher at Canterbury College of Technology, passing on the building skills he learnt as a very successful builder, continually in demand for his craft for which he had a natural talent, running his small business on a reputation of really sound hard work and recommendation. I often think how satisfactory it must be for him still living in an area where he has personally built or extended so much property; an artist surrounded by his work, he has certainly left his mark. Married to Clare a clever, patient and loving mother and hard-working home-maker on the 22nd September 1989, we are blessed that they have given us three fine grandsons – Ben, now in his first job, Joe and Lee all doing well at school and all seemingly to have inherited the hard-working ethics of their parents. Clare, a Legal Secretary by training, dedicated her early married life to her family staying at home to care for them during their formative years, giving the boys a warm and secure home life. Later she returned to work first for the local District Council before changing back to her more familiar role as a Legal Secretary, when Neil changed to the more secure but less lucrative world of teaching. They are a happy, close-knit, outwardly affectionate family. Neil bought his first house while in his twenties, a house close by on the estate where we lived at the time but now the family live in a much more substantial property which he has expanded as the family needs demanded.

Ben, a quiet serious boy and the eldest of our five grandchildren, is also like his cousin into IT and builds his own computers as well as being a talented craftsman working in wood and other materials to his own design. He bought and paid for his first car – a highly polished and immaculate classic Mini Cooper – and passed his driving test by working as a waiter in a fine local restaurant. Now having successfully sold the classic Mini he has bought a possibly more modern car exchanging modern design for vintage nostalgia in order to have a reliable car to get himself to work at the local academy where he has been fortunate to land himself a job in the IT department of an establishment partly funded by Microsoft.

Joe, undoubtedly academic, plans a career in engineering and is taking Pure Maths and Science and hoping for a University place this next year. The sportsman of the family, he takes every opportunity playing cricket where he excels with both ball and bat and in the winter playing football.

He has bought a car saving up working as a gardener's assistant whenever he is given the opportunity.

Lee, the youngest, is also doing very well at school where he has developed considerable musical talent as a drummer reminding me with his drum kit of a budding Eric Delaney and causing Neil to build an extra soundproof block onto the house. Sadly, however, his music tutor moved on to pastures new; but every cloud has a silver lining, for Lee has now taken up the piano and seems to have inherited my own mother's musical genes. Lee appears also to have inherited my love of history and at the time of writing is looking to a career in teaching.

Matthew now lives in Florida employed by a company in the communications industry, working long hours with responsibilities and company clients all over the USA; encompassing the time zones from east to west coast. He works from home and lives alone with a small pug dog he has named Louis. Although he has made a number of good friends since first going to the United States, his current lifestyle means he leads a very solitary lonely life with little opportunity to make new friends. Life for him has been hard with tremendous highs and lows and over the last few years worrying ill health. His life story so far would make a first-class novel full of absorbing stories sometimes heart wrenchingly sad, sometimes exciting, and often dramatic. His life is filled with travel and tales of expensive hotels in Venice, Hong Kong and Paris; glittering social occasions, coupled with a desperate struggle for economic survival. He has had, on different occasions, cars to drive ranging from company Bentleys, Cadillacs and Mercedes 500SLs to old clapped-out Volvos and vintage Toyota Celicas of his own. He has lived in London's Harley Street, somewhere around Sloane Square, Brixton, and Folkestone. He has rented homes in Florida at St Petersburg, Largo, Palm Harbor and Clearwater, all in the Tampa area. Generous to a fault with a caring and loving nature he has always preferred to live in some style, renting good property rather than putting down permanent roots in something less pretentious. A series of financial crises, mainly brought about through his exploitation by others, and his own ill health have dominated the last few years.

Growing up at school his musical talent brought him to the fore in the school amateur dramatic productions and gave us great pride on many occasions. Matthew really wanted to become an actor but he was frustrated when he and I clashed as to the method he thought might fulfil his dreams. The details are no longer relevant but Matthew decided to leave the security of home and went off to London to seek his fortune.

From that day to today he has supported himself, starting first of all working for a consultant using his fluency in both French and German. Unfortunately his employer was not doing well and he could not afford to pay a living salary and Matthew moved on. A number of jobs followed before he found employment with a small London-based publishing company where soon he found himself the chairman's PA and when the company and chairman moved to Florida, so did Matthew complete with Green Card. The company prospered and picked up some valuable clients and Matthew became a Vice-President but unfortunately the chairman appears to have been ill advised by his local accountants as to just what was allowable and what in fact was considered tax evasion. When the IRS arrived in force the company folded as clients and staff abandoned ship and the chairman headed rapidly back to the UK. Left in the lurch with salary owing and no job, times must have been desperately hard, harder than I can possibly imagine but his friends rallied around and helped out and eventually he landed his current job.

Life was to be lived at a very different level and then ill health hit and he became a participant in the lottery of American general medical practice. Fortunately he is currently insured but sometimes I wonder if the care and diagnosis he has received and the sheer number of tests carried out, has more to do with monetary exploitation than real need or good medical practice. Fitted with a heart pacemaker at 39 years of age and in receipt of what appears to me a dubious earlier diagnosis for another unrelated but life affecting ailment, he lives what to me is a thoroughly undeserved struggle to just exist; rather than being able to live life to the full. One of life's real survivors, Matthew currently lurches between highs full of laughter, good humour and enthusiasm and lows of loneliness and despair which reminds me of that heart-rending small figure sitting silently by himself on the staircase of the home in Ramsgate.

We keep in touch regularly at least once per week by telephone or visually on the computer with our children Nicola and Matthew in North America and of course are able to see Neil and his family regularly as they live locally down the road. Travelling long distances by air is getting more difficult and more expensive as we get older but it is such a great joy to be reunited once more and the experience is always something positive with which to look forward. We will continue to travel as long as we can, but I guess we may reach an age when the children will need to come home to visit us.

Meanwhile the world has become so much smaller in the fifty-three years since Sally and I got married; when parting meant almost complete loss of contact. Except of course by the expensive vagaries of the shaky hands of strangers on a Marconi wireless Morse key, prone to atmospheric conditions; or the very unreliable ship's postal system where letters could be lost for months. Today, with a click of a mouse, the computer screen can be filled with the images and voices of love ones in real time speaking from the other side of the world and I am filled with delight and relief.

Coincidence and Premonition

My mother was not a practising clairvoyant, although for a time as a child I do remember her reading something (in the days before tea bags spoilt that bit of harmless fun) of the future, in the shapes of an individual's tea leaves left in the bottom of a cup. However she did seem to have uncanny premonitions which sometimes turned out to be accurate.

Just before Sally and I departed on a holiday touring California in 1991 I went to visit my mother, who by that time was living in a Nursing Home at Chislehurst. My mother looked at me with a sense of finality and said dramatically;

"Good bye Son."

I sensed she thought this was to be our conclusive meeting and enquired why? She replied to my utmost surprise that she thought she was going to be run over by a motorbike! I did not take her seriously for she lived in a sheltered community, well looked after and at the age of eighty-seven rarely went out.

Before we left, we met our daughter's father-in-law, the late Peter Trimble, a lovely bearded man with a twinkle in his eye and a soft melodious Welsh accent who, discovering we would be in California at the same time, said;

"We'll see you there then."

"Fat chance," I replied.

The 3rd October 1991 was a beautiful warm sunny day in Yosemite National Park as Sally and I parked our hired Buick at what the Americans call a 'vista position' and began to take the obligatory photographs of the mountain El Capitan. A tour bus pulled in and off stepped Peter and Marion Trimble.

"There, I told you we would see you and you didn't believe me," he said, accusingly, as only the Welsh can do. Turning serious he then announced;

"By the way I have some bad news – your mother has been run over by a motorbike and is recovering in hospital."

Poor Mother, she had apparently treated herself to a day out and got off a bus in Chislehurst only to be run over as a motorbike unexpectedly came around a corner. She had a broken pelvis and other bones and recovered very slowly. She was only ever able to walk again with some difficulty but sadly she lost her independence and confidence that day and spent her final five years confined to the home.

Premonition is certainly difficult to explain but undoubtedly we all experience extra-sensory perceptions and I know that after fifty-three years of marriage, Sally and I are usually conscious of reading each other's thoughts.

On the morning of the 16th November 1996 my busy twenty-four hour watch came slowly to an end and I was relieved at the Coryton oil refinery. I had worked through the night berthing and un-berthing three large tankers and was tired and ready to go home and sleep when I had a premonition that on the way, I should call in to see my mother, although I had spoken to her the night before to find she had been entertaining the other residents on the piano.

I arrived just in time to find her being lifted into the ambulance on her way to hospital suffering from pneumonia, from which she died two days later. How can one explain that premonition?

On a lighter note and to complete the story of the meeting in California, we must revert back to 1991. We had arranged to meet up with the Trimbles in San Francisco a few days later following our chance meeting in Yosemite National Park. While the ladies went shopping in San Francisco, Peter and I drove out on Saturday 5th October 1991 to see the baseball game between San Francisco *Giants* and the Los Angeles *Dodgers* at the 57,500 seat stadium Candlestick Park, for which he had the tickets while I had the car. The *Giants* won 4–0, if I remember correctly, but I found the game somewhat slow and the play of some two hours forty-five minutes boring. I left my numbered seat to queue for some beer and frankfurters when after a long time without any score, somebody hit the first home run – I had missed it. When I returned to my seat the neighbouring crowd were quite excited, telling me I had won one of the prizes drawn every quarter based on the seat numbers. I rushed back to Peter and he confirmed my number had come up. Now I have to say the prizes had been well worth having and included such items as motor cars, motorbikes, household furniture and white goods, lawn mowers and airline tickets. I was excited; the winner had to report to an office with his ticket on the other side of the stadium on a particular mezzanine deck. I asked what I had won. Peter replied, laying on his Welsh accent with a trowel and in retrospect, a sly grin;

"Well I think he said you have won a B-you-ick."

Excitedly I thrust all the beer and frankfurters into his hands and rushed off to the other side of this vast stadium, bursting in breathlessly to the appropriate office waving my ticket.

"I've come all the way from England and I think I have won a prize."

Carefully examining my ticket slowly the large man confirmed my win and not sharing my enthusiasm ambled off ponderously to get my prize. Well obviously it wasn't going to be a Buick but it could be something equally worthwhile.

After a short while of excited anticipation the man returned clutching a large brown paper parcel.

"What is it?" I asked curiously.

"Tee shirts and sweat shirts," he replied bluntly.

Well a prize is a prize and perhaps I should have been more grateful for although the sweatshirts were of good quality and together must have been worth well over $100, they had been designed as an advertisement for the town of Stockton, California apparently famous for underground caves; complete with stalactites and stalagmites. The artist's depiction on the shirts unfortunately gave the impression one was looking into a giant mouth with rows of crooked teeth – it was hideous. The beer and frankfurters were gone when I got back and we soon gave the tee shirts away, although I seem to remember, Neil did wear one when he was employed deep underground on the England to France Channel Tunnel construction.

So that is the home front, we have been blessed with a family of whom we are incredibly proud but I do not want to 'gild the lily'; we, like all families, have had our difficulties and disagreements and I am sure this chapter will not find complete accord with all members either due to omission, imbalance or error but it is my personal recollection of family relationships and mine alone; as are all individual memories. It is also far harder to write than tales of the sea.

Chapter 25

Master Pilot Relationship

Turning back to the main theme of my book I will now write of the peculiar relationship between Pilot and the Master of the ship to which he has been appointed.

RFA Olmeda replenishes Canberra
One of a set of ten paintings to commemorate RFA service
during the Falkland War

A marine pilot needs to develop a great deal of diplomacy building a rapport as rapidly as possible between him and the Master of a ship, but it is not always easy. In a non-compulsory pilotage district the Master has the choice of whether he uses a pilot or not; the pilot providing a service which the Master uses out of personal choice. In a compulsory pilotage district the situation is very different for the Master has to accept the services of a pilot duly qualified by the local pilotage authority; in the UK that now means the local Harbour Authorities and has to delegate control of the navigation to the pilot.

The Master, knowing the limitations and abilities of his own ship and reasonably familiar with a port, often is consequently of the opinion that he really does not need the services of a pilot. Always under pressure from his owners to avoid pilotage costs; in a compulsory pilotage district there is always room for tension.

The Master, faced with a complete stranger coming aboard to take over the navigation of his ship, must quickly assess him, discuss with and agree with him the proposed plan of action for the safe arrival or departure of the ship. This is something called a 'passage plan' but at the end of the day he has no choice but to trust someone over whom he has little control and, being human, may not have immediately taken to because of his looks, opening remarks, attitude or perhaps previous experience.

According to British law, the position of a compulsory pilot, which was my position except when using my Deep Sea Pilotage Certificate, is that I was solely in charge of the navigation of the ship. According to law, I superseded the Master in all matters connected with the navigation of the ship. I was entitled to have my orders promptly and diligently carried out; and, over my pilotage career of thousands of ships, I can only recall ever having my orders queried on three occasions. One was a genuine misunderstanding; one was ignorance of the depths of the local water and the other sheer arrogance.

The last one, the Master of a smallish UK tanker only just of a tonnage requiring by local regulation the services of a Berthing Pilot, was confrontational from the start; probably because he objected to having to make use of a Berthing Pilot. In any case it was soon apparent that if I was to say white, he would say black. When I presented my plan for departure (which was to kick the stern off and turn short around to starboard using the tide, bow thrust and tugs) he decided against my advice not to use the tugs provided and paid for by his company. His plan was to just let go his tanker moored stern to a spring tide and turn to port using his bow thruster and single-screw main engines only. I explained this would put the ship in great danger of the stern being set upriver by the flood tide to strike the lower end of the berth, while he was attempting to lift the bow off to port; my advice was ignored.

With the ship 'singled up fore and aft' the silly obdurate man set his plan in motion, letting go all the lines and using his bridge controls he attempted to swing to port directly off the jetty; he was soon in trouble. Realizing that my predication was about to be fulfilled, at the last moment he handed over for me to 'pull his chestnuts out of the fire' and take emergency action as the tide did indeed sweep the stern up towards Bravo Jetty. The stern barely cleared the downstream end of that jetty as the ship now on Full Ahead with the helm hard to starboard, slowly gathered way. Further collision was only avoided with Alpha jetty close upstream, by turning short round to starboard dangerously close to the jetty and by going full astern on the engines, using a tug to push on her port bow and the thruster full to starboard. There were shouts of alarm coming in at different times from the mooring parties, both fore and aft, and warnings from the tug Masters watching with incredulity at what they presumed to be my moment of insanity. It was in retrospect my own fault for allowing the Master to go against my advice but the only way I could have prevented his action was to involve the Harbour Master and have the ship, which required permission from the VTS centre to move, denied that permission. What had been a simple little job had turned into a nightmare and I dreaded meeting the culprit again but fortunately he completely disappeared from the scene and hopefully was given a job as far from the sea as possible. But I digress...

My job was to navigate the ship, manage the arrival time directing the course and speed of progress, obey the international and local collision avoidance rules, order necessary sound signals, control the tugs and watermen running the moorings, communicate with the harbour authority and vessel traffic services and agree on a safe anchoring position when required.

The master and or officer in charge of the navigational watch was required to ensure that the ship responded efficiently to the pilot's orders and gave the necessary support co-operating with the pilot and maintaining an accurate check on the ships position and movement using the engine controls, navigational assistance, lookouts when underway and sufficient men and equipment when anchoring or mooring the ship. He was also required to have rigged and manned the pilot boarding ladder or have boarding arrangements which strictly complied with the safety requirements of international law; failure to do so very often meant the pilot, having risked his life boarding the ship with what turned out subsequently to be in the dark unsatisfactory or downright dangerous boarding arrangements, arrived on the bridge angry and contemptuous of the Master responsible.

The Owner was supposed to provide a properly equipped ship maintained in an efficient state and competently manned in terms of numbers, skills, experience and the prevailing circumstances but while continually there has been international pressure to improve standards and indeed the ships of today are of a far higher standard to those I was to pilot in my earlier days, both the Master and I too often had to make do with the very poor tools we were given. It was no good blaming the poor Master when too often he needed sympathy and understanding of his difficulties; we needed to work together.

The rules were there but my view was that regardless of my position of strength as a compulsory pilot I had a contract of service to the Master and felt that he was ultimately responsible and exercised that responsibility by employing me and taking my advice. I needed him and he needed me. To build confidence and a rapport between us I was writing and preparing a basic passage plan for the Master long before it became the accepted practice or requirement. I endeavoured to buy the Master his national newspaper on the way to the pilot station and when, as sometimes happened, he had been kept waiting due to delays caused by other traffic ahead of him at the pilot station, I tried to avoid rising to the angry and often sarcastic remarks by pacifying him and making the point that I could make up any lost time on passage.

If he was late on arrival I tried to avoid complaining about bouncing about in a lively pilot boat unnecessarily for a couple of extra hours. One had to remember that in the early days when radar was less efficient, a passage up channel or across the southern North Sea in unfamiliar waters, past many known shipping hazards and in poor visibility was very tiring for the professional Master who would have invariably been on the bridge for many hours and possibly through the night; he may be tired but he was usually very pleased to welcome me aboard. Should the boarding arrangements require comment I tried to wait until we had exchanged information and commenced our passage inward before having a quiet word; if they were bad I would refuse to board and have to face an irate Master when finally boarding after the situation had been rectified.

Sometimes the master/pilot relationship got off to a bad start which I tried to placate with humour. For example, one day I boarded a small German Schuyt off the NE Spit buoy and was greeted by the Master with a question. Did I know what special day it was? I replied that it was a Wednesday but what was so special? To which came the reply;

"Today is Adolf Hitler's Birthday."

Inwards at Knock John Channel

Not wanting to rise to the bait I said nothing but walked to the other side of the wheelhouse thinking, did we have a real bastard here or was he just trying to be humorous? The little ship plodded on inward through the Princes Channel steered by her automatic magnetic compass with two silent figures sipping strong black German coffee staring ahead out of the forward windows; the air was silent and very disagreeable.

Suddenly the Shivering Sand Towers came into view and the Master stirred and possibly feeling somewhat guilty attempted to make conversation.

"Vot is this, Meestir Pilot?"

He asked speaking as they do and referring to the Maunsell Forts built in 1942 for the Army anti-aircraft units to defend London from the bombs of German aircraft. My reply went something like this;

"Strange that you should ask that, Captain, but they are a relic of the Second World War, you do remember the war?"

"Ja of course, but what were they," he replied somewhat irritably.

"Well, Captain they were built as an experiment for the monkeys," I started to explain.

"MONKEES? Vot kind of experiment?"
He exploded, his large florid face deepening in hue.

"Yes monkeys, Captain," I went on to explain...

"You must understand we had many very valuable monkeys in our world famous zoos at Regents Park and Whipsnade and these animals were frightened by the bombing during the blitz; so the authorities decided to build a safe haven for them here out on the water, but unfortunately the monkeys were bored! Now there were no toys for the monkeys and they were too impatient for fishing but by 1942 we had plenty of bofors guns and as an experiment it was decided to teach the monkeys to fire these guns and do you know these monkeys were so successful – they shot down 95% of Hermann Goering's Luftwaffe!"

With that the miserable German Master exploded with laughter, his bright-red face beaming with appreciation and he promptly called down to the mess boy to fetch a couple of beers in order that we might celebrate our good master/pilot relationship. He had of course been lying – it was not Adolf Hitler's birthday, for he was born on the 20th April 1889 and it was not even April but midsummer.

I too had been lying, for the Maunsell Forts had not been manned by monkeys but perhaps I can be allowed a little literary licence for they were indeed manned by soldiers; who were referred to by the sea going fraternity as 'pongos' or performing monkeys!

That fragile relationship could sometimes be destroyed beyond redemption. I remember during my training period taking passage outwards from Gravesend to the NE Spit buoy with a pilot who told me of his experience with a small Dutch Schuyt when turning into the Princes Channel. In dense fog without radar he was navigating just using dead reckoning and the occasional sighting of a large buoy looming up alongside him and the sound signals of the buoys when so fitted.

On the ebb tide he misjudged the entrance to the Princes Channel and the ship overshot and ran into the Shivering Sand Towers, causing one of the Maunsell Forts to come crashing down on the foredeck of the little ship. The collision crushed the foremast and caused the crew of three men a boy and a dog plus pilot to rapidly leap into the small wooden boat kept on the poop for just such an emergency, rowing clear as the ship slowly began to turn over. They rested on their oars within sight until low and behold the Fort slid off the ship into the sea. With a shrieking of grinding metal a considerable groaning noise and clouds of rust to penetrate the gloomy dank seascape, the little Schuyt bobbed pluckily up from underneath the large black monster.

Quickly they rowed back and re-boarded, setting off to seaward having more than firmly established their point of departure and with no more damage to the ship than a flattened foremast and deck fittings. The Master/Owner however refused to speak a single word to the pilot for the remainder of the passage, not even a 'goodbye'. The Master/ Pilot relationship was irreconcilable.

The Miners' Strike

This is the record of an occasion when the experience of daily developing a rapport under somewhat difficult circumstances served me well.

On the 12th March 1984 a National (though arguably illegal) Coal Miners' Strike began that came as no real surprise to those of us able to see the tremendous build-up of coal that had been deposited at the power stations around the coast, as obviously the industry was being prepared to do battle. Miners from Kent were among the first to answer the call to strike from Betteshanger, Tilmanstone and Snowdon Collieries. Betteshanger miners were often regarded as the most militant in the country but certainly in Kent probably because Betteshanger attracted a lot of the hard-line union men blacklisted in their home areas after the General Strike of 1926 and because Betteshanger was the only pit to strike during the Second World War, resulting in three union officials being imprisoned and over 1000 men being given the option of a fine or hard labour. They had a history of being militant.

Having personally visited a deep coal mine in the Ruhr and crawled along the working cutting face more than a thousand metres below the surface prior to passing out through lack of oxygen in the narrow return tunnel, I had every sympathy for anyone working down a mine; a place I would never willingly visit again but I could not imagine I would become in the least bit involved in their struggle to keep the mines open. That is until the 26th June 1984 I was called to bring out of Richborough a small Swedish fuel oil tanker the *Fajal* 363 grt, 7 feet 6inches draft which had been chartered to bring in oil for Richborough Power Station from oil storage tanks in the Thames and Medway. Chartering in a foreign ship had become necessary when the National Union of Seaman vowed support for the miners and it was considered there was some risk of the berth being blockaded by one of the regular British flagged NUS manned oil barges that regularly supplied oil from the Thames Estuary.

'Mighty Servant '1 with 'Glamor Labrador 1' at West Dunkirk

The Port of Richborough was being picketed and naturally I was worried about driving through the picket lines to park my new car at the quay. But as pilots we had another problem, for few if any of us had actually had opportunity to pilot a ship into or out of the port; although Richborough appeared on our licences. The river Stour cuts a small visible winding channel in the shiny wet sand that fills Pegwell Bay at Low Water, a channel which was marked with unlit wooden beacons.

Being unfamiliar with the entrance and having plenty of time before the ship was due to sail I thought I would go down at Low Water and check the navigable courses in the channel and the relative transit positions of the wooden poles being used as beacons. Rumour had it that the miners had been moving the beacons under the cover of darkness and Kent Police had been forced to bring in an inflatable dinghy manned by police frogmen to prevent further disruptions in the safe navigation at the port. All seemed well to me and with sufficient time to find some lunch, I entered one of the local watering holes.

As I walked in wearing my Trinity House Uniform with its shiny gilt buttons, I found the pub full of grim-faced men in groups engrossed in conversation seemingly bereft of humour; the conversation died as I approached the bar.

"Are you still serving meals or am I too late?"

I asked the young lady behind the bar, trying not to appear uncomfortable with the atmosphere in the smoke-filled old room. She passed me the snack menu and I ordered a toasted sandwich and a pint of beer. Noticing the very unfriendly challenging looks of a large man standing next to me wearing a National Union of Miners lapel badge I offered him a pint of beer, asking him which colliery he was from and quickly told him of my Ruhr experience and subsequent sympathy for anyone working in a coal mine; he accepted my beer and I managed to avoid the expectant looks of his cronies rapidly emptying their pint mugs.

Recognising that I was the Pilot for the tanker *Fajal* he asked why if I had such sympathy for the miners I was going to cross the picket line. I explained that if I wished to retain my licence to work and support my family I had no choice, for refusing to Pilot the *Fajal* would be a breach of the Pilotage Act and that as a self-employed Trinity House Pilot the Authority would without doubt suspend me without pay. My colleagues with whom I shared my income would have little sympathy either, and ensure that any such misdemeanours on my part were brought to the attention of Trinity House.

The large Miner looked at me with some scepticism, not entirely I felt convinced until I mentioned that there was, in fact, another side of the coin. If I was to be prevented from carrying out my duties as a Marine Pilot, such action was in law a much more serious offence; one of criminal law rather than civil law. There had in fact been no threats or implied threats just genuine curiosity as to our relative situations, a civilized discussion over lunch. I refused his offer of a beer on the grounds of duty calling and during the following months piloted the *Fajal* both into Richborough at 9 or 10 feet draft and out at 7 or 7 feet 6 inches, according to the tide, without a single incident despite the large police and picket presence. We shook hands, parted with mutual respect and I drove down to the ship. How ironic that Margaret Thatcher, having put the Miners to the sword, then turned on the country's Marine Pilots just two years later; but that is another part of this story.

It was in fact an interesting little bit of pilotage, feeling our way through the changing bends until we reached the strait and a turning basin into which we ran the bow into the mud bank before backing around to face seawards and berth at the Power Station Terminal.

Pilotage Training

Throughout my Pilotage career I was heavily involved in trying to improve the standards of training for Marine Pilots and in particular to improve Master/Pilot Relationships; despite the more humorous anecdotes mentioned earlier. I prepared detailed Passage Plans for the Masters of large tankers long before they became a requirement and I worked hard at being as professional as possible when piloting. Acting as a consultant for Videotel, a private company specializing in training videos for the maritime world, I remember fighting a continuous battle with the many Shipowners and Master's representatives; each with total recall of instances where obviously matters had not been satisfactory.

Sally Viking Ramsgate Ferries at Dunkirk

It was agreed that a video should be filmed of pilots in action – on ships where possible and on the new ship simulator at Warsash, demonstrating not only the ability of the new technology available but best Master/Pilot practice. A Master and Bridge Team of officers were flown in from India to bring a simulated tanker, to be piloted by me into the simulated Thames Estuary. The Master and I did not meet prior to my walking into the simulated chartroom; the Bridge Team had prepared their Passage Plan and I had mine.

We filmed it as we thought it should happen completely without a script on the 21st June 1993. The Master asked questions as he thought appropriate and I briefed the Bridge Team on matters of importance to me. Whether the draft film was originally planned to be used as a basis for further improvement I never knew, for the other consultants were evidently happy with the result. The video became an industry standard for a number of years as part of a series on Bridge Procedures marketed by Videotel.

The only hitch we had while filming was that once the simulator was started the pre-set flood tide set in and the simulated tanker behaved naturally setting in to the south west in the dark as expected. This would have been fine if it had not been necessary for the film makers' requirements to adjust lighting and profile angles requiring a number of re-takes. Every time we restarted, the ship had moved further off the required track and my first order had to be "Hard to Starboard" to try and regain control. Eventually not wishing to be filmed even on a simulator grounding in a large tanker, I called a halt and we started afresh. Looking at the video today I imagine after fifteen years there may be a new edition for Passage Plans have become far more formalised, Electronic Charts and Automatic Identification Systems have all been incorporated into the equation; but basically the message remains the same and has stood the test of time.

Chapter 26

Unexpected Mechanical Failures

Engine failures can come at any time and the pilot must always be ready to act quickly. It was my experience that such failures are more likely in the initial stages of manoeuvring, having just left a berth or got underway from an anchorage; and indeed this incident took place halfway on passage in from Folkestone to Tilbury, following a few hours' wait in the Margate Roads anchorage.

Ramsgate Ferry, Le Mans, at Dunkirk

The *Hoegh Beaver*, a Norwegian cargo ship of 7,273 gross tons, bound inwards from Freetown rolled heavily as she turned seawards. The Master made a good lee a mile off Folkestone, despite the south-westerly gale driving the large breaking seas and heavy swell crashing up the English Channel. After a short uncomfortable passage out from Folkestone in the heavy weather the Trinity House Pilot boat *Lodesman*, with a short burst of correcting power appeared suddenly out of the darkness to arrive alongside the floodlit port side of the ship in relative shelter and I made my way out of the warm cabin into the elements. Carefully I waited with a spray-drenched seaman at my side to assist my boarding and secure my sea bag to the heaving line which dropped with a thud from above to the pilot boat foredeck beside us; the pilot boat itself dipping into a large wave cascading water over our shoes. We waited for a lull, a quieter moment in the residue of swell spilling under the stern which, from experience, I could feel the launch responding to through my legs before I stepped quickly through the driving rain onto the wet rungs. I climbed swiftly – using the pilot ladder, floodlit by a ring of intense brightness breaking the coal-black darkness of an early winter's evening – aboard.

The evening of Saturday 27th November 1976 was a foul and dirty night, but the ship was early with the wind and sea behind her and not due at Tilbury until 10:00 hours the following morning. After a brief discussion with the Master it was agreed to proceed as quickly as possible up to the shelter of Margate Roads and get some rest at anchor before picking up the berthing programme in the morning. This went well; traffic off Dover, as we passed inward a mile off, was light and the weather meant we passed only two large piloted ships in the Downs. The anchorage off Margate was full of small ships sheltering from the weather but we found a reasonably sheltered position north east of North Foreland and safely anchored.

It was still blowing, south-westerly gale force 8, with moderate to good visibility and heavy rain squalls when we got underway at 06:00 hours, to the first of the ebb tide. With a maximum draught of 18 feet, we planned our passage inwards via the Princes Channel and with a considerable number of small ships coming out and mostly peeling off to the south, we approached the channel on the charted recommended track to pass fairly close south of the Tongue Sand Towers. The wind and tide were trying to set us north of the line but at a speed of 15 knots track was maintained until we were about 8 cables south-east of the Towers. At 06:46 the vessel suddenly lost all power and the lights went out. I immediately ordered the helm hard to port and asked for someone to go forward and standby the anchors.

Unfortunately the helm only went as far as 10 degrees of port helm before all the power was lost. There was no emergency steering immediately available and the ship, rapidly losing way, immediately began to set up towards the Tongue Sand Towers. I carefully watched the bearing of the Towers and was relieved to see that we still carried sufficient way to clear the large steel and concrete gun towers but the Southern Towers Buoy was another matter. There was no doubt we were going to hit that. If I let go the anchor which by then was manned, I judged there was a strong likelihood that the ship would bring up and swing violently with wind and the ebb tide onto the solid tower.

'Hoegh Beaver' just misses Tongue Sand Towers

I therefore decided to let the ship run over the buoy, passed my thoughts to the Master who was in agreement and who quickly rang the engine to 'stop' in case the struggling engineers managed to start up the brute just as we passed over the buoy.

The banging and crashing was horrendous as the ship rolled to wind and swell and the buoy flashing merrily crashed about seventy-five feet down the starboard side before disappearing under the hull, only to reappear on the port quarter still flashing merrily.

We cleared the Towers on the western side and the engine was restarted without further delay. We had only really lost a few minutes but it seemed like hours. With dawn breaking we proceeded on time to berth. I never did find out if in fact there had been any damage to the buoy or ship, my report was received by Trinity House without comment and I heard no more of the incident.

Norwegian Lash Ship North Edinburgh Channel

On the 18th November 1972 I shipped off Folkestone into the Norwegian LASH (lighter aboard ship) *Atlantic Forest.* She was bound for the Medway where buoys had been laid in deep water in the river for her to flood her dock and discharge loaded barges instead of containers, to start a new service between the Mississippi USA and Europe. At 35'6 draft and 36,870 gross tons she was quite a heavy lump but very manoeuvrable. The bridge was situated right on the forecastle, not an ideal position for the heavy swells of the North Atlantic or for conning the ship through bends in a narrow channel, but she was a new well-equipped ship and I expected no problems.

Passing Dover and east of the Goodwin Sands, we dropped anchor at the Outer Tongue Anchorage for a few hours to await the tide for entering the North Edinburgh Channel and to make her required ETA at Garrison Point. When we got underway the weather was superb with the sea clear and like glass as we headed due west from the anchorage, to pass close north of the *Tongue Light Ship* before swinging ninety degrees to starboard, across the bar and into the North Edinburgh buoyed channel before curving back round to port to the south west.

The tide ran strongly south west across the narrow entrance to the channel and I increased speed to ensure a good response for the manoeuvre but as we came abeam of the light ship, the wheelhouse filled with the sounds of alarm bells and, as the power started to go off the board, I instinctively called for the helmsman to put the wheel 'hard to starboard' watching the wheel indicator anxiously. I was very lucky for as the power died completely and we lost the engines, the helm indicated 'full starboard helm'. Slowly she started to swing away to starboard towards the sand and we warned the anchor party, still cleaning up below us, to stand by to let go again.

Going out on to the port bridge wing to watch the speed of the swing aft, I was relieved to see despite a complete loss of power we were turning rapidly. Passing through north we kept swinging away to the north east until we cleared the shallow water running down our port side but it had been close, so close in fact we could see the bottom clearly under the port bow. We now had to stop the swing before the ship's length behind us kept going and put the quarter ashore. Fortunately at that moment the engineers reported normal service resumed and we were able to steady her up on an easterly course and steam away from the sand before turning back to enter as originally planned. We made up time and arrived on schedule, despite the fact that the gyro compass took some time to settle down and I found myself continually facing aft to ensure the ship was following me on course.

Had we not managed to initially get the starboard helm on, the ship would have grounded somewhere south of the Edinburgh Channels towards the top of the tide – but luck was on my side once again.

"Master of the Sea Lanes"

Much to the amusement of some of my colleagues the above title was given to an article written by the author John Dyson for the *Reader's Digest* and published in January 1984 about a single day in my piloting life. The story should have been of several days' duration to show the variety of ships we piloted to match a similar article that had been written about a Rotterdam Pilot for the Dutch Edition of this famous magazine, but John Dyson had such an exciting time with me he produced the article after just the one single act of pilotage. Well he would wouldn't he, I hear my colleagues muttering.

Why I was approached to have my work scrutinized I am not sure, but some time before the approach I do recall I had met a man at a Charity Fund-Raising party who seemed very interested in my job as a Marine Pilot and having "swung the lamp" a little, I then discovered he was Michael Randolph, at that time Deputy Executive Editor of *Reader's Digest International Editions*.

John Dyson however had everything going for him – wonderful dramatically changing weather, and a superb modern well-run large containership and, as a result of a power failure, the near collision between two other ships (which I hasten to point out was nothing to do with us but a near miss) which we witnessed. The ship I was to pilot was the Dutch container ship *Nedlloyd Tasman*, 27,613 gross registered tons, 743 feet long, Speed 19.5 knots, Captain Evert Feenstra. It was a well-written article describing the whole process of bringing a ship into the Port of London, the sea marks, other shipping, the scenery and weather, what I did and what was said, plus a description of my lunch! There were a couple of minor errors which my colleagues noticed but which I had ignored prior to publication because I felt they would not have been noticed by the general public and therefore correction was unnecessary.

The main publishing problem however was the objection by the owners of the ship – which had a power and sub sequential steering failure when passing a colleague of mine in a loaded bulk carrier full of sugar – to having their ship actually named. My late colleague Captain Charles Jacklin, who sadly died a very premature death a few years later, saved the day by taking emergency avoiding action to avoid collision. Action which almost grounded his own ship the *Rajaan*, as what was described as the "large white painted ferry bound from Flushing to Sheerness," scrapped by a mere twenty feet off his starboard side. According to my log the incident took place on the 9th December 1982 but was not published until the January edition of *Reader's Digest* 1984 just over a year later.

Fanciful Accountability

I was deeply honoured when on the 7th May 1998 I was elected to serve as the President of The Nautical Institute, for the period of two years, at the AGM held in conjunction with the Maritime Excellence Exhibition at the Guildhall in the City of London. The importance of the post and the respect with which the Nautical Institute was held and I was therefore treated within the Maritime Industry came as a surprise when I first attended several important functions but I never thought at the time just how holding such a position might affect my piloting. I was, after all, just an ordinary PLA Thames Pilot; surely nobody expected me to suddenly turn into something special – or did they?

Just two months later on the 9th July 1998 events conspired to cause me considerable concern, for what if far from the high expectations of a few, I had a serious maritime accident? The act of pilotage concerned the large container ship *City of Durban* (Draft 11 metres, length 258.6 metres, 52,055 gross registered tons) bound from the North Fleet Hope Container Terminal to sea via the Sunk Pilot Station. On the inward passage I knew the ship had developed engine trouble with her starboard engine and therefore naturally my first question to the Master as we went to stations with the ship moored head down on the flood tide, was a query as to whether the problem had been resolved and I was assured by the Master that the Chief Engineer had informed him that both engines were now in full working order.

It was a nice summer evening as at 23:15 hours, with the Voith Schneider tug *Sun Thames* secured on her towline forward and the *Sun Surrey* secured on the starboard quarter, we checked with Port Control as to any other traffic movements out of our sight in Gravesend Reach and were informed that the large car carrier *Asian Vision* was to move from Tilbury Landing Stage and proceed in to take our berth. We were given permission to proceed and slipped our moorings, moving out into the river to clear the shoal water off the Tilbury Lock Bell Mouth. We started to move slowly ahead and I slipped the stern tug but retained the forward tug secure on her long towline by instinct rather than normal practice. The river, just 500 metres wide, bent around Tilburyness ahead of me as I prepared to turn the ship to port through an eighty degree turn, using slow ahead or more on the starboard engine and just dead slow ahead on the port engine. We were aware that the *Asian Vision* was moving and that we had to pass at least 1.2 cables distance off Imperial Wharf to clear a set of mooring buoys.

The telephone to the engine room rang suddenly and ominously, shattering the quiet in the darkened wheelhouse as the bow of the ship came abeam of Tilburyness and the Captain told me we had lost the starboard engine, the very engine I was relying on to assist in the turn to port. The starboard telegraph rang to stop and a mild expletive escaped my lips for which I apologised to the couple of passengers standing quietly watching the operation. The *City of Durban* was now running straight for the south bank as the flood tide began to take effect on the port bow, resisting our efforts to turn into it with the helm hard to port, the bow thruster full to port, and fortunately the tug *Sun Thames* which immediately on my request had started towing to port. I reported my problem by VHF Radio to Port Control anxious that the *Asian Vision* was aware of my difficulties.

The ship continued relentlessly and directly for the south shore and I was suddenly disturbed by the thought that "This is not going to look too good for the Institute"! I checked that the anchors were cleared for use and stopped the port engine, then put it astern. Slowly and reluctantly the bow started to move to port and the ship came around late into the bight of the river to line up for passage down Gravesend Reach. The only problem I had now was that in order to clear the mooring buoys off Imperial Wharf, I had to get back into the centre of the river and head directly for the *Asian Vision;* which was coming up with the flood tide under her. Fortunately all went well and we passed very close, but clear to proceed to the Southend Emergency Anchorage Z3 where we swung to port into the first of the ebb tide with little difficulty, in order to carry out two hours of engine adjustment before proceeding without further incident to sea. Fortunately throughout the incident I had not incurred the name of the Nautical Institute adverse publicity but I had felt probably unwarranted extra responsibility.

Chapter 27

Incidents in Fog

On the 20th December 1972 I was the Pilot of the Finnish cargo ship *Rekola*, a motor ship of 2731 gross registered tons and 300 feet in length, bound inward to Victoria Deep with a draft of some 17 feet. She was not a large ship and we were making a good passage inward, for she was equipped with what was for her era fairly good radar; despite the dense fog which had persisted all the morning. However, about midday we were informed on the half-hourly Thames Navigation Service Broadcast that due to the dense fog and the presence of a large LASH (Lighter Aboard Ship) ship moored just upstream of Gravesend Pilot Station, causing a radar blind spot in the river, the Gravesend Pilot Cutters were not working and services promptly stopped for all ships requiring a pilot. We anchored off Southend to await improvement which came about 20:00 hours that evening. Being a handy ship I was able to weigh anchor quickly and soon found myself leading a stream of traffic up the Sea Reach Channel. There were a number of ships with pilots from the Southend anchorage, including the *Hornland* and *Neptune Topaz* and a number of unidentified smaller exempt ships without pilots following behind, the closest being about ½ mile astern of the *Rekola*.

At the time of leaving the anchorage I was aware from the previously transmitted broadcasts that an unknown ship had anchored in the middle of the narrow channel south of Mucking No.1 buoy. The visibility which had improved to about 3 cables shut in again dense as we passed the Mid Blyth Buoy at around 22:00 hours with the tide flooding at about 2 knots.

The cold dank air took on an eerie green hue to the north as sounds of escaping steam and weird creaking noises, accompanied by the occasional striking ring of hammer blows on metal, marked the presence of the giant unseen oil refineries in full production; close by on the starboard side. The bridge rails and rigging ran with water, leaving one with wet coat sleeves as we listened and peered into the cold thick gloom for a sign of anything. Preceding at reduced speed through the still night I had the radar set on the 3-mile range and identified the echo of the 'unknown ship' which appeared to be stopped in mid-channel, ahead of me and south of the Mucking No.1 Buoy.

I then became aware of the echo of a following ship emerging astern onto the 3-mile range of my radar gaining on us as we endeavoured to creep slowly between the ship and buoy ahead. At about 22:13 hours Thames Navigation Service broadcast that the anchored vessel was named *Tamora*, that she was not fitted with either VHF Radio or Radar but she now had a PLA launch alongside which was so equipped and would shortly be moving out of the fairway. As the lead ship I immediately replied to TNS that I intended to pass very close to the north of the *Tamora* and requested that she remain anchored until I had passed clear. I was told they would pass this on to the PLA launch and I heard no more.

Channel 12, the TNS VHF Radio working channel, was busy but I was becoming concerned that the ship closing me from astern was either unaware of the situation or simply going too fast; I reported my concerns as soon as possible to those watching the port radars in the operations room at TNS Gravesend and heard them request the vessel identify herself and instruct her to ease her speed. A displeased voice from a small exempt British coaster identified his ship and passed a message to the effect that he was following 'the Tug' and that he was not going too fast but was only on 'dead slow ahead'. He was wrong on two counts – the *Rekola* was not of course 'a Tug' but a cargo ship some 300 feet long and in light of the subsequent incident his speed may well have been considered excessive.

I never did see either the launch or the *Tamora* or Mucking No.1 Buoy, as I further reduced speed and slid between the two a matter of feet away, just maintaining steerage way; but as we passed I could hear voices in conversation and her bell ringing as her windlass worked at the same time. Was she in fact ringing the regulatory signal for a vessel at anchor in fog, the rapid ringing of a bell at intervals of not more than one minute or was the fact that her anchor was now aweigh and off the ground being indicated by those on her forecastle to her bridge, by the traditional rapid ringing of the same bell?

It was really no longer of concern to me *Rekola* was past the bottleneck and my concentration was to round the Lower Hope Point; turning to port my focus of attention was ahead. Fortunately at that time the river was completely devoid of outward traffic, for at 22:27 hours, just a few minutes after the exempt coaster was requested to ease her speed, the same voice from her bridge now somewhat dispirited came up on the VHF to report that he had been in collision.

Upon learning of the collision and with a view to rendering assistance, I brought the *Rekola* round onto a downriver heading using what is described in the text books as a "Williamson Turn"; that is a turn designed to bring a single-screw ship around onto an exact reciprocal course. It was the first and only time that I was ever called upon to carry out the manoeuvre in earnest and, despite the dense fog, it worked perfectly for as we came around and stemmed the tide, manning the decks with lookouts, floodlights and cargo nets in case there were survivors in the water, wreckage was reported flowing up on either side of the *Rekola*. We could not see any swimmers and were pleased to have it confirmed shortly afterwards that all the crew of the sinking Tamora had been rescued by the Duty Tug from the Shellhaven refinery, close by the scene of the collision.

With one ship sinking and the Gravesend Pilot Station going off station once again, we anchored just out of the Lower Hope Channel between Numbers 5 & 7 Mucking buoys. The *Hornland* anchored further downstream from me, while in endeavouring to anchor clear of the channel the *Neptune Topaz* found the ground. It was turning into quite a long tiring night for all concerned but there was more to come.

The fog was still dense in the Lower Hope Reach and the Gravesend Reach where the problem still existed some twelve hours later but, as breakfast came and went, one could hear by changing VHF channels the traffic way upriver reporting improving conditions of visibility and we knew it would probably not be much longer before traffic would get back to normal.

However the late Daniel Ivor MacMillan was quite a forceful character; a Trinity House Thames River Pilot and official Representative of the Thames Pilots and one time Mayor of Gravesend, he was particularly annoyed that the LASH moorings should lead to the disruption of Pilotage on the Thames in fog for what ever reason, and that morning he decided to force the issue. As he sailed down the clearing upper reaches of the river in a small 499 grt Schyt, outward bound for the North East Spit, he declared to TNS on the VHF for all to hear that if the Gravesend Sea pilots could not get off to relieve him at Gravesend, it was his intention with the agreement of the Master to take the ship through the Sea Pilots Compulsory District to the NE Spit buoy off Margate. One could cut the silence on the radio with a knife as the listening pilots, their thoughts perhaps concentrated not so much on the fact that his violation of the sacrosanct pilotage boundaries might bring back work for all the pilots but on the pilotage dues he would be 'stealing' from their common purse. Whether he had expected the fog to be clear at Gravesend the end of his district or not, we will never know; but it did not and he was committed to his proposed course of action. Once passing Gravesend and commencing his outward passage he was continually harassed by the Gravesend Duty Fog pilot persistently claiming poor old Dan was off track etc.

Meanwhile well aware that the fog was clearing in the upper reaches of the Thames, I discussed and agreed doing the very reverse with the Master, assisting him with his own passage up above Gravesend to Victoria Deep Water Berth; a berth very familiar to this particular Master. We waited until Dan had actually passed our position in the anchorage before I went up on the air.

"Gravesend Radio, Gravesend Radio, this is the Finnish Ship Rekola at anchor in the Lower Hope, Draft 17 feet 6 inches. We are about to weigh anchor to proceed inwards for Victoria Deep."

Mid morning at Gravesend, the significance of my statement must have raised a good number of questions. Did the port have the authority to stop me? What cargo was I carrying? Could the River Pilot Cutter Serve the ship? What had Dan started? Is the Harbour Master here? How much more is he going to take from our Common Purse than the amount Dan will be paid? There was a considerable pause before Gravesend Radio responded apart from the initial;

"Wait one."

Then, *"Rekola, Rekola this is Gravesend Radio, do you realise we still have dense fog here and the pilot service is suspended?*

"Gravesend Radio, yes that is understood but in view of the fact there are no pilots available, the Master who has already been delayed 24 hours is opting to proceed to the berth without a river pilot. He has asked for my assistance in the river, the berth being well known to him. We will be at Gravesend in thirty minutes and I will stop and make every effort to give the River Cutter radar assistance to embark a River Pilot but if none appear, we will continue on passage."

With that we weighed anchor and proceeded in slowly to Gravesend Pilot Station where the fog was so dense we could not see the water from the ship's bridge, but I recognised a small target moving away from the Royal Terrace Pier downriver towards me and I was able to confirm the coxswain's questions as to our relative positions and courses. Hearing the cutter's engines as she came alongside, I went to the port bridge wing and, peering downwards, could just see her shape safely alongside – but what were all those white shapes? She seemed to be covered in seagulls, but they soon turned out to be the white cap covers of the many River Pilots who were either seeking passage to the Tilbury Landing Stage or perhaps intent on 'tarring and feathering this young upstart' who had nearly got away with a considerable sum of their pilotage dues. The Master was delighted and wished me a cheerful farewell but the handover to the River Pilot was somewhat frosty and aboard the River Cutter I was greeted with a not unexpected disagreeable silence but an amused smile from the coxswain on receiving his gratuity; when I remarked that I had nearly avoided paying him.

Daniel Ivor MacMillan and I had many a chuckle about that day as the years went past but he did rather better financially out of it than I did, for pilotage earnings made outside the district were never shared. My mistake was to even suggest stopping, if I had known nobody would thank me – I would have carefully avoided the cutter, but I never got another opportunity.

On the 24th April 1973 Dan MacMillan was serving as Mayor of Gravesend when he relieved me at Gravesend on the bridge of a regular visitor to the port, a Greek spirit tanker by the name of *Violetta*. With a draft of 31 feet 7 inches and of 11,624 gross registered tons, the ship was I imagine getting towards the end of her working life and had at that time what I considered to be very poor radar plus a full cargo of volatile petrol which appeared to be barely contained within her old corroded worn plates.

The Master, a delightful hospitable man, always ordered his London pilot from the port of Antwerp and I had been across to the continent for her on a number of occasions, given the opportunity by the pilots ahead of me on the roster who, knowing the ship, had declined the job. It was a long tiring and at times worrying trip from the Belgian pilotage district across the traffic lanes in the poorly marked Southern North Sea to the Thames Estuary and inwards via the North Edinburgh Channel to Gravesend, but it paid extra money which I never declined. We had dense fog leaving Antwerp and for most of the night-crossing but on arrival off Margate the fog had cleared and we commenced a clear run-in, bolstered by the stimulant of copious small cups of strong black Greek coffee accompanied by the obligatory glass of dubious looking water. Breakfast arrived and the Master, pleased with our progress, had the cook produce egg, bacon and toast for his English guest – breakfast by way of reward. The breakfast I thoroughly enjoyed despite the pervasive strong reek of petrol fumes which drifted along in a cloud surrounding the ship and to which I had become accustomed. It was however a little alarming when members of the crew wandered out onto the wing of the bridge lighting up cigarettes despite the large no smoking signs about the ship.

It was a time when there had been a number of high profile shipping accidents and growing public concern about lax rules and regulations. There were a growing number of ships being put under flags of convenience in order to avoid the stringent high standards expected by the traditional maritime nations and a general feeling there was a need for tighter regulation. That feeling had manifested itself in new Port of London Regulations, largely driven by the concerns of Gravesend Council that dangerous goods should not be permitted above Coal House Point and therefore past Gravesend during the hours of darkness or in fog.

It was clear visibility as the dear old *Violetta* wafted past Coal House Point, in a cloud of petrol fumes, to pick up her Trinity House River Pilot inward bound for one of the oil storage tanks nestled steamily on the northern shore of Long Reach at Purfleet. I was pleased to be allowed that far up the river, for I had been listening to the radio reports from the upper reaches and was conscious and wary of reported fog further up. The River Pilot Cutter arrived alongside and the nimble smartly-dressed figure of Daniel Ivor MacMillan shortly stepped into the wheelhouse. I quickly introduced him to the Captain and handed over the ship's con, pointing out the one poor radar on the 3-mile range, the screen protected from the daylight with a plastic visor. I say quickly for I had noticed a fog bank moving across the Tilbury Dock and almost immediately the Tilbury Landing Stage disappeared as the fog rolled over the roofs to spill right across the river ahead of us. Remembering Daniel's involvement with the new regulations and pondering on his predicament I could not help saying;

"She's all yours, Mister Mayor."

I landed and headed for the railway station and the train home; the Mayor, now committed, skilfully negotiated the next three bends in the river and berthed thankfully without incident.

Chapter 28

Command Experience

When I left the Royal Fleet Auxiliary to join the Trinity House Pilot Service, my career had taken an unplanned change of direction for my lifetime ambition had always been up until then, to have my own command, to be the Master of a ship and be responsible for the well-being of the crew, cargo and safe navigation of that ship, through a diversity of weather conditions, on voyages across the oceans to unknown foreign lands of different cultures.

The winter of 1974/75 had seemed incredibly cold, wet, windy and long. I had been piloting for eight years and was by then licensed as a First Class Cinque Ports Trinity House Pilot of unlimited tonnage based at Folkestone, serving the London District from the south. But although I had by then piloted my first VLCC, the larger ships which I preferred were few and far between; when along to Folkestone on the 23rd February came the MV *Somersetbrook,* another small but newly built British cargo ship of the middle trade. During the passage inwards to Gravesend the Master was complaining to me bitterly that due to a shortage of qualified Foreign Going Master Mariners in the market place, he had been unable to get leave. This time however he would have to be relieved on arrival because the ship was to load for the Mediterranean, a Deep Sea voyage which would require a Foreign Going Master's Certificate of Competency for those waters, rather than the Home Trade Master Mariners Certificate which he held. He told me that his company up until that moment had been unable to find such a person and I saw the opportunity to fulfil my ambition.

I asked how long the projected voyage was to be and was told probably about six weeks, a round trip to the Mediterranean. The thought of the warm sunshine of the Mediterranean appealed to me instantly as I peered again out in the failing daylight at the familiar five flashes every twenty seconds of the North Foreland lighthouse, appearing once again through the driving rain. The wheelhouse windows rattled with the freshening wind as we approached the North East Spit buoy and the wide estuary of the

River Thames on that cold February afternoon; I shivered and thought of warm sunshine and the clear blue Mediterranean of my earlier life. It was a pity I did not take the opportunity to find out a little more about the ship before making an offer which was difficult to withdraw.

Now this was at a time when there being a general shortage of deck officers in the British Merchant Service, a small number of pilots had been using their leave to sail on ships for short periods of time adding extra money to their income. Usually however they did not sail as Master, and were from my experience generally considered with some disdain by their colleagues and regular shipping company staff for shipping as mere watch keepers; just to ensure a vessel could sail. I certainly would not have considered such a position feeling that it was demeaning but I did feel that to sail in command, especially as I had not had that experience, would be appropriate and complete my career. A number of London Pilots had also about that time worked in Jeddah as pilots, clearing a backlog of shipping at the Saudi Arabian port; something which I had considered but rejected. My fear was of the consequences of the risk of having a minor road accident in that country, only to find my Mr Fixit was less influential than the other persons. As a result of which I might not get home and could possibly put in jeopardy the wonderful job I already enjoyed!

However, this time I was tempted and told the Master that I had sufficient leave to be able to take a couple of months if necessary. We were in late February and approaching the end of the financial year, thus allowing me to use up outstanding leave from the current year and break into my leave for the next year. The Master said he would pass on my details to his Owners but I seriously thought nothing would come of my offer; which I had not in any case discussed with my lovely wife Sally – how would I explain my sudden wish to return to sea, albeit briefly?

The following day, the 24th February, I had just stood off in the morning to join the MV *North Isle* off Folkestone for pilotage into Garrison Point and the Medway, when the telephone rang and a voice asked; if I was serious about my offer would I come straight up to the company offices in London before joining the ship in Newport? Being already committed to an act of pilotage I had to decline, but confirmed my interest after having discussed the idea with a very surprised and less than enthusiastic Sally. In order not to delay the ship it was arranged that MV *Somersetbrook* would sail loaded from Newport to round Land's End and anchor in Mounts Bay off Penzance where I would join on the evening of the 26th February 1975.

It had been a long and tiring day when the train finally pulled into Penzance and I made my way to the small harbour at Mousehole, to take the boat out to join the ship when she came into the Mounts Bay anchorage. Grabbing a quick evening meal while waiting for the ship to arrive, I discovered that the day had been marked by the memorial service for all those lost aboard the British coaster *Lovat* which had capsized with a cargo of coal slurry earlier in the year with the loss of thirteen lives; I hoped not a sad and ominous omen of things to come.

The boat standing by in the pretty little harbour turned out to be the old pilot boat from the River Medway. I was immediately reminded how often I had been asked by the Medway Pilots to round Garrison Point with a ship because this same boat was considered unsuitable by them for the prevailing weather that particular day off the point; yet here she was in a new role running up to ten miles offshore, putting pilots aboard large bulk carriers bound for Port Talbot and elsewhere. Well, to be fair, the big long Atlantic swells rounding Land's End were probably more comfortable than the short vicious wind against tidal seas experienced at Garrison Point and why in any case risk getting wet when there was a safe alternative.

The *Somersetbrook* looked low in the water as we approached in the darkness and perhaps I should have checked the draft before I boarded; given the opportunity again I certainly would do just that but I was on unfamiliar ground, apprehensive as a new Master not knowing exactly what to expect. It was many years since I had qualified as Master Foreign Going and in any case I came from a regime where a Purser had always been responsible for the wages and accounts as well as much of the routine ship's business. While passing through London I had quickly bought the latest edition of Kemp and Young's *Business Notes for Shipmasters* and was somewhat relieved to read in the Preface to this 1972 Revised Edition that; "*In a world of change the shipmaster, and others connected with shipping, have, so far, escaped very lightly.*" Apart from the Rochdale Report, Decimalisation and changes to National Insurance Contributions, little had changed in the years subsequent to my examination in Shipmasters Business; although of course up until this moment I had not been called upon to use much of that detailed knowledge. Kemp & Young's little book, a mere 125 pages long, which I read avidly on the train to Penzance, was to serve me well together with the *Handy Book for Shipowners & Masters by H. Holman,* published by the United Kingdom Mutual Steam Ship Assurance Association Limited; a legal reference book which I had bought earlier in my pilotage career.

How lucky I was, for shortly after my command experience the floodgates opened and today's Master is faced with a raft of complex regulatory mechanisms as society attempts to satisfy and balance the needs for cheap efficient transport with the demands for safety and environmental protection. In such a dynamic situation with new legislation and penalties for infringement coming out continually, the 2003 Edition of the *Nautical Institute Shipmaster's Business Companion* by Malcolm Maclachlan runs to some 900 pages having grown from 470 pages just seven years before and weighs 2.5 kilos. I certainly do not envy the Master of any merchant vessel today a further seven years on.

The MV *Somersetbrook* had "cleared outward" from Newport with a Home trade Master and a full cargo of grain for Torre Annunziata situated on the mainland in the bay just south of Naples, Italy to pick up a Foreign Going Master off Penzance – me. The handover of this small ship and her mixed crew took considerably less time than I imagined, while considerably more time seemed to be spent quite literally accounting for the Master's bonded stores. I was warned by my predecessor that I probably had two men with a serious drink problem among the total compliment of twelve, although three of the crew were Cape Verde sailors and strictly teetotal. He advised me to avoid selling any spirits to the officers and crew. My heart sank, a great start this was turning out to become, what a pity I had not picked up on this problem during the pilotage into London or were in fact the poor unfortunate men new replacements signed on in Newport?

Watching the small pilot boat chug cheerfully off into the night towards the twinkling lights of the rugged Cornish coast, I gave my happy colleague a reluctant farewell wave and, deep in thought and worried, I concentrated on weighing anchor and the beginning of my adventure; for this my one and only voyage in command was indeed going to turn out to be a testing experience.

With the anchor aweigh I moved slow ahead onto a southerly course with the Chief Engineer operating the engine controls from the wheelhouse beside me. Finally, with the anchor stowed and secured, I then set course passing abeam of the Wolf Rock Lighthouse and out on a direct course across the Western Approaches and Bay of Biscay. Heading for Cap Finisterre at our full service speed of twelve knots, we needed to make up for lost time and satisfy the high expectations of the charterers who were based, I seem to recall, in Amsterdam.

There was little traffic around and with the Second Mate taking the first navigational of the six-hour watches, I inspected the navigational gear before finally turning in for a fairly sleepless night as the ship gently rolled her way southwards in reasonably good weather. My night was to prove sleepless because it was soon apparent that as I looked around with the fresh eyes of the responsibility of command on passage, I soon noticed aspects that had been of little concern to me when acting as pilot. It was immediately obvious that the ship had been very sparsely equipped with the barest minimum of navigational aids and I realised that my two navigational watch keepers were both elderly gentlemen in their sixties and close on retirement. Not a real problem unless one of them slipped and fell climbing the wet vertical ladder to the monkey island in order to take a bearing from the magnetic standard compass high up in this lively little ship. The problem was that although she was equipped with a gyro compass to run the automatic steering, the ship was not equipped with wing repeaters for navigational use and the only means of taking a visual bearing in order to ascertain the vessels position was to climb to the top of the wheelhouse. True she had the one good radar and was fitted with a Decca Navigator which had obviously proved sufficient for fixing the ship's position when trading around the United Kingdom and North Western Europe, but we were bound to the Mediterranean and the Decca coverage ran out at Lisbon, leaving us very reliant on that one radar set.

I was awake early and made my way immediately to the bridge where, despite the good weather, my attention was drawn to the amount of water washing occasionally over the main deck, feeling instinctively that the ship was indeed too low in the water. I checked with the Chief Officer on details of the cargo plan and the soundings in the ballast tanks and discovered that the grain cargo virtually filled number two hold, while in number one hold bagged grain had been used to top off the bulk grain. The Bosun, he told me, was just about to sound the ballast tanks as part of the daily routine and indeed shortly afterwards the East German Bosun appeared on the bridge with his sounding book. On inspection nothing appeared untoward to the chief officer who was, unlike me at that moment in time, aware of the supposed current condition of the tanks. I resolved to have a look after breakfast at the cargo to ensure all was well there, not wishing to make a fool of myself, for maybe this ship was always that wet.

After a good enjoyable breakfast, I had a quick look around the accommodation and introduced myself to the remaining members of the small crew as I familiarised myself with the ship. I then proceeded forward with the help of one of the Cape Verde sailors to inspect the holds; only to find that all was well with the grain cargo which was, as far as I could, see well stowed. We were just in the process of closing up number one hold when the fire alarms started to go off in the engine room; I ran for the bridge to join the chief officer and an angry looking chief engineer telephone in hand.

"Where is the Fire Chief?" I gasped breathless and anxious; this was my first day dammit!

"It's alright, Captain, the Second Engineer has put the fire out," came the prompt reply, and I was greatly relieved but puzzled that everything had happened so quickly?

"That is great, Chief, we obviously have a good second engineer," I continued in my relief only to receive the comment back from the Chief that we certainly did not in his opinion have such a person; for it appears that the hero of the story had in fact inadvertently sprayed diesel fuel over the main exhaust when topping up the settling tank, a careless action which had caused the fire in the first place.

"The problem is that the damn fool did exactly the same thing last week," the chief remarked quietly with concern. Fortunately the fire had been minor but it still involved extra paperwork and the overall responsibility began to quickly come home to me and I began to doubt the wisdom of my decision to volunteer for this particular albeit brief career move.

I was still not happy with the feel of the ship and I decided therefore to get the Bosun to re-check the soundings while I at the same time could further familiarise myself with that part of the ship; for I was sure I could feel the free surface effect of liquid moving somewhere beneath my feet. Lo and behold we soon found slack water in the double bottom tanks which suddenly and mysteriously had appeared but which, on reflection, must have been creeping in as the ship worked in the seas on the passage around Land's End to Mounts Bay and beyond; further inspection indicated that when the ballast had been pumped out prior to loading, the sea valve had not been securely closed. The unwanted sea water was soon pumped out and the ship riding a little higher felt far more comfortable as we proceeded south on that first day with two problems overcome and my confidence growing.

Later that first morning there was a knock at my cabin door and the small wiry Glaswegian Cook/Steward arrived to discuss his menus and likely store requirements before disclosing the real purpose of his visit. Would I sell him a bottle of whisky? I declined, being very much aware of the warning from my predecessor, only to be given a long spiel about how difficult it was to sleep in this class of ship rolling and pitching heavily in the Bay of Biscay, without a wee dram as a night cap; I did not think we were in fact in heavy weather. I stuck to my guns offering the cook beer but not spirits which I made clear I had no intention of selling to anyone aboard. He was not a happy man and went off muttering words to the effect that "the last Captain sold me a bottle of Scotch every day"; a statement that somehow did not ring quite true. He was however, despite a weakness for his native tipple, a superb cook who in all weathers and under the most difficult of conditions produced really fine food throughout the voyage and it was a real pleasure to have him aboard despite the odd moment of weakness for which I seem to remember I forgave him.

The ship was fitted with a small VHF Radio and a mains Radio telephone transmitter which operated somewhere between 1605 – 2850 kHz with a Distress and calling frequency on 2182 kHz and was our method of communications with the outside world. Being more familiar with the VHF I struggled at first with my first calls to the company and charterers via Brest and then later via Lisbon using the main MF transmitter; but fortunately both the Chief Officer and Second Officer were familiar with the equipment and I soon became fully competent. Rounding Cape Trafalgar I headed for the Straits of Gibraltar and was pleased to pick up Gibraltar Radio on the VHF. It crackled into life and I received immediate orders to put into Ceuta for bunkers just a few hours away, I quickly consulted Kemp and Young, realising I had much paperwork to prepare as we adjusted course for Ceuta and needed to make contact with that port to order a pilot and give my ETA. I had been caught on the hop and had to sit down and type out crew lists and stores lists, something easily done in today's computer age but in those days it meant fiddling with a manual typewriter, carbon paper and a worn-out typewriter ribbon – damn I would not be caught again.

We made Ceuta and after a brief wait off the breakwater our pilot appeared and we proceeded inwards to the bunker berth; my first experience of the Master/Pilot relationship from the Master's perspective. I found I had to ask relative questions as to the berthing arrangements rather than be provided with a plan of action, but in all other respects I soon realised that this particular pilot was a fine ship handler and I started to relax; which proved to be a mistake. As we glided inward through the blue Mediterranean waters to approach the bunker terminal in the warm sunshine of the North Africa coast to berth portside to the quay, the pilot suddenly blew a pea whistle twice presumably to attract the attention of the mooring gang ashore. To our surprise and horror there was a roar from the forecastle head and a cloud of rust particles and dust drifted up towards us on the bridge wing as the Chief Officer, perhaps imagining this to be a signal or possibly responding to earlier practices in his life, let go the port anchor without instruction and let it run beneath the ship as we gradually lost headway. Fortunately no harm was done; the water was deep and the pilot's responses were swift, so swift in fact I wondered whether this was not the first occasion an anchor had been let go as a response to his wretched pea whistle. In retrospect I do remember instructing the Chief Officer to have both anchors ready for use when he went forward, perhaps I should have stressed that they were to be prepared only for emergency use and not necessarily as part of the berthing plan which I had not ascertained at that time.

Finally and successfully the ship was moored alongside without further incident. Port Officials then poured voraciously through my cabin door and gradually the ship's business was carried out begrudgingly to varying degrees of expectation of reward from the Master's Bonded stores; I had always known that such was the custom in many parts of the world but never really appreciated the extent to which the practice was common or for that matter had been personally responsible for the largess. The bunkers were duly loaded under the calm and careful scrutiny of the Chief Engineer and within hours we were to put to sea and continued on passage along the Barbary Coast.

Sadly unbeknown to me my embargo on the sale and consumption of spirits had been breached by opportunists at the bunkering jetty, and on sailing I discovered I had a number of casualties incapable of performing their duties. Their tasks were undertaken by the rest of us until some hours later the guilty had sobered up sufficiently to return to their respective duties but it was a nightmare scenario and I longed for the completion of the voyage and a return to the folds of my family and the relative civilized world of pilotage.

Just on a thousand miles to the east north east, past the southern tip of Sardinia and across the Tyrrhenian Sea, the small port of Torre Annunziata nestled in the Gulf of Naples close to the ruins of Pompeii, and under the still but menacing presence of the volcano Vesuvius awaited our cargo of grain. The month of March in the Mediterranean was not as warm as I mistakenly remembered and we plodded along as fast as possible under a leaden sky and threatening rain, something else likely to cause concern, delay and dissatisfaction with the charterers. We passed the pretty island of Capri on the 3rd March and made contact with the port authorities at our port of destination but although we arrived on our ETA, we were forced to anchor outside the port as a considerably larger ship was seen to be entering ahead of us to take the only berth. As we lay at anchor that night the wind freshened, and one of my two experienced watch keepers soon called me before the ship started to drag anchor onto the lee shore with the rising ground swell. Working on the wet forecastle was difficult for the anchor party but we successfully weighed anchor and moved further out into deep water to ride out the bad weather. Fortunately it did not last long and soon it was our turn to take the berth, a manoeuvre which this time went without any drama. The usual voracious officials piled through the door as the ship's business was fulfilled.

It was the 8th March before we set sail for Taranto via the Straits of Messina to load steel coils for Newport. The passage took only about thirty-six hours and here we were again picking up a pilot, somewhere off the extensive mussel beds visible to the south side of the harbour entrance. It was here that the VHF in the wheelhouse once again burst into life filling the small space with a voice calling the ship's name. I answered and was put through to the Charterers in Amsterdam who, stressing the importance of saving time, wanted an ETA for Newport. Much to my embarrassment and to the amusement and considerable speculation of the several officers in attendance, I was offered – for all those present to hear – quite a substantial bonus if I could have the ship back in the UK by the 25th March. Well at this stage we were yet to pick up the pilot, to berth or find the cargo; and had I turned around and sailed immediately without the cargo it would have been unlikely that we would have made that deadline. The offer sounded generous but they must have known their money was safe.

We waited and waited, first for a berth and then for cargo and then for more stainless steel cargo to come off the mills while we lay idle alongside; all the time voracious officials and ship chandlers made their appearance. One morning up early I noticed the young Cape Verde night watchmen head for shore on the completion of his night watch, wearing a rain coat in the warm sunny weather, and my curiosity was aroused. I met him at the top of the gangway on his return and asked where he had been. To the post office came the hesitant but probably truthful reply. "You are not bringing any whisky on board are you?" I asked, pointing at his bulging pockets. Quietly without a word he produced two bottles of Scotch but loyally did not tell tales on the real culprit who had ordered him on the errand or paid for them in the first place. Not wishing a repeat of the Ceuta fiasco, I knew I had to stamp out such activity and that I did by dropping both bottles onto the concrete quay below, where they shattered with a loud bang thus draining the neat whisky into the harbour. The frightened young sailor promptly burst into tears, although I reassured him that I knew that he had not bought the whisky for himself or paid for it. After ensuring the broken glass was swept away I then summoned the three sailors and the Bosun to their mess room where I told them forcefully and loudly enough to be heard throughout the accommodation, that if I found any of them trying to smuggle alcohol aboard again I would sack them all and send them all home instantly. Although I was doubtful whether my owners would have approved of the expense and I was bluffing; fortunately I had no further trouble from alcohol.

In Taranto I took the opportunity as soon as possible, while lying alongside still without cargo, to conduct a full fire and boat drill and actually put a lifeboat into the water as required every two months and as the circumstances permitted. On the passage outwards we carried out a fire and boat muster and that had, I remember, appeared to take everyone a little by surprise; but to actually consider putting a boat down, well here was a novelty. That statement is not meant to be a criticism of those previously employed to run the ship, for aboard running hard around the North European coast there obviously had been little time in port and where, in any case, fatigue was always a major consideration to encroach on such a procedure. In a system where the two deck officers worked six hours watch-on watch-off and all hands constantly were being turned out at night as the vessel visited sometimes more than two ports in twenty-four hours; opportunities for such procedures were few and far between while fatigue was the major issue. Fatigue which fortunately on the longer ocean passages to the Mediterranean I was able to alleviate somewhat by regularly spelling the two watch keepers.

The problem we had in Taranto was that it was discovered that the inflatable life rafts had been, I imagine, retrofitted and secured to the deck in their large metal housing brackets, too close to the after davit handles for winding out the boats; thus not allowing a complete turn of the handles once fitted. It came as a surprise, for the ship had been issued with her Safety Equipment Certificate earlier that year following her first two years in service. But what to do; it was my responsibility and of real concern. The ship had sufficient life saving capacity in her inflatable life rafts and so that was not a real practical concern but swinging out the life boats would not be easy. Moving the life raft brackets would be a major disruption to the accommodation below involving the cutting of the welds and dockyard intervention, with surveyors and possible delay to the ship. I got out my two books and reading of the legal merit and authority of a Master's Letter to his Owners, I sat down and spelt out the problem in an official letter and told them I intended to sail for home with the situation unresolved and asked for arrangements to be made for the situation to be rectified on our return. Fortunately we were to proceed home without requiring the use of lifesaving equipment but there were still to be a couple of incidents when this knowledge was not far from becoming just a little more than a vague possibility.

The days passed slowly in the warm sunny port of Taranto as we awaited production in the local steel mill of the stainless steel coils we were supposed to be loading for Newport, a process which I had attempted to speed up with the help of the ship's agent and the usual voracious officials streaming aboard without effect. The delays of course involved investigation into the amount of lay time allowed in the charter, that is unnecessary delays to the ship for which the voyage charterers would have to pay the ship owner demurrage at a daily rate once the lay times allowed had expired. It was to me an unfamiliar and complicated aspect of the business and I was glad I had brought with me my two reference books and pleased to have an experienced chief officer, who had himself served several years in command and had indeed a valid Foreign Going Master's Certificate of Competency. Sadly the company had decided not to allow the man command of their ship but brought me in instead; he was however to me an asset to be managed that I on several occasions had cause to appreciate.

Walking ashore one day in Taranto I found an art shop and bought a couple of cheap canvases, pots of acrylic paint and brushes, together with a cheap folding easel. I had set up the easel in my cabin looking out over the foredeck and set about painting the view when, on the second day, I was disturbed by sudden movement in the ship. Movement which stopped abruptly when my poor little ship, lying quietly and innocently alongside the quay without power on the main engines, was pinned hard against the quay forward by a large Italian freighter which, passing up our port side from astern and until that moment out of sight to me, was now attempting to berth alongside ahead of us. My paintbrush and I were pushed off balance and a nasty inappropriate and unplanned brown line of wet acrylic paint appeared in the sky of my painting.

Worse still the little ship's forward bulwark rails appeared to be damaged on the port side. I ran forward to join the Chief Officer who, surveying the damage, had wisely and fortunately had a couple of the sailors in position with fenders which had been used to prevent more serious damage; but still I found the bulwark rails had been inset over several feet and damage had been done. Lloyd's surveyor would have to be called and no doubt the ship would be listed as having been in collision in Taranto and my colleagues at home waiting at pilot stations for ships and with nothing better to do but daily scan the list would have a field day. Well of course that goes with the territory and although my officers had been alert to the dangers suddenly developing and had taken the only action available to them, we had indeed been in collision and I called the agent in order to inform Lloyd's and my owners.

Now on inspecting the ship's papers during my first few days aboard I had come across a company pro-forma that was obviously designed for just such an occurrence as had now happened. It basically was an admission of full responsibility for an accident to my ship to be signed by the Master and Pilot of any other ship causing damage to the Company's ships. I had looked at it in amazement at the time and thought – heavens, just who would be gullible enough to sign such a document? Now was the time to find out.

I sent my Chief Officer, who was a great raconteur with considerable Irish charm, to invite the Master and Pilot of the large Italian ship aboard to inspect the damage to my ship and when they surprisingly arrived almost immediately into my cabin, I was able to demonstrate just how their action had disfigured my painting, indicating the brown smear of paint in the azure blue sky. However, I said, while I was prepared to over look this minor inconvenience, my Owners were somewhat less forgiving. As I pointed out it was obvious I could not be held responsible for the accident but my Owners did expect me to request in such a situation as this, that they both should sign the appropriate admission of responsibility. Now I had always been taught to avoid signing any papers admitting liability and particularly documents in a foreign language, but these two delightful gentlemen signed without hesitation. When the Italian Lloyd's surveyor arrived he was astonished to find me in receipt of the signed document; "How did you get the Italian Master and Italian Pilot of an Italian ship in an Italian port to sign such an admission of responsibility?" he asked and, pointing to my easel, I started to tell him the story of my damaged painting! The Italians are of course art lovers.

Somersetbrook in Taranto

Finally we completed loading the cargo of all the stainless steel coils that were available but found that the charterers had incurred deadfreight charges, a payment in lieu of the freight the ship owner would have earned if the full cargo had been available, which it was not. Out came my two books again and more paperwork to be done before finally we set sail for home on the 25th March 1975.

Pleased to be on the last leg of my experience I set course to pass south of Sicily on what appeared to me to be the most direct route and quickest route home; it was a mistake, for on the south side of that island we ran into a deep depression which being wise in retrospect I may have avoided the worst of, if I had diverted north through the Straits of Messina before turning to the westward for Gibraltar, thus running along the north side in the lee of the island. On the south side the wind howled and shrieked in the rigging as the little ship rolled stiffly and violently and the seas rose and the swells grew ominously, breaking heavily over the fore deck. I was forced to reduce speed and took the con myself, allowing my two elderly watch keepers time to attempt to get some rest in the safety below, while the Chief Engineer and I nursed the little ship through a very long day.

Despite the very worst of the weather the little Glaswegian cook managed all the time to produce excellent delicately prepared meals – large Italian tomatoes stuffed carefully with minced beef I remember being particularly good, and I was pleased that I had purchased from the ship chandler at great expense the very best ingredients and roasting joints of fresh meat. We dinned well but then I certainly had no intention of volunteering again.

The bad weather soon passed and we found ourselves somewhere off Algiers. One sunny afternoon, I was sitting at my desk working on the Portage Bill, which was basically my account with the owners showing crew wages, overtime due, expenses incurred and paid on the voyage, monies advanced to crew members and calculations for national insurance, union dues, radio messages and postage, canteen bar and tobacco costs for the voyage. I was working to the predicted time of our arrival home to payoff in pencil, allowing myself time to pre-work several days thus allowing for possible delay.

The late afternoon sunlight streaming in the cabin windows behind me over my shoulders onto my desk, started to move across the desk and I thought the Second Officer was probably altering course to starboard to avoid another ship on this lovely calm day and I ignored it as I got on with my calculations. A few minutes later the sun went across the desk in the same direction and I was immediately alert realising we were now turning in circles. I raced up to the bridge to find the Second Officer at the chart table busily engrossed in correcting a large folio of Admiralty charts, completely oblivious to the fact that the gyro compass, following an apparent failure of electrical supply, had collapsed on its side gently winding itself down as the automatic pilot tried to keep up with its spinning dial, the alarm quietly buzzing to itself.

Surprised to see me and horrified at what had happened on his watch, he was full of apology. Poor man, overworked and out of his familiar Home

Trade waters, he was desperately tired and merely trying to catch up on his many duties. There were no ships in sight and no harm had been done but there could have been. I asked him to put the clamps on the gyro and go into hand steering, calling for an AB to take the wheel and steer by the magnetic compass. Sadly the so-called AB could not steer and the Second Officer, who confessed to never having even looked at the gyro compass in all the months he had been aboard the ship, was unable to clamp it; so took the wheel instead. The gyro was not one I was familiar with but with the help of the manufacturer's excellent manual of operation and with the power supply checked out by the redoubtable Chief, I soon had the little beast up and running again but it took what seemed for ever before it settled down sufficiently accurately, in order to reconnect the auto-pilot.

As we approached Gibraltar in fine weather, the skies away to the west of the Straits were getting darker. Gibraltar Radio warned of strong electrical storms and freshening winds to the west of the region in the Atlantic approaches. We passed Europa Point, Gibraltar as it was getting dark and the lights were beginning to come on in that old familiar port and I felt a touch of nostalgia for my days in the Royal Fleet Auxiliary but I was concentrating on the violent lightning over Tarifa and the Punta Marroqui as we steamed out from the relative tranquillity of the Mediterranean into the threatening darkness.

Suddenly the ship's lights went out and the air was filled with alarms, the gyro compass once again fell over and the main engine stopped in the narrowest part of the Straits of Gibraltar. It was before the implementation of the IMO Routeing Scheme and I had kept fairly close to the north shore and out of the path of much larger faster overtaking ships, but that now put us onto a lee shore with a freshening wind. We put on the emergency NUC lights and awaited anxiously word from the engine room.

My mind raced as to all the precautions I could take and I needed to take to prevent a grounding such as clearing away the anchors for the most obvious remedy, notifying Gibraltar or even calling for assistance if all else failed, but the Chief called to say he was confident we could get under way again shortly. In the meantime, standing on the bridge wing I was sure I could hear the sound of breaking surf in between the claps of thunder and see the dark forbidding black mountains to the north lit by the forks of lightning. The Chief however was good at his word and soon we had power and were able to proceed on course for the port of Newport three days to the north without further incident. Very soon we cleared the electrical storm and trundled up the Spanish coast to round Cap Trafalgar; after all the excitement it was with some relief that we were now clear of the Gibraltar Straits.

Having the radio situated in the wheelhouse without any privacy meant that calls to the owners were difficult unless I was alone. In my letter from Taranto I had (together with a general report of the progress of the voyage to date) requested immediate relief for two of the ship's complement and this had obviously been duly noted for on approaching Land's End I received a call from the owners. The conversation with the office which apart from assuring me of my relief in Newport, confirmed that Mr......... and Mr.......... were also to be relieved as per my request. Sadly one of the men was standing next to me at the time and up until then he was unaware that his services were no longer required, for although I had warned him that his lapses of conduct could not be tolerated and therefore he should have known dismissal was on the cards, I had been waiting for confirmation from the owners that they were in agreement before I told him to pack his bags. Naturally he was displeased and our relationship deteriorated rapidly; a sad ending for me but not entirely for him for I subsequently learnt that he had been re-employed on another of the company's ships.

We arrived in Newport with a cargo of steel the very day news had been announced of sweeping reductions of steel production and the closing of local plant at nearby Port Talbot; not a very popular cargo or arrival.

Mindful of the bad weather we had experienced south of Sicily and the heavy seas that had pounded our steel Macgregor Hatches, my last act as Master before finalising my Portage Bill and handing over to my relief, was to attend with the agent a local Notary Public and register a standard Note of Protest. This being a declaration that damage may have been caused by stress of weather outside the ship's control. It was a good move, for despite the use of sealing tape at the joints some leakage of water had taken place through the rubber seals of number one hatch and although no damage to the stainless steel coils was apparent; by Noting Protest hopefully I had given my owners some form of protection against claim.

The whole experience of that one exceptional voyage had been far more of a challenge than I had anticipated or at the time desired, but it gave me a far greater appreciation and understanding of the daily problems faced by those in command of a merchant ship; knowledge and experience which was certainly beneficial in my own future Master/Pilot relationships as my career developed. I returned to the fold of my family and the Cinque Ports

Pilots, having attained a lifelong ambition but now completely contented and convinced that I was indeed highly privileged to be a pilot; able to manoeuvre a ship safely to the berth while enjoying the sense of achievement and job satisfaction that came with the challenge but once there, to be able to walk away from the ship and all the daily problems inherent with command.

Chapter 29

The Beard Must Go

Just before Christmas 1987 when serving as a Trinity House Cinque Ports Pilot I was berthing a car carrier in Ramsgate. The wind was fresh and I had removed my uniform cap so as not to lose it over the side. I was, however, wearing the prototype red Seasafe Pilot's Coat I had bought from the late Stan Coe – a Gravesend pilot who, with a great interest in pilot safety, had set up a company manufacturing purpose-built protective clothing to bring pilots into the twentieth century. The Company, still going today, now has an International clientele.

Looking down onto the quay from the bridge wing at Ron Cannon, the local coxswain of the RNLI lifeboat, who was running my mooring lines to thank him, I was greeted with the cheery response of; "Mr Russell you look just like Father Christmas!"

Now at that time I had a full beard which I had first grown some twenty-five years earlier – but was it really getting that white? On arriving home I studied myself in the mirror and decided, no surely it looked distinguished but alas a seed of doubt was sown to come to fruition just over a year later.

On the 25th April 1989 I was called to pilot a fairly large Finnish paper product carrier from Gravesend to the sea. The MV *Pokkinen* was 522 feet

long, with a Gross tonnage of 12,400 tons and at 16 knots she was a good job on the ebb tide. Despite the poor weather, a strong south westerly wind and lumpy sea, we romped along but I was somewhat disappointed to learn from the Ramsgate pilot office covering the NE Spit Pilot Station, that although I was obviously the fastest outward ship and would arrive first; I was going to have to wait in the pilot boat while those behind me on outward ships were rounded up before the boat

would run the eight miles back to Ramsgate. It meant I was to spend at least an extra hour and a half bouncing about in the rough waters around the North East Spit buoy, instead of a nice quick run home.

I had just come to terms with sod's law, when the VHF radio crackled into life on VHF Radio Channel 16 and a voice from a Sea King helicopter on exercise from RAF Manston, called the ship by name. I answered and we moved to a working channel. The Captain of the aircraft asked if, as an exercise, he could land a man on our after deck while we proceeded. I asked the Finnish Master and he immediately agreed.

Now at this point I suppose I should have remembered that I was now an employee of the Port of London Authority and not a self-employed Trinity House Pilot but I was used to making my own decisions and I didn't. I had been self-employed for twenty-one years and only a few months before I had, thanks to Margaret Thatcher, lost my independence as a result of pilot re-organisation but it would take some years before the attitudes of the old Trinity House men were to change, if ever.

Faced with a long delay in the boat I wondered if the pilot of the Sea King would be willing to land me at the Ramsgate Pilot Station. I quickly consulted the Master who was happy, providing no extra costs were incurred before I replied;

"Yes, the Master is quite happy for you to put a man on the deck but if you would like a real exercise, how about landing me at Ramsgate?" It really had never occurred to me that the pilot might say yes but back came a prompt; *"Yes I would be delighted to do so."*

It rapidly came to me that I had set myself an adventure I might well regret but I now had to work fast. The ship was on her final leg to the NE Spit buoy; I quickly called the pilot boat to tell him his services were not required and, before anyone ashore could query my actions, I said my farewells to the Master. He took me by the arm, looked anxiously at my white beard and muttered,

"Please be careful Mister pilot and good luck."

The roar of the Sea King helicopter was deafening as it hovered close overhead the small group of us on the after mooring deck in the failing light of that early spring evening. The Loadmaster came spiralling down on what looked an incredibly thin piece of wire. I tucked my uniform cap and radio inside my coat and followed the instructions carefully, putting the lifting harness over my head and under my arms before we lifted off the deck of the MV *Pokkinen* as the helicopter rose with us on a static wire. To my surprise the Loadmaster was secured to the wire above me with his legs wrapped around my middle. It all seemed somewhat undignified but I had little time to think about that as the ship rapidly got smaller as we rapidly gained altitude, the radio sticking into my ribs as the harness came tight.

While the Sea King helicopter maintained a hover some height above the sea, I was glad to have my heavy issue PLA shoes on to keep me vertical in the strong wind, until eventually we were winched into the open side door. I slid across on my backside and took off the harness when invited to walk through to the flight deck.

MV. "Pokkinen" outward bound at NE spit 25th April 1989

Landing by Sea King Helicopter

Now after my experiences flying in Lynx and Wessex helicopters, the Sea King was huge. I walked through to the flight deck and was greeted by a figure in the right-hand seat outlined against the light and coast of North Foreland. I looked twice, for I was shocked – the aircraft was being flown by what looked to me to be a boy. He stared at me in turn for I must have looked wild and dishevelled from the wind and his face went pale. I guess he must have thought he had picked up Methuselah; and I knew, this white beard really must go.

We soon arrived at Ramsgate Harbour and with a roar of echoing sound around the Edwardian Terraces, did a circuit of the harbour coming into the hover over the top of the pilot station, which at that time was situated on the end of the Eastern Arm. It was dark but the ground below was illuminated by a large floodlight as I sat on the floor of the helicopter with my harness on and feet dangling below, the Loadmaster directing the pilot into a position above the office. A large foot in the middle of my back propelled me out and I commenced my descent, my feet feeling for the ground. I arrived on terra firma some fifteen minutes after leaving the ship. What a great adventure I thought, but others were less impressed – the Pilotage Manager for one, my wife for another.

I was to arrive home after driving across east Kent, the build-up of adrenalin slow to abate and still full of myself only to be pulled up sharp. I spilled out the story to my wife Sally and the expression on her face rapidly turned to one of horror. "You silly old fool," she said; "Your daughter is getting married in a week's time. What if you had had an accident? We would have had to change all the plans!" I quickly realised where the priorities lay and that I was in the dog house.

Within the year I shaved off my white beard and found beneath the growth the handsome face of a relatively young man.

Chapter 30

Very Large Crude Carriers in the Thames

VLCC Al Haramain awaits tide in Black Deep ∠age

This chapter is based upon a paper I originally wrote for the Honourable Company of Master Mariners in London, updated and revalidated for presentation to a number of seminars around the world; I have however taken out most of the more technical elements for fear of boring the reader. This is about the practical problems my colleagues and I experienced handling VLCCs in the years before my retirement, my views at that time on the need to improve the training of pilots, and how we in London were managing and assessing risk for what remains an international challenge today. Written in the nineteen-nineties, the situation has changed somewhat and thankfully much has been improved but it was an important part of my life bringing me great satisfaction, considerable stress and some frustration. The views and recollections of events expressed are of course my personal views, they were not necessarily recollections held by some of my colleagues or employers but they were mine and they are on record and as such they are a historical fact.

VLCC Chios at Number 4 Berth Coryton

On the 7th February 1997 the last Very Large Crude Carrier (VLCC) to be programmed to the Shellhaven refinery on the River Thames, brought in a part cargo of 150,000 tons of Arabian Crude and so ended for Shellhaven an era, which began in 1968. The name of the ship was the VLCC *Mariner* with a length of 344.4 metres and deadweight of 267,038 tons; the author was the berthing pilot and sitting in the front row for my presentation in Athens as I opened with this paragraph; was the Master. Thankfully he greeted me warmly and assured my audience that it had been a 'lovely job'.

During the last 16 years of my 32 years service as a pilot, I had been either the pilot responsible for the safe sea pilotage or berthing of many VLCCs and hundreds of large tankers.

Professor Michael Disney, in a paper which raised the question as to whether tanker disasters were merely instances of bad luck or bad judgement, asked whether in fact they did not indicate something more fundamentally wrong? Were the ships simply too large and under powered? He wrote, "Disasters are averted only by skilled pilots making precise and infallible judgements of current, tide and wind for miles ahead of their vessels." He raised the question, "how precise and how infallible have we any right to assume that human beings will always be?" Stating that, "The bigger the ship, the narrower the channel, the lower the vessels power-to-weight ratio and the faster the tide, the more exquisitely accurate we must expect the pilot to be." He asked, "But how fair and how naive is it of us to expect superhuman capacities of ships' pilots? Given the possible stakes how fine can we allow the margins for error to be?"

Certainly the pilot handling such vessels has to develop an acute sense of situational awareness probably best described by Endsley & Jones in 1997 as:

"The perception of the elements in the environment within a volume of time and space, the comprehension of their meaning, and the projection of their status in the near future."

Professor Disney was not the first to raise such issues, for as long ago as 1978, in a "Human Factors Study of Marine Pilotage," sponsored by the UK Department of Industry, it was suggested that a close and detailed study of accidents to ships and workload as indicated by heart-rates may be of value. Stating that "pilots may be working from time to time at the limits of their skill" and "It is possible that 'human error' as an explanation may mean 'human overload'." One cannot help but wonder whether the first chapter of this book dealing with my subsequent heart problems was really about the consequences of such overload.

Scientifically the bumblebee should really not be able to fly but it does. VLCCs from a scientific view we have been told, need the power of a Saturn rocket to stop them; but, as you read this, VLCCs are being berthed successfully without incident, and as a matter of routine in ports around the world.

At the time I questioned what could be done to improve the safety margins and improve the training and support for the pilot, post the Sea Empress grounding at Milford Haven; the industry was attempting to address the issues needed to avoid further such accidents. Within the United Kingdom, there has been a review of the Pilotage Act 1987 but some pilots remain, even today, of the opinion that the act, which was commercially driven, contributed little to safety. Perhaps in retrospect a harsh judgement and a generalisation as the ports now responsible for pilotage have carried out those duties with a wide range of success.

Professor Disney however made the suggestion that, "Since VLCCs (Very Large Crude Carriers) had been in operation for some twenty-five years by the time of *Sea Empress*, the "professionals" in the trade had colluded in it too long to take a really objective view of whether the business was safe or not."

Fore deck of VLCC Clio at Coryton 4 – the Agent comes aboard
(Photo PJDR)

He may well be right in his opinion, certainly a pilot has little margin for error or omission, the job can be highly stressful and particularly so in the UK, since the 1987 Pilotage Act with the threat of "criminal proceedings" in the event of an incident. Hardly the sort of encouragement one needs to take on the extra duty of care and few friends if things go wrong. Yet possibly because piloting these very large ships requires a high degree of competence and experience, and there is a calculated risk, there is also a considerable element of job satisfaction and an adrenalin buzz that appeals to many pilots. Certainly there has been no shortage of pilots willing to take on that extra responsibility in the past. Times however were changing and it was noticeable as the twentieth century came to a close, that where choice was available, an increasing number of pilots had begun to decline the opportunity.

Modern economies have an insatiable thirst for fuel, which Governments exploit by taxation. To remain competitive and keep their costs down, the oil companies and ship owners scaled up their ships to enormous size and particularly so when in the 1970s a VLCC could pay for itself in one voyage.

A situation that returned in the few years prior to the current recession, causing massive over-ordering and the building of such ships. But one cannot scale up any design and expect it to work exactly like a larger version of the original because as Galileo long ago pointed out, when you double the linear size of any system, its weight will increase 8 times over, but its surface areas will only increase by 4. At the end of the day somebody somewhere has to manoeuvre the result of those market forces safely to berth, and God help him if he makes an error of judgement or omission.

The majority of the tankers bringing into the port North Sea crude were about the size of the *Sea Empress*, while those bringing in Arabian crude were much larger VLCCs which had lightened at an earlier port; where, often before re-organisation, I was to join them prior to their passage through the Dover Straits into the Thames Estuary. Over the years I was to join VLCCs at Antifer and Le Havre on the French coast, Finnart in Scotland and at Milford Haven in Wales.

Whether of Panimax size or a VLCC, a tanker would usually arrive loaded to the maximum draft the tidal constraints for the day in question permitted and therefore there were common considerations of shallow water. The common factors of large turning circles, squat, bank effect and tidal influence, give the pilot few surprises because from his training within his own pilotage district he had learnt from experience what to expect and where to expect it.

The size of the ship affected the number of tugs required, the requirement for sufficient water at the berth on the falling tide and mooring points of sufficient strength. It required both a safe tidal and weather window and planned escape holes, with sufficient depth of water in the event of the need to abort a passage. The passage of these large ships required risk assessment by the Port Authorities and sometimes traffic management to allow a Planned Passage to be maintained. It required risk assessment by the terminal and by the Pilot in consultation with the Master. It required very careful planning incorporating accurate hydrographical information and accurate tidal information; together with a warning system of any tidal surges. It also required the experience of a well-trained and confident pilot. I say confident with some trepidation because over confidence is one of the greatest problems in pilotage, but believe me those brutes were unforgiving and really no place for the faint-hearted.

The passage required very accurate weather forecasting and safety parameter outside which berthing was prohibited and although these were in place before I retired, there was a lack of clarity as to who actually took the decision to abort. Far too often a Berthing pilot was faced with wind in excess of the agreed parameters, or fog at the berth because the ship had been committed to the final approach on existing conditions, rather than an imminent weather forecast. It may have been because a refinery was short of crude oil and nobody was prepared to accept the expensive responsibility of delaying the ship and particularly so the port operators. It was the author's opinion expressed loudly and clearly on a number of occasions that the pilot, who was expected to perform the berthing, should make that decision and that it was one decision which even the Master could not overrule. To expect a pilot to perform a berthing operation with one of those ships against his professional judgement was a recipe for disaster.

With a tidal constraint of 13.5 metres (+ or -) in the Thames Estuary, the older generation of VLCCs had a freeboard that was slightly less than the draft (11.5: 13.5 Metres). This huge freeboard at (345 x 11.5 metres = 3967.5 square metres) results in a considerable amount of windage. The new generation VLCC post 1990, with segregated ballast tanks and double bottoms, have an extra 5 metres freeboard which at (345 x 16.5 = 5692.5 square metres) when berthing and more than 7000 square metres when sailing. Thus pilotage in wind has become yet more demanding because some efforts to reduce risk to the environment by way of hull construction, while without doubt successful in one way, have caused handling difficulties. i.e., these vessels may well be less likely to spill oil if they go ashore but their sheer size when arriving part-loaded, makes them more likely to go ashore due to their increased windage and increased kinetic energy. These vessels are so large now that at high water on a spring tide the chick sans on the terminal have to be disconnected and discharging stopped.

Problems relating to: maintaining track in an approach channel without tugs and the maximum amount of wind that can be worked in that channel. The number of tugs required to berth safely, in even light breezes. Just how effective the tugs can be when their tow lines have to be secured as high as 23 metres above the water (car carriers use bits set into the hull to which and from which the tugs secure themselves) and the time taken to secure a tug, from that height; are not new problems, but ones which have become worse since 1990.

Navigation in the Thames Estuary

The sheer size of the Thames Estuary required that the VLCC leave the outer limits of the port, with her pilot embarked, not much after low water in order to be up at a moderate speed and swing to the Flood tide before high water. Ebb tide berthing at Shellhaven was too late should a problem develop that would require the vessel to abort her berthing through weather, tide, shortage of tugs, or mechanical defects; there simply was insufficient time to get out again down the Sea Reach Channel to deep water.

Another problem was the size of the pilotage area and the large number of pilots required to service so many ships and berths within the port. With so few VLCCs to give experience to pilots, that was about one every two weeks before I retired, and with only one or two per week during the busiest periods in the late 1970s; to be shared amongst several hundred pilots then, nobody could claim to be an expert if, every first class pilot was authorised to handle these ships. So these were just a few problems, which had had to be solved during that era – but when did it all begin, what measures have been taken to address the perceived needs and practical problems which evolved?

The Route

The first problem the Inner List Sea pilot had was to pick up the Deep Water Route running south westerly through the shoal area close east of the Trinity Buoy. This was a critical area because the vessel was usually underway from the Sunk Deep Water Anchorage when the pilot embarked and setting to the Southwest towards the shoals on the Flood tide. Unless the Bridge Team had recognised the need to prevent the charted approach being jeopardised or recognised the route they should be taking, then it was not uncommon to have to abort the approach and start again. Apart from a small dogleg the route was straightforward from there down the Black Deep Channel. The approaches to the Knock John Channel required careful positioning and timing, then it was straightforward to the Southwest Oaze/West Oaze area where the first really critical timing was important. The vessel also had to be brought around to starboard for about thirty degrees before putting the helm over to port to pick up the centre line buoys of the Yantlet Channel at Number 1 Sea Reach.

The vessel then entered a 10 miles long by 152 metre wide by 10.2 metre datum depth channel and was therefore unable to abort until in the slightly deeper and wider waters off the refineries. The Berthing Pilot and four tugs would join a VLCC bound for the Shellhaven Refinery at No.7 Sea Reach and for Coryton Refinery at No.6 Sea Reach; which is 5 miles from the respective berths. The programmed speed at that time was around 5 knots through the water. The speed was then progressively reduced until just short of the berth when, at less than 3 knots over the ground and with the vessel virtually stopped in the water, she could be swung to starboard into the flood tide off the berth.

Mobil VLCC at Jetty 4 Coryton

Speed was reduced by stopping the engines and maintaining course with a kick ahead on the engines or by use of minimum pitch ahead and by use of a Voith Schneider tug on the centre lead aft. At such slow speeds a Doppler-type ground log was essential, the "experienced mark one eyeball" may be good in clear visibility and daylight but with such slow speeds and such large ships and with lateral movement, even the experienced eye can be deceived. Sadly with the advent of GPS which can give a fairly accurate though historical speed when travelling in a straight line there has, it seems, been a reluctance to have the Doppler log repaired or even fitted. It was the author's opinion that the carriage of a Doppler-type log should have been mandatory for all large tankers.

Evolution

Many solutions were developed in reducing risk and improving safety margins within the author's pilotage district during those early years of development of the VLCC. Following the 1967 Arab/Israeli war the Loadline Zones were changed and in 1968 the first very deep draught tankers began to arrive in the Thames Estuary. They were not unexpected and considerable work had wisely been done to assess the risk and make preparation for this new generation of ship. The Port of London Authority had examined the depths in the approaches to the port and come to the conclusion that more accurate surveys were required and that those surveys should be repeated at intervals of not more than six weeks for the most critical areas. The Port Hydrographical service was expanded and took on a new and very vital role. In order that accurate knowledge as to any difference between the rise of tide on a particular day and the predicted value for a given time could always be established, automatic tidal gauges were established throughout the estuary. The technology of these gauges and the display of the resulting information have of course improved over the years.

The oil companies at the same time had been seriously studying the effects of squat and the minimum under-keel clearance that could be obtained with safety. The financial considerations being that a 200,000-ton tanker had the additional earning capacity of £25,000 per annum per foot of draught in 1967. Whatever the motive, by filling tankers with ballast water and running them into and out of ports at all states of the tide and weather conditions and repeating the operation in one port as many as 200 times, a criteria was established. I was told that this operation was carried out in London but I have seen no written evidence. Certainly the criteria of a minimum under-keel clearance of 3 feet (0.9 metre) in the final approaches and 4 feet (1.2 metres) in the outer estuary proved to be adequate over the last 32 years of my career as a pilot in the reasonably sheltered waters of the Thames Estuary, providing the ship did not exceed the programmed speed.

Under Keel Clearance varied from port to port, depending upon the exposure of the planned passage to wave and swell effect. In London no allowance was made for wave response for the simple reason that most of the estuary is protected from the heavy swells which would greatly increase the draft of the vessel should she roll heavily? The Deep Water Route (232°) at the Sunk was the only exposed area where the pilot might need to abort a passage due to rolling, but this was highly unlikely because the predominant winds tend to be south-westerly where there is virtually no fetch and north-easterly which is right astern. Should the weather be that severe, then it was unlikely the vessel would have been brought into the port in any case.

The designated berths were another thing. At Shellhaven Bravo there was insufficient water for these tankers and therefore provision had to be made. This was done by dredging a box at the berth down to 14.5 metres where the datum depth was about 9.5 metres. The boxes were and remained 370 metres long by 65 metres wide. The VLCC, once alongside, floated in the box as the tide falls as much as six metres around her. Despite quite steep sides, the box proved in practice to only require a small amount of dredging every six months in order to maintain the advertised depth, while the contractors carried out regular monthly surveys. At Coryton the situation was not quite so severe in that the berth specifically built for the new generation was established in deeper water but dredging and surveying still took place regularly.

The pilots at the time were self-employed and licensed by Trinity House. There were separate pilot stations at Folkestone and The Sunk (off Harwich) working inwards in competition and one at Gravesend working outwards. There were at the time two choice Shell pilots at Folkestone but neither of these pilots or any of the pilots on the ordinary sea roster initially had experience of the new deep tankers they were to be expected to pilot safely to the berths. Training was not given, and in fact training for this kind of new venture was probably not available at the time. The pilots themselves recognised this and also the fact that it would be irresponsible if the safe conduct of these ships was left to the first class pilot who happened to be on turn to work, when there were 100 pilots on the station. Protracted negotiations took place between Trinity House, the oil industry and the pilots until a system of select pilotage called "The Inner List" was established. At the beginning and until North Sea crude started to be imported in the late 1970s most VLCCs were piloted initially from the south and west after lightening at an earlier port, using the Black Deep Channel. Eventually more and more tankers were to use the Sunk anchorage as a waiting area, and today all VLCCs are piloted in from the north.

The pilots trained themselves; the most experienced being the Shell Choice pilots who initially took the next man on the "Inner List" with them and always to gain experience two pilots boarded each ship, the first to actually conduct the vessel, the second to understudy. This had the added advantage that in the event of fog or illness there was always an additional pilot. This was in the early days before Passage Planning or Bridge Resource Management when the pilot could expect little help from those on board, although right from the beginning Shell produced a very basic printed Passage Plan, which the pilot completed. They were exciting times with often inadequate radar, steam turbines giving a delayed response to engine orders, single-screw propulsion and conventional tugs only and very often poor communication and astonishingly declared draughts which were on occasion far less than the actual draft as a few unscrupulous individuals attempted to save their owners money.

The pilots learnt the hard way. On one occasion I believe the *Magdala,* which at just over 105,000 gross was one of the largest at that time, turned short when altering course at the centre line buoy Number 3 Sea Reach; she dug her nose into the mud and sand and came to a stop rather quickly. The ship however was only ashore for some 20 minutes before proceeding to the berth. The sea bed in the Thames Estuary is kind, however the incident led to improvement with the provision of the Southeast Leigh buoy, which was positioned to allow the pilot of a VLCC to know exactly when to put the helm over and turn with confidence onto the next course.

The same unfortunate ship had a far more serious incident when she arrived late to berth at Bravo Jetty Shellhaven on another occasion and did not manage to get fully into the box before the tide came away and part of the ship took the ground. The initial cause was, it is believed, an engine defect which delayed her; she certainly had a record of boiler feed problems on other voyages. A decision was taken to berth to the Ebb tide but she gradually dropped back and eventually did not make even that in time. Apparently there was no sign of damage at the berth but, on the outward passage when the tanks were entered after cleaning in the Bay of Biscay, severe hull damage was discovered. Needless to say VLCCs were not allowed to Berth at Shellhaven on the Ebb tide any more.

Several vessels overshot Alfa berth Shellhaven and went ashore on The Mucking flats due to engine failure and one which came to grief when attempting to swing off Shellhaven before her tugs were on station; the tugs having been delayed on another ship. As a consequence Alfa jetty was no longer used for large tankers and the tugs were to meet all large tankers bound for Shellhaven Bravo with a berthing pilot as early as Number 7 Sea Reach. Over the years the conventional single-screw tugs were gradually replaced by Voith Schneider tugs which gave far greater control over the manoeuvres.

The "Inner List Pilotage Service" piloted the ships from the outer limits of the district or the previous port in most cases, which meant that on arrival the pilot had been on his feet for a considerable length of time when he then had the most difficult part of the voyage to perform. This clearly could not continue but it was only after protracted negotiations that a separate "Berthing Service" was agreed. Pilots were recruited from "The Inner List "and one pilot of the new service was to remain on watch at the refineries to berth and un-berth all tankers over 11,500 tons. The fact that only one ship over that size could be moved at a time was agreed with the oil companies and made it considerably easier to supply the necessary tugs and watermen.

In 1988 Pilotage was reorganised nationally and the London Pilots lost their self-employed status and became employees of The Port of London Authority. Pilots then began to work both inward and outward throughout the whole district and the sea pilots retrained above Gravesend to Crayfordness and the River Pilots retrained to Number 1 Sea Reach. The effect of this was twofold. The disadvantage was that it diluted the practical experience of each pilot in that his district was vastly expanded and the chances of him going to the same berth often was greatly reduced. The advantage, apart from a commercial one to the port and its customers, was that most ships had one pilot between the sea and the berth and thus each pilot was given more opportunity to develop his berthing skills.

Quite rightly I think the PLA and the Oil Industry decided to retain the Berthing Pilot scheme as it existed and continued with an Inner List for all vessels of over 270 metres in length and 12.3 metre draught. The existing Berthing Pilots remained in position and vacancies occurring through retirement and sickness were replaced as before from the Inner List, which was itself recruiting post 1988 First Class pilots to become the Berthing pilots of the future.

Personal Experience

These enormous ships give tremendous job satisfaction when everything goes well but there is sometimes a challenge, the unexpected, which can demand even greater concentration than usual. This is the tale of just one. It is included because in one incident it highlights the dangers when a large tanker was allowed to move into a dangerous situation. It shows that sometimes the Master/Pilot relationship, despite the pilot's efforts, can be very difficult and far from the ideal being urged by some; and what can happen when the ship has no Passage Planning or Bridge team. The following report was written as a warning to colleagues and the Port Authority.

The Berthing of the very First New Generation VLCC in 1992

The crisp November morning was bright and sunny as I made my way downriver from Coryton Jetty number 4 aboard the duty tug to rendezvous with a brand new VLCC of just on 282,000 tons deadweight and 328 metre long, at Sea Reach buoy number 6. Unbeknown to me at the time, the published deadweight did not reflect the increased kinetic energy of this ship which, being fitted with segregated ballast tanks and I believe double bottoms, had a much larger moulded depth and beam than earlier VLCCs. On this particular morning I was conscious of the fog I had seen when driving to the refinery and the radio reports to and from The Thames Navigation Service (VTS) of the dense fog in the river above Gravesend.

The climb to the bridge is a long one, first up the side of the ship using a combination of pilot ladder and accommodation ladder, because the climb exceeds 9 metres; then along the main tank deck and up six decks to the bridge. I climbed quickly and arrive on the bridge slightly breathless, taking over from the sea pilot; I establish the present position, course and speed over the ground and positions of the other shipping. The sea pilot introduces me to the Master, an elderly looking oriental gentleman. I look ahead along the 850 feet of ship ahead of me to see if the crew has gone to 'stations' to make my four tugs secure. I can see nobody.

The Master tells me nothing about his ship, which appears to be on her maiden voyage. The sea pilot quickly supplies the facts that he has learnt on her inward passage. She has a single screw which is right-handed. The large diesel engine gives a quick powerful engine response. She is equipped with two good radar sets and Doppler log etc.

Ahead, the oil refineries start to disappear in the fog. I must get the tugs made fast before we run into poor visibility which will make it difficult if not impossible for them to secure without considerable danger to themselves; for without them I will be unable to swing the ship to manoeuvre for the berth or to abort the berthing. I ask the Master if the crew is standing by ready. He bobs his head in the affirmative and mutters "yes, yes, standby." Still I see nobody forward!

The sea pilot warns me that little English appears to be understood. I am concerned that the Doppler log indicates a speed over the ground of 7 knots and more concerned to find that this is the lowest speed the sea pilot, who is also a very experienced berthing pilot, has been able to achieve. Each time the engines are stopped, the vessel, unusually for a VLCC, quickly loses directional stability apparently moving away from the nearest underwater patch forward. Possibly she is trimmed by the head. To maintain course the engines have to be put ahead again.

A container ship requests permission to pass inwards on our port side and is given approval with a reminder of the reduced visibility ahead and a warning to watch out for our four tugs manoeuvring to secure at each quarter.

> *"Fear born of the stern matron Responsibility, sits on one's shoulders like some heavy imp of darkness, and one is pre-occupied and possibly, cantankerous."*
> **William McFee**

Approaching Sea Reach 7 buoy some 15 minutes after boarding, still without sign of the crew on deck and with the fog slowly rolling in and the tugs yet to be secured, I lost patience with the Master. Raising my voice I shouted at him, "Crew Standby fore and aft," and gesturing at the tugs, the fog, the chart and the Doppler, I graphically got the message across to him that all was not well and that if "he" did not co-operate there would be a disaster. He spoke into a hand-held radio and one man ambled along the deck. Seeing him I shouted again, and at last the urgency of the situation seemed to dawn on the Master.

At 7 knots, with a container ship passing ahead of me under the port bow, we slid into thick fog at Sea Reach No.7. We had yet to make the tugs fast but we were committed, unable to stop or manoeuvre due to the limitations of channel width and depth of water. There was a distinct danger that I was going to run ashore with 160,000 tons of sticky black crude oil to pollute the Thames Estuary; unless I could control the situation. I began rudder cycling using full helm first one way and then another. The engines were stopped and put ahead again to maintain directional control.

Surprisingly I felt curiously controlled although the Doppler cried out to me that the speed was far too high; fog shrouded the shoreline as we went past the Canvey Gas Terminal at 7 knot and my visual warning system, without a reference point, failed to trigger a rush of adrenaline. At that moment my one Voith Schneider tug reported he was secure on the centre lead aft and was immediately instructed to "lean back". A second very powerful conventional tug reported he was secure on the starboard bow and I knew I had the ability to swing if I could get sufficient speed off.

The thoughts raced through my head. What was I doing here? Should the vessel have been programmed in if the fog was expected? I thought of the time I had aborted safely a large North Sea crude carrier at Sea Reach No.7 in clear visibility, rather than attempt to manoeuvre in dense fog off the refineries, and found I was criticised for my action. This time I had no choice. The ship was committed to the Sea Reach Channel before I arrived on watch; she could not abort without tug assistance and was in any case far too large to abort in the Chapman once in the fog, even if I could have got the way off and secured the tugs. Briefly I wondered whether in the event of an accident, a court of law would consider my actions exemplary or in any way negligent? The criminal negligence section of the Pilotage Act 1987 hangs like a dark cloud over those placed in the position of responsibility for implementing the commercial desires of others. Certainly whatever the professional opinion of my peers, a major disaster and consequent environmental pollution of the Thames Estuary would create a media circus of Roman proportions, calling for someone to be sacrificed to the lions! Almost certainly me!

I recalled the advice I had written for the Nautical Institute book on Pilotage in a Chapter on "Stopping Ships in an Emergency". Was I doing all that I advised others? Would I be 'hoisted by my own petard'? I had certainly warned of the dangers of attempting to use anchors, unless one could make quite clear the necessary instructions to the anchor party; the absence of English meant I had little chance of doing that here.

At Holehaven all four tugs reported they were secure. The fog remained thick but I had managed to reduce my speed to 6 knots, still too fast to attempt to swing. I was committed to going on although I was now passing the position I would have chosen to abort.

As the bow came level with the end of Occidental Jetty, with only just on one and three quarters of the ship's length to run before I came abeam of my own berth and with a channel width of 600 metres, I sent my two heavy forward conventional tugs over onto the port bow and helm hard to port and kicked her ahead. As soon as the sea pilot, who was monitoring the manoeuvres on the other radar and who had given invaluable help watching other shipping and distance to go etc., confirmed my observation of a cut of the bow to port, I warned the tugs and returned the helm to amidships and went full astern on the engines.

Unable to see the shore and with my eyes focused on the Doppler log, I appealed to higher authority! The speed began to drop far more quickly than my experience told me it should be doing. Was the Doppler being rendered inaccurate by the underwater turbulence created by maximum engine power? I looked at the surface of the river 90 feet below me on the starboard side and decided to trust the Doppler.

I informed my tugs that the speed appeared to be down to 5 knots and that it was safe for them to take the ship around to starboard while I continued to go Full Astern. The VTS was informed that I was swinging off Occidental. Slowly she started to come around and as she did the fog began to break and there clearly visible was our destination Coryton Jetty No 4.

As the Doppler dropped to zero, I suddenly found myself ideally positioned for berthing. I informed the VTS that I could see the jetty and intended to berth. This was done without further difficulty, in fact the ship ended up stopped in the water in exactly the right position to drop in on the tide and run the first lines.

In a total time of approximately 1 hour 15 minutes from the time of boarding at Sea Reach 6, the vessel had come 5 miles through the fog, swung and berthed exactly in position without need to be adjusted even a single foot to line up with the manifolds. The Thames Waterman Colin Barker coming aboard to get his bill signed by the Master looked at me with what appeared to be new respect, for conducting an operation in which probably there was more luck than planned skill remarking:

> "Mr Russell if you do another 27,000 ships, you'll never do one
> again as well as that. We could not even see you in the fog."

He was right of course, but to me the whole job had all been far too fast, although time waiting for an expected response had seemed interminable, a sure sign of stress. Heart Rates as high as 157 bpm were registered on a pilot berthing a VLCC during one study. I now wonder just how much damage this particular incident did to my own system. The sea pilot and I were both conscious of how close we had been to a serious incident and how fortunate we had been to have luck on our side. I was grateful that the Duty Officer at the Thames Navigation Service had not burdened me with unnecessary enquiries and had left the decision making to me on the bridge. I was glad also that there did not appear to be a bridge team monitoring the movement and distracting my concentration with alarming information of which I was only too aware. I left with a tremendous feeling of job satisfaction without a word of thanks from the Master whose total lack of awareness had astonished me. Pilotage could have stressful moments but it really was a lovely job.

Passage Planning

It was mentioned earlier that right from the beginning the Shell Company had a basic Passage Plan as indeed did the PLA and the Pilot. Such plans were concentrated on areas of critical depth, predicted tidal and passage times; they were fairly basic and really remained little changed except that as the years progressed calculations tended to become computer generated. The fact remains that the pilot did his own calculations and the Duty Port Controller independently produced a basic plan on a pre-programmed computer. Some regular North Sea Large Tankers and some VLCCs also did their own independent calculations. The plans were therefore subject to confirmation and double scrutiny but plans were merely plans, they could not foresee the future or what exactly would happen on a long pilotage and they may require a great deal of flexibility depending on traffic, weather conditions and as we saw earlier with one ship, the ability of the vessel itself to maintain the plan. They also require that the person producing the plan have adequate notification of his or her task and time in which to make the plan.

The author produced personally for all Inner List ships not just the basic plan for that particular tide but also a more detailed navigational plan giving water depths, parallel indexing opportunities, light buoy characteristics, distance to go, emergency anchorages, etc. But for those pilots who had moved into the 1990s and had computers at home.and had the ability to do such things at the touch of a few buttons, it was easy. Such a plan however was too complex to discuss and agree before the passage commenced, as some would suggest. The pilot, on boarding a VLCC approaching the Deep Water Route at the Sunk, did not have time to agree in any detail either his plan or the ship's as the vessel moved onward towards the shoals.

When I was acting as a Berthing Pilot the Master was given a plan of the berth if he was not a regular visitor. The manoeuvring characteristics of the ship were checked and the planned manoeuvre and the speed at which it was planned to swing, the position and type of tug and their deployment and why, and the moorings and anything else we might expect were discussed and agreed. As previously mentioned such an exchange requires an understanding of language and a degree of knowledge of the expectations of what was about to happen.

Training

In retrospect the author's training was quite inadequate for the responsibility that he eventually accepted; accepted because service in the Inner List and Berthing Service had always been voluntary in London and it maybe that many of the pilots who did not volunteer were those that recognised that inadequacy. Certainly most pilots had relatively little large tanker berthing experience until they actually took on the job because the system did not allow it. The volunteer watched and learnt rapidly when second pilot in the Inner List and then as the Inner List Pilot. The author was more fortunate than most in getting a place at Port Revel the Ship Handling School at Grenoble, France on an advanced pilot's course but he was by that time already handling VLCCs. All pilots were naturally grateful to the best of their senior colleagues who passed on their skills and through whom most was learnt but even they could not prepare one for some of the situations one was likely to confront; pilots needed better training.

During my last three years of pilotage service as the Senior Pilot in the Port of London, and as Chairman of the United Kingdom Marine Pilots Association Technical Committee, I did my best to support those trying to improve standards of Pilotage Training in the United Kingdom; finally using my authority as the elected President of the Nautical Institute to persuade recalcitrant people to at least listen to our arguments for improvement. I wrote and contributed to the increasing debate and was pleased to learn recently that much that I and my colleagues had written about has since come to pass, but whether it is actually working I cannot tell; the reader would need to ask a serving pilot for one view and a serving shipmaster for another. I doubt if they will ever agree.

Chapter 31

Piloting in Heavy Weather

The weather at sea was ferocious for Christmas 1997 and the New Year of 1998 came in violently with both the Sunk Pilot and North East Spit Pilot stations being unable to work because of tempestuous north-easterly winds and heavy breaking seas. The first period of dirty weather had started around the 18th December, a day when I was asked to board and pilot into London the MV *Buxcrown* an 18,000 ton bulk carrier, with a draft of 9 metres and length of 175.6 metres waiting west of the port of Dover and sheltering from the northerly winds.

It is ironical but it had taken nearly nine years for a severe disruption to the Pilotage Services at the Thames and Medway to happen, a prediction which as Cinque Ports Pilots opposing the re-organisation of Pilotage in 1988 we had imagined might be far more common. Before re-organisation in severe weather we always had a choice of the Pilot Station at Folkestone in strong northerly weather and the North East Spit and Margate Roads in southerly and westerly weather. The Cinque Ports London Trinity House Pilots had a proud record of never failing to serve a ship and were reluctant to accept a situation which was inherently flawed and where pilots were being expected to work more exposed waters. Following 1988, certainly on occasions, dirty weather meant that either or both the exposed stations were briefly unworkable but in the main these were brief periods; this spell of seriously turbulent weather was something else.

On Christmas Day a weather window was forecast and I was stood off for a large tanker inwards for Coryton Berth 4, the *Alandia Pride,* Draft 12.7 metres, 44,109 GRT, Length 245 metres; the family who had all arrived for lunch were not very pleased but delighted when the ship was cancelled due to the high winds. Their pleasure was ephemeral for on Boxing Day I was to stand off for the same ship and left by taxi for Harwich before lunch, joining the deeply laden tanker following a violent passage in the pilot launch as she rolled in the heavy swell five miles east of the Sunk Light ship, spilling seas and spume across the main tank deck in the fading light of a dark winter's afternoon. Carefully timing my climb on the lee side, I managed to escape a drenching from the sea water flowing with the movement of the ship from the weather side across the dark deck towards me, but unhappily I could not avoid arriving on the bridge with shoes full of water. However, my main concern was to get the ship onto a course for the Deep Water Route with the stern to the wind and swell and avoid the heavy rolling which was dangerously increasing the draft in relatively shallow water. With my adrenalin pumping I soon became oblivious to my wet feet and with the ship on course and with a cup of strong black coffee inside me I soon forgot the least of my worries. The inward passage went without incident, the berthing being carried out at the limit of our wind restrictions before the next weather front arrived and the bad weather continued.

Three days later I managed a quick run into Coryton with a small LPG carrier before once again the weather caused the closure both of the outward stations. In the meantime Pilots were bringing ships outwards from London and the Medway to be 'over carried' with the ships to Scandinavia, the Continent and British ports around the coast. On New Years Eve I thought it was to be my turn for pastures new when I joined a large Russian tanker – the *Kapitan Koziar*, 45,353 GRT, Draft 12.7 metres, Length 243 metres – at Shell Haven Bravo Jetty where she had been loaded with a highly inflammable cargo of 60,000 tons of export leaded petrol bound for New York. With the whole ship and surrounding area reeking of petrol fumes, we left the berth at 23:30 hours and headed for the open sea; the Sunk Pilot station was not working but the wind had come around to the west and it was hoped that by the time I got there service would be resumed, at least I was promised they would send a fast launch out to review the situation.

As the New Year came in we slipped our tugs and started to slowly increase speed. Ashore people were celebrating the New Year with fireworks, fortunately well away from us but alarmingly as we built up speed, more and more red hot sparks were discharged from the funnel abaft the bridge and being blown directly ahead of us to cascade around us on the bridge wings, down past the bridge house front painted with large 'NO SMOKING' signs and onto the main tank decks. Had we been at sea, a large alteration of course would have allowed the sparks to fall harmlessly over the side clear of the vessel but we were in a narrow channel and compelled to proceed almost on the same course for the next fifteen miles.

Recalling memories of seeing the wreck of the *Stanvac Japan* in my early career I held my breath and pointed out to the Captain the possible danger of our becoming a particularly large New Year's Firework somewhere off

Southend – a likely situation if we did not get the engineers to control the situation. He spoke quietly by telephone to someone in the engine room and carried on smoking his cigarette apparently unperturbed. For the next hour and a half or twenty miles, the bulk of the sparks continued to cascade through the petrol fumes to fall prettily onto the main deck covering 60,000 tons of unleaded petrol bound for New York; I prayed the pilot boat would resume service and I could get off at the Sunk and that I did, landing at 05:45 hours at Harwich.

The next four days produced severe weather with winds of ninety knots and one hundred and fifteen knots in the south-western English Channel, through which my comrade was outward bound; but by then I had some leave, was curled up in front of the fire with a glass of seasonal cheer and was not called upon to venture out again until the weather moderated. The fate however of my Russian colleague remained not far from my thoughts and certainly I did not envy the crew of the *Kapitan Koziar* punching her way across the North Atlantic to New York with 60,000 tons of export unleaded petrol; for which incidentally the New Yorker would only pay $1.25 maximum per gallon while, thanks to UK tax, we were paying just on $5.00 per gallon.

As a pilot, heavy weather was part of the job and one soon learnt boarding techniques, climbing swiftly in stages possibly as high as nine metres up the side of a rapidly rolling ship as it rolled away from the pilot on the ladder with that ladder firmly against the ship's side, only to hold on grimly as the ship rolled back and the pilot ladder left the side to hang momentarily in space. One soon learnt to wait patiently, usually cold and dripping wet in a heavy swell for an extra large wave that would lift the pilot boat high up the ship's side before stepping across to grab the ladder and then climbing rapidly as the pilot boat dropped heavily away. One also had to learn when to refuse to board until the Master manoeuvred his ship to give the pilot launch the shelter of a better lee.

In particularly heavy weather if the climb was long, I preferred the pilot launch to pull away from the side providing the ladder was clear for departure and for the coxswain to wait motoring parallel with the ship in order to watch my progress until I was seen to be safely aboard; preferring to fall into the water rather than onto the hard unforgiving deck fittings of the pilot boat with the risk of serious injury. With a short climb I preferred to have the boat remain alongside.

Landing was somewhat different and again a matter of preference; I liked the boat to be alongside and moving at the same speed as the ship before stepping down onto the ladder, thus ensuring that the ladder did not become entrapped between the boat and ship causing it to break with the weight of the boat. The calculated risks became routine and I can never remember being fearful of the task, although at times it could be frustrating and particularly annoying when quite obviously due care and attention had not been paid to the condition of the pilot ladder or a Master failed to give a decent lee.

The most dangerous moment in the whole operation was undoubtedly stepping from the ladder backwards onto the moving boat for the pilot could not see or gauge clearly the exact time to take that step as the boat rose and fell behind and below him and therefore a pilot had to rely heavily on the seaman standing on the pilot boat deck to talk him down; telling when to stop or go.

The oddest most risky and stupid boarding I ever made was to a small Dutch Schuyt which was bound for the Granville Dock Dover from off Folkestone in a south-westerly gale Force 9, using the heavy weather pilot boat *Lodesman*. I was particularly keen to get aboard for it was a nice short job for me and paid a small extra fee to add to my small basic sharing turn. We tried to board in the traditional manner but the ship rolled so violently we could not get alongside without damage and we were about to give up when the coxswain suggested that if he could persuade the Master to put the heavy weather on his port bow and maintain minimum steerage way, he was sure we could lay the port bow of the *Lodesman* with its heavy fenders against the starboard quarter of the ship and push sufficiently for me to step across. Well I was young and fit and perhaps conscious of the crowds of people on the Leas at Folkestone watching with curiosity; I decided to give it a go but much to my surprise the manoeuvre went perfectly. The Coxswain brought the *Lodesman* slowly and skilfully up to the stern of the heavily pitching Schuyt and the two vessels hardly touched on her starboard quarter as I swung myself over her rails from the port bow of the pilot boat to the quarter deck of the small coaster, arriving outside the galley door in time to startle a large wide-eyed black cook emerging with a bin full of steaming vegetable peelings.

Boarding a ship in bad weather was a problem but actually manoeuvring large ships in strong winds could be a nightmare, the storms of 1987 being a particularly well-documented occasion. I, of course, over 32 years had my fair share of wind; my most worrying times being when berthing large tankers at the Thames oil refineries at Shellhaven and Coryton with the wind gusting to our maximum considered limits of 30 – 40 knots and with open boats running lines between ship and jetty in danger of being trapped, if one was unable to stop a ship being blown onto the berth. Risk assessment was carried out by the oil companies and tables of permitted wind speeds were produced but wind speed was difficult to predict in my days and one could very often find a dangerous situation developing. The rules however did not always suit everyone as we shall see with the following anecdote.

You Can't Sink a Rainbow

Towards the end of March 1983 I stood off to join the VLCC *British Ranger (130,145 GRT, 269,882 DWT, Length 338 metres, Draft 35'7")* in the French Port of Antifer, where she was to discharge part of her cargo before proceeding to Coryton to complete her discharge of Liberian crude oil. We always sent two pilots in the interest of safety and familiarity to these VLCCs, one to understudy and support the other. I was lucky to have John Foot as my colleague for we had shared interests, he now being a painter of some repute with a couple of published books under his belt but this was some time ago.

It was in fact a time when the Government of Margaret Thatcher, in response to the Ship owners who were purported to be the Conservatives' main financial supporters, was seriously considering the re-organisation of pilotage at the request of the Chairman of the Ship owners' Pilotage Committee, a man whose family-owned company mainly ran a fleet of British Coasters not subject to compulsory pilotage unless they went on a voyage outside the Home Trade Limits. He, we understood, considered the regulations to be archaic, pilotage too expensive and overmanned. Well to a certain extent he was right, there was need for an overhaul, but when you open up a can of worms you do not always solve the problem. He was to admit to me some years later that he thought maybe he had shot himself in the foot, as I stepped out of my brand new Lexus expressing to him delight at my new working conditions, for which I thanked him.

It was not a happy time for the Cinque Ports Pilots faced with the possible disembodiment of a system that had developed over some five hundred years. We were very angry and pilotage was becoming of great media interest, but did the public know what was meant by pilotage and just who were these pilots? The BBC decided to find out and Radio 4 was tasked with recording a programme about pilotage and of a pilot at work. Of course a VLCC was not typical of our work but it was probably the most impressive and would be of most interest to the vast majority of people, many being completely unaware that such ships regularly entered our ports.

The BBC Radio 4 Team joined at Antifer and appeared immediately surprised at just how long the job would take and concerned that they would meet their deadlines. We sailed from Antifer and the French Pilot disembarked dramatically in a small helicopter from the main deck. Although I had a Deep Sea Certificate issued by Trinity House to pilot from Lands End to the London Pilotage District and from Cherbourg to Rotterdam to the London Pilotage District and my services would have cost his company no extra, the Master chose to take the ship through the Dover Straits and across to the London Pilotage District without my assistance, as was his right. Deep Sea Pilotage is not compulsory and considered unnecessary by many Masters as experienced as the Master of the *British Ranger*. After travelling by train to Le Havre and faced with a long day ahead I was pleased to get some rest as the ship moved north along the French coast before crossing to enter the London District at the Sunk. During this time the BBC carried out several interviews with the Master and his bridge team and John and I were left wondering what was being said and just how much the team valued our expertise, if at all.

Prior to arrival at the Sunk and the beginning of our pilotage, I updated my passage plan, which John double checked for me and discussed and agreed it with the Master. Basically we knew the time we had to arrive at Sea Reach Number 6 buoy to embark from a tug, one of my colleagues acting as the Berthing Pilot. The plan was a calculation backwards from that time of the speed and positions the ship would need to adhere to, allowing sufficient rise of tide to give always slightly more than our under-keel clearance allowance. These large ships were usually programmed in at a maximum speed of twelve knots through the outer estuary where the minimum UKC was 1.2 metres, gradually reducing to five knots when embarking the Berthing Pilot, where the minimum UKC was 0.9 metres.

The ship arrived on time at the Sunk and I started inwards through the Deep Water Route; the BBC producer asking me if they could record a long steady blast on the powerful steam whistle to introduce the programme. It was an impressive sound, implying the enormity of the ship and the nautical flavour of the programme. The questions were never intrusive and great care was taken not to interfere with my concentration at critical points on passage or when I was speaking or listening to the VHF Radio.

I was monitoring two radio channels throughout. The general call and distress frequency, *"North Foreland Radio"* on VHF Channel 16 and *"Gravesend Radio",* the Thames Navigational Service at Gravesend on VHF Channel 12.

As we steamed steadily inwards down the Black Deep Channel I sensed the wind increasing and the skies beginning to darken in the west. I was not surprised therefore when *"North Foreland Radio"* burst into life to issue a Gale Warning;

"South Westerly Gale Force 9 Imminent
Sea Areas Thames and Dover."

Now this was unpredicted and could have serious consequences if we attempted to berth in weather outside the safety parameters; but the decision was not mine and I called Gravesend to ask the Duty Officer to check with the Refinery and Berthing Pilot if, in view of the imminent force 9 gale warning, we should abort the passage plan. The reply was swift;

"Gale Warning, What Gale Warning?
We don't have a Gale Warning."

I replied; "The one currently being issued on North Foreland Radio."

There was a stunned silence and I suggested we conversed on a private VHF Channel where I reminded the Duty Officer that we had a BBC Radio 4 Team aboard recording the more interesting conversation and making the point that currently I was committed and would need time to abort, get the speed off and preferably swing to the flood tide, before either anchoring or coming out again. Awaiting a reply we steamed implacably on but it did give opportunity to answer questions stressing the safety precautions we took to protect the environment, the ship and the berth. Of growing concern to the producer were the issues of time we might lose if aborted and the subsequent re-scheduling that would be required at the BBC.

At this point having swung into the narrow Knock John Channel, the reporter asked exactly how much water was under the keel. When I replied that it was only just over the 1.2 metres he appeared stunned, looking forward pensively from the bridge as the 1,000 feet of hull slid ahead of us between the buoys of the narrow channel, guarded by the rust-streaked sentinel of the old Knock John gun tower. Looking back I think he remarked that 1.2 metres was not very much, only about as high as his waist which gave me the opportunity to remark words to the effect that; *"This was when we really earn our money."*

Clearing the Knock John Channel we received instructions to abort this tide and plan for the next, some twelve hours later. After consultation with the Master it was decided we would use the last of the flood tide to swing into Whisky One Anchorage off Shoeburyness, not an easy manoeuvre but one which with the help of John Foot and the efficient bridge team and under the watchful scrutiny of the PLA Radar at Gravesend we achieved to everybody's satisfaction; except of course the BBC Team who were straining at the leash to get off.

The following morning was clear, bright and sunny with a fresh breeze as we prepared to get underway. I obtained permission to weigh anchor from TNS Gravesend, gave details of my revised planned passage and a clear warning of my intentions to shipping in the vicinity. Several ships replied with assurance that they would keep well clear of me in order to give me plenty of room to manoeuvre. However as the anchor came aweigh and I started to turn this large ship short around to starboard, one small ship continued to close my port bow coming out from the Barrows Channel quite oblivious to my sound signals and radio warnings. Closer and closer she came until we could identify her as the *Rainbow Warrior,* while on Full Ahead and Hard to Starboard I attempted to turn the *British Ranger* short around, staying clear of the shoal water on the Oaze bank. Such a large ship does of course take considerable power to pick up speed and with the wheel hard over, the kinetic energy is largely absorbed by the turning moment, so that such ships can be turned from stop almost in their own length. We were barely moving through the water ahead and must have looked at a glance from the *Rainbow Warrior* as though we were still at anchor, perhaps an easy mistake when tired.

There was considerable excitement on the VHF, in the Port Control Room and on our bridge – everywhere it seems except on the bridge of the little ship dedicated to saving whales and the environment, which momentarily disappeared out of sight close under our swinging bow, only to reappear unscathed plodding wearily inwards for London.

The Duty Officer at Gravesend asked me on the private VHF Channel if I wanted, in light of the obvious breach of the Port and International Regulations, to take further action but some years earlier I had been asked to submit a report when a feeder container ship passed similarly close ahead under the bow of a VLCC on which I was the second pilot. I did as asked and was horrified that on the strength of my report and corroborating evidence from the TNS, the flag state of the feeder ship subsequently took away that Master's Certificate; I certainly did not want a repeat of such action. I suggested that perhaps one of the PLA Marine Officers might have a quiet word with the miscreant and make the point that his, or it might have been her actions had been witnessed by a BBC News Team and that while I was prepared to take no further action, I could not guarantee that *Greenpeace* might not find itself the subject of an unfavourable news story. In the mean time I appealed to the better nature of the Radio 4 Team to be content with the story about Pilotage and not do damage to an organisation trying to do good as they see it; they obviously kept their word for not a word appeared in the press.

Sadly, although I only "nearly sunk" the *Rainbow Warrior,* just over two years later at a quarter to midnight on the 10th July, 1985 there was an electric blue flash and what sounded like an explosion and the same little *Greenpeace* ship began to sink at her mooring in Auckland harbour, New Zealand. It appears that rather than allow her to disrupt nuclear testing at Moruroa, French secret agents had used explosives to blow her up.

British Ranger berthed that day almost without further incident, despite quite strong winds which caused me great difficulty as at slow speed we crabbed up the Sea Reach or Yantlet Channel and, at Number 3 Sea Reach, very nearly clipped the South East Leigh Buoy. Being unfamiliar with the Whisky Anchorage which I was only to use a handful of times in 32 years, I had misjudged the time necessary to weigh anchor and swung into the channel and committed myself far too quickly and was consequently running ahead of time. At very slow speed the wind on the port bow was trying to push me out of the channel to the north, but we made it safely and the Berthing Pilot arrived with his four tugs and I handed over to him.

But we were not there yet, for one of the tugs managed to get the towline around his propeller. The Berthing Pilot called for another tug for, certainly with the wind freshening again, we could not risk berthing with just three tugs, two of whom were conventional single-screw tugs.

The BBC Producer asked me quietly;

"What happens now?"

I replied that in the interest of safety we would have to abort and go to sea again. His expression clearly indicated his opinion of pilots, ships, the weather and all things maritime but fortunately we either got an extra tug or the fouled tug managed to clear his tow line. If needed to take the ship to sea again, I knew somebody would soon call me, in the meantime I went down for lunch while the ship berthed safely.

Chapter 32

Unnecessary Risk

The seamen of the nineteen fifties would have been astonished not only at the sheer size tankers had become but as to just how small the total complement of a VLCC was just a quarter of a century later. Yet today, a half a century later, the average complement is down to a mere twenty-five persons of a multi-culture divided by language and expectations. Fortunately before I retired in 1999 International Regulations and systems of ship management had, through the work of the International Maritime Organisation and stakeholders, been considerably improved in response to a number of shipping casualties but a mere decade before all kinds of odd things happened.

On the 12th May 1986 the VLCC *Al Saqr Al Arabi,* (Draft 38 feet, 144,264 gross tons, 285,452 Deadweight, 339 metres overall, built 1976) arrived on time at Sea Reach Number 6 buoy inward for Coryton 4 with approximately 150,000 tons of crude oil. The ship was well found and had been inspected and approved by the Mobil Superintendent at her lightening berth in France for acceptance at Mobil Coryton. The sea pilot had experienced no difficulty on the passage and all seemed to be well when I took over for the berthing.

Fortunately the weather was fine and clear with very little wind when at 00:30 hours I deployed my four tugs, one at each quarter, as the VLCC slid slowly inwards on the flood tide. I gave orders for the tugs to be secured on their towlines and concentrated on the speed and course as I waited for confirmation that the tugs were secure. The operation seemed to be taking an inordinate length of time and my patience was wearing thin as we passed the Scars Elbow buoy. I enquired of the tugs by VHF as to their progress in securing and was alarmed to learn, from out of the darkness, that nobody had appeared on the decks high above them to send down a heaving line with which to pull aboard from each tug, first a messenger line and then finally the heavy wire towrope.

I stopped the large steam turbine and expressed my concern to the Greek Master, who began a shouted conversation in English on his portable radio to the officer in charge on the forecastle head. His raised voice was not one of anger but the natural explosive delivery that I recognised as that of someone from the Mediterranean area; but, nevertheless, I found it difficult to either understand his instructions or hear what was being relayed in response. Eventually I was told that the ship's heaving line was of insufficient length to reach the deck of the tug some thirty-five metres below.

"Get two heaving lines and tie them together,"

I replied, as the very young third officer from the Philippines (obviously fearful of the wroth of his Captain taking the opportunity while the Master was busy) quietly whispered to me that this enormous ship had only three seamen on deck forward, of which one was the officer and one a young cadet. I asked about aft and was told again only three, of which one was a young ordinary seaman; I was horrified and immediately realized that we would not be able to secure the tugs in sufficient time to swing on the flood tide or secure the moorings, before the ebb tide came away.

It was fortunate that I had already stopped the engines, for it took nearly one and a half hours to finally secure all four of the tugs. I enquired of the Master as to why the job was taking so long and not wishing to betray the young officer to his Captain, enquired as to whether he had sufficient men for mooring.

"Of course we have enough men, Mr Pilote,"

was the prompt reply of the Master, irritated that I should imply otherwise. I reported to the Gravesend Radio that I was still attempting to secure the tugs and intended to abort the flood tide berthing and berth to the first of the ebb tide. Using my private radio I contacted the Thames Watermen at the berth waiting for me and knowing the ship's agent would by now be in attendance, explained the delay and asked if it could be arranged for extra watermen to board the ship to assist with the moorings. It was possible and the ship behaved impeccably, running off her speed while maintaining directional stability, to berth to the Ebb tide without further incident at 02:40 hours. There was an internal enquiry following my report and it would appear that the ship did have a full complement of officers and seamen, of whom a good percentage had been allowed to sleep in, rather than I imagine be paid overtime; but I was never party to the results of the enquiry and can only guess at why I was put to so much stress by such unnecessary risk.

As a Berthing Pilot I received nothing but the full co-operation from ship's Masters, Agents, the Tug Masters, the Thames Watermen and the Marine officers at Port Control and of course the Refinery Superintendents and Duty Staff. Berthing a VLCC we always used four tugs to swing and berth head out to the flood tide and only three tugs for unmooring when head down.

The *VLCC Grand Lady* (281,794 tons deadweight, draft 11 metres and 328 metres length) had for some unknown reason arrived late and been berthed head in, when I was tasked with un-berthing her and swinging her on the ebb tide at 13:30 hours on the 3rd February 1995. The weather was reasonable but the wind was beginning to freshen in the morning and I called the agent to ask for a fourth tug in view of the need to swing on the ebb tide. Not unreasonably being aware of the extra cost, he asked if in my professional opinion another tug was really necessary for the ship. As soon as I explained my concern he replied;

> *"Pilot, if you consider an extra tug to be necessary,*
> *I will order a fourth tug."*

There was no hesitation and he was true to his word, calling me back a few minutes later to confirm I now had four tugs available; it was lucky that we had both been successful, for events were to conspire to demonstrate the need. Coming off and stemming the ebb tide parallel to the berth with the conventional single screw tugs *Sun Kent* and *Formidable* on the port and starboard bows and Voith Schneider tugs *Sun Mercia* and *Sun Surrey* working aft, I positioned the ship in the middle of the available water and started to swing to starboard. As she came around, the ebb tide and wind caused her to begin to drop rapidly sideways down the river, the stern being reluctant to come up into the wind. Athwart the river there was a loud bang and I lost my largest tug when the tow line to *Formidable*, parted on the starboard bow; but fortunately we had the extra tug available and by pushing and pulling the after end of the ship, she came around on to a course to take her safely to sea as *Formidable* recovered her broken tow line. It would have been a nightmare without that extra tug and the extra expense was never queried.

The Danger of Complacency

On the 11th December 1994 I very nearly came to grief through my own complacency, the outcome of over familiarity. The Pilot Co-ordinator, the term used for a dispatcher, called me early one morning to order my services for a tanker berthed at the Isle of Grain Power Station to take it from the Medway up the Thames to the Littlebrook Power Station, just above the Queen Elizabeth Bridge in Long Reach; announcing;

"I've got a nice little job for you."

Meaning in retrospect I suppose it was a 'nice short job' but the 'little' clicked in and the fact that it was a 'United' tanker was synonymous with his use of the word, for that company did tend to operate a number of fairly small coastal tankers at that time.

The *United Moonlight* (draft 7 metres, 29,649 grt, length 207 metres) was however one of the company's bigger sisters. My problem was that this was my first ship back on the Sea Roster after a prolonged absence when, due to a colleague's illness, I had just completed two months' continuous work as a Berthing Pilot at the oil refineries, handling much larger ships including VLCCs. Thus I allowed myself to become complacent; this ship was not bound for the refineries but much further upriver where she was to prove somewhat demanding.

Stepping aboard at the IOG Power Station I should have been alerted, for the ship was using three tugs to un-berth, while I knew that I had been only given two to swing in less room. I queried the situation with the Medway pilots and was told that 3 tugs was their requirement. I was not impressed and foolishly thought them over cautious; things were like that on the Medway, I thought, after all at one time they would not handle large tankers at night – how did they get away with it! I was to learn a lesson and bitterly regret my unkind thoughts.

All went well, the *United Moonlight* swung easily from the Medway to the Sea Reach Channel and I proceeded inwards passing the refineries, up through the Lower Hope and around into Gravesend Reach where, somewhere off the Tilbury Landing Stage, the ship took on a new persona becoming larger before my very eyes as she seemed to gallop along on the flood tide. I swept around Tilburyness and dropped my speed well down on sighting a small spirit tanker discharging at Wouldhams Jetty (GATX), Greys. My two tugs had been in contact by VHF Radio earlier, to find out where in the river I wished to make them secure for berthing and I had replied rather over confidently; that the lower end of Long Reach would be okay and they had consequently run on up the river ahead of me.

Approaching Broadness inwards at slow speed I started to make my turn to port and watched as the bow came slowly around the sweeping 110 ° bend in the river. Suddenly I realised all was not well and the adrenalin started to pump; we were going too slowly and as we turned to port the flood tide, gaining in strength on the port quarter, was pushing the stern around fast to sweep upstream towards the coasting tanker sitting directly in its path on Wouldhams Jetty, gently emitting clouds of vapour into the cold dank still air.

I put on more speed but my experience told me that we were not going to clear the small tanker where people slept or worked below, blissfully unaware of impending disaster, unless I could reduce the speed the stern was swinging towards the north bank. I put the engines full ahead and the wheel hard to starboard and the swing to port slowly stopped, as we kicked the stern just clear of Wouldhams Jetties and, rapidly gaining speed, started to swing back towards West Thurrock Power Station. The Scandinavian Master stood stoically on the starboard bridge wing, apparently unperturbed by the manoeuvre, as I reversed the helm and slowly reduced speed and once more brought the ship back on to the correct course.

I had given myself quite a fright and should have known better but the *United Moonlight* was the first really large ship I had piloted around Broadness, although it was not to be the last and I am pleased to say I never repeated my error. Quickly calling the tugs to come back and make fast before I turned into Long Reach, I was relieved to have them secure at each end when the wind started to freshen on the port beam as we entered that final stretch, struggling to remain in the middle of the river. Passing under the Queen Elizabeth Bridge she turned easily to port into the wind and was berthed at Littlebrook Power Station without further incident.

Chapter 33

Published Papers and Committee Work

The Trinity House Cinque Ports Pilots, being self-employed, to a certain extent ran their own business affairs and governed themselves subject to Bye-Laws approved by Trinity House and regulated by the local Trinity House Superintendent of Pilots. The Pilots were represented by an elected First Class Pilot acting as 'Representative', an 'Honorary Secretary' and of course 'the elected committee'. There was a great deal of extra curricular work to be done by these individuals over many difficult years negotiating with The Corporation of Trinity House London, the Chamber of Shipping the owner's organisation, the Department of Transport and the Government of the day, other Pilot Stations and outside bodies. Not everybody volunteered for this unpaid work, although most did their share over the years but usually the work tended to fall on a few stalwarts willing to give of their own spare time to serve their colleagues. Pilots were, by the very nature of their profession, used to having their own way and were strong-willed, making it difficult to obtain a consensus; and sometimes, as a consequence, we were our own worst enemies. Into this mêlée I innocently stepped when I volunteered to serve as the Under-draught committee member and soon found myself confronted by what I considered to be archaic thought and petty rules and regulations, causing me to act the angry young man. I had to leave the Committee on my elevation to First Class but returned later to serve eight years in all, two years of which I did as Honorary Secretary.

I was not however a 'political animal' and apart from the daily internal problems and constant external battles, which involved representation at meetings and subsequent reports and letter writing, I tended to concentrate on the technical aspects and professional role of the marine pilot. I subsequently became heavily involved in the Technical Committee of the United Kingdom Marine Pilots' Association; which I chaired for the final three years of my career. Because of the threat of traffic diversion to the future use of the brand new Trinity House Pilot Station at Folkestone, I subsequently became involved and after studying the provisions of the International Maritime Organisation Guide to Ships Routeing, served as a

UKPA Technical Adviser and then as one of the UKPA Representatives on the United Kingdom Safety of Navigation Committee (UKSON) for seventeen years.

Following an extensive oil spill after the loss in March 1967 of the VLCC *Torrey Canyon* on the Scilly Islands and the VLCC *Amoco Cadiz* in March 1978 on the French coast, and following in 1971 a series of accidents in the English Channel which led to calls for immediate action, considerable change was being promulgated in the maritime world. The serving professional mariners lacked an open forum to present their views, arguments or suggestions for improvement and warn of dangerous practice that was developing. Fortunately a forum was provided when a number of concerned professionals got together and formed The Nautical Institute, which I then joined as a Founder Member, going on to help establish the Dover Branch in 1975.

In 1978 the Dover Branch of the Nautical Institute held an extremely well-attended and well-reported international seminar concerning *"The Practical Problems of Navigation in the Dover Strait"*, at a time of mounting tension between the stake-holders; my humble contribution being a paper dealing with *"The Practical Problems of the Pilot"*. The seminar raised many issues that led to better understanding between the Authorities responsible and the Mariners using the area, and common sense prevailed. Some new navigational aids were established; pending prosecutions for alleged breaches of the regulations were dropped; the Anti-Collision Regulations were clarified and ultimately revised; and from then onwards steady improvements were made in the interests of safety. More importantly we had proved that, with a professional approach and recognised forum, practical solutions could be achieved; the mariner on the bridge did have a voice to which the authorities would listen.

How ironic it is today that despite all that has been achieved and continues to be done to improve safety of navigation; there is a marked similarity between the 1971 incident and another one some years later. In the first multiple accidents the tanker *Texaco Caribbean* was sunk in collision with a freighter off the Varne bank and the following night the wreck was struck by the freighter *Brandenburg*, which also sank. Some six weeks later, the freighter *Niki* struck the wreckage and sank, with the loss of all 21 people on board.

Another multiple accident took place thirty-one years later when the Norwegian car carrier *Tricolor* collided at 02:30 hours on the 14th

December 2002 in the English Channel with the Bahamas-registered container vessel *Kariba*. The damage was so extensive that the vessel sank at approximately 05:00 hours local time in 25 metres depth leaving her resting on the bottom of Channel, but only partly submerged because of the low tide. The *Tricolor* was carrying 2,862 luxury cars and 77 units of Ro-Ro cargo on its way from Zeebrugge to Southampton when the collision occurred. *Kariba* was damaged above the water line and headed for Antwerp under escort.

Vessels using the Straits of Dover, claimed to be the world's busiest shipping lane, were warned by regular radio broadcasts of this sunken wreck blocking the route. A UK Coastguard tug remained alongside to warn other ships to the 50,000-ton, 200-metre ship obstacle. Yet despite this the newly built 95 metre Dutch Antilles registered 3,000gt MV *Nicola*, from La Corunna in N. Spain for Rotterdam with 7 crew, ran down the sunken *Tricolor* on December 15, 2002. The *Nicola* was stuck on top of the *Tricolor* for several hours before being pulled free by two tugs on Monday December 16. Finally the wreck of the *Tricolor* was struck a third time when the Turkish-registered 800-foot MT *Vicky* (built in 1981, and bound from Antwerp, Belgium for New York with 2 million gallons of kerosene and 24 crew) inexplicably struck the wreckage of the sunken car carrier, despite all the warnings on 1st January 2003. Fortunately she was also pulled clear after a couple of hours.

Accidents will be impossible to eliminate completely, but there is no doubt that the safety of navigation generally has been enhanced considerably in the last twenty years. With advanced technology bringing in the advent of Global Positioning Systems (GPS) and the fitting of Transponders to all ships for the Automatic Identification System (AIS), as well as the use of electronic charts, there should be no excuse for those on the bridge to be uncertain of their own position or the position, course, speed and name of ships around them. Lack of training and misuse of that information or over-confidence and fatigue, coupled perhaps with adverse weather and wind in particular, may remain the major cause of maritime accidents.

Electronic Charts

Quite unexpectedly at a UKSON meeting in the 1980s, I was asked by a Government representative to write a paper under the title "*User Requirements for Electronic Charts*". I was surprised and puzzled.

"*Why ask me? Why not a Master from one of the top British Shipping Companies?*" I enquired.

"Because firstly we would get a Company approved specification from people probably as yet without any experience of using Electronic Charts. While secondly as a Pilot you obviously, from your contributions to the debate so far, have experience of using a number of different manufacturers' products and can probably better understand the international manning element. Finally I think you have the imagination."

I was extremely flattered to be asked and duly wrote a paper which was considered by the UK Marine Directorate Working Group on Electronic Charts in full and published in précis in the International Journal of the Nautical Institute *Seaways* in December 1987, entitled "ECDIS". Sometime later I sat in as IMPA representative at a Working Group at the IMO where a number of my suggestions surfaced and were discussed, although my paper had not been officially tabled. There were a couple of thoughts the UK Authorities did not agree with and a couple the manufacturers felt challenging, but happily the general response had been complementary.

The icing on the cake was on the 6th June 1999, when I walked on the bridge of the new German-built cruise liner, *Super Star Leo* in Singapore, to find that she and her large sisters had all been fitted with the very type of equipment I had been proposing. It was a rewarding experience.

The Channel Tunnel

Over the following years I was to write a number of papers on different subjects, written in my own time but also without financial reward; however in January 1985 a request came in to the UKPA from a firm of Parliamentary Lobbyists. My name was passed to The Channel Tunnel Group who were looking for a qualified mariner to examine all the competing plans for the fixed channel link, before the final decision was made by the French and British Governments for approval. Somebody had very kindly thought I might fit the bill. The task was very interesting and not too difficult because the two governments had asked their respective maritime directorates to produce a set of 'Maritime Requirements' the contenders would have to satisfy and these had been agreed and set in stone. As a mariner totally familiar with handling large ships in all weathers in the area, I was asked to review the plans of each project and comment as to whether I thought the maritime requirements were sound and whether in my opinion the contender's plans complied with those requirements.

Of course I was merely looking at the competition, which in each case had a maritime component, while the proposed Channel Tunnel had none.

There were without doubt some wonderful ingenious projects but sadly all of them seemed to me to have a flaw or infringement of those strict and comprehensive and well-conceived rules, when I came to review them. My paper was published in the NI Journal *Seaways* in August 1985 and a further six hundred copies were sent to every Member of Parliament by the Parliamentary Lobbyists, in case they missed my presentation in Committee Room 8 of The House of Commons, which most did! However it was an interesting experience and for once I was wined, dined and paid for my intellectual efforts.

Chapter 34

Pilotage Re-Organisation 1988

Pilotage Re-Organisation was a traumatic experience for pilots throughout the UK generally, but here I will address the experience as I witnessed the change as a Cinque Ports London-based pilot. Other pilotage districts may have had a smoother experience but a number had a far worse experience than we did and my sympathy goes out to all those who lost their jobs, homes and were forced to change their careers.

During the reign of Margaret Thatcher the ship owners were financial supporters of the Conservative Political Party and consequently had the ear of the Prime Minister, despite their decline as they abandoned ship, sunk by rising costs and the falling freight rates, which decimated the country's Merchant Service. The Pilotage Committee of the General Council of British Shipping was being chaired by the owner of a famous British Coastal Company still going strong but a company which rarely, because of the nature of their trade, required the services of a pilot but whose principals objected strongly to some of the archaic regulations that did affect them and which were, in their view, in need of revision. Who better to bring about that necessary change than the person indebted to them; Margaret Thatcher in her crusade to drag the UK screaming out of a land of petty bureaucracy.

The battle was joined and at Folkestone our elected Member of Parliament, The Right Honourable Michael Howard, seemed to be fighting our corner particularly well, defending our four hundred and fifty year service to the safety of shipping in the Dover Straits; that is until he was suddenly promoted to the front bench and appeared to me to become too busy to give our problems his full attention. Maybe I do him injustice, but it was a decision which in retrospect I wondered if Margaret Thatcher was to live to regret.

It was a long battle which the pilots were bound to lose, particularly so when in order to obtain expensive legal representation and the legal services of the Transport and General Workers Union (TGWU) to fight the detailed legislation before them. The pilots of the small but independent United Kingdom Pilots Association (UKPA), voted to join the TGWU and their hitherto professional arguments were subsequently considered by some tainted and promoted as left wing unionism. The Conservative Government's resolve for change was consequently strengthened and our battle was lost.

The 1987 Pilotage Act and its Outset

I always imagined a major role of the House of Lords was to study and amend poor legislation sent up to them from the House of Commons. A wise Council of Elder Statesmen, able to see the folly of their youthful colleagues. This Bill, after a quick read through in the House of Commons, was mainly debated in the House of Lords; where it is true to say the pilots' views were well-expressed but in the main ignored. It was then returned to the Commons where a little debate took place on the first few clauses and virtually none on the others. The vote was supposed to be a free one but in fact, probably because few understood the implications, the members lined up in party order. There were but few amendments at the Committee stage and pilots certainly got the impression that their sincere views for the safety of shipping or the provisions for an adequate pilotage service, had been to a large extent ignored.

The Act, which transferred responsibilities for pilotage from the existing pilotage authorities to Certain Harbour Authorities (CHAs), was passed onto the Statute Book and the "Appointed Day" hung over the negotiations like a black cloud. The "Appointed Day" was that day when the changes were to actually take place and was not immediately announced. The earliest it could have been was nine months after the Act was passed. There appeared to be a difference of opinion as to just when that appointed day would be. One view was that there could be no appointed day until the negotiations between the pilots and the CHAs were completed and then been referred to the Arbitration Panel for a decision requiring Ministerial approval.

The other view was that the appointed day could be announced at any time.

What was clear was that on the Appointed Day all existing requirements for pilotage to be compulsory would disappear, together with the existing pilots' licences and the qualifications of pilotage certificate holders. The ports would then be responsible for authorising who would be a pilot and what pilotage was to be compulsory, if any, and what exemptions there would be, if any. The pilot boats and pilot stations, some newly built at vast expense like my own at Folkestone, some wonderful old buildings with years of tradition around the country would also be passed gratis to the CHAs.

History

One might question why pilotage needed re-organisation and why this particular solution? There have been pilots for London in the Dover Straits since Henry VIII gave Trinity House a Royal Charter in 1516 and probably some two hundred years before that. In the 1913 Act, pilotage became compulsory and trade boomed in London, except for the war years, and particularly so with the construction of the 1950s. Pilots were recruited to serve the growth in shipping. Following which a combination of developments; the growth in size of tankers and reduction in their numbers, the switch to containerisation for many cargoes and again larger but fewer ships, industrial disputes and the eventual closing of many of the London docks and a failure to meet the challenge of the changing times and revoke legislation which meant pilots were being employed in circumstances where arguably they were not necessary; such as foreign flag ferries. For a number of years, as the required numbers declined, new recruitment was unnecessary and gradually the average age increased.

After the *Torrey Canyon* and *Amoco Cadiz* accidents, there was much concern about pilotage in European waters and the 1979 Act envisaged that compulsory pilotage would become the norm. That Act failed to bring about substantial changes, all the accidents were soon forgotten and that assumption ceased to command general support. Unlike France and Germany where the pilotage services gained in importance, here, cost-cutting had become of paramount importance.

The 1983 Act merely consolidated the 1913, 1936 Acts and the pilotage provisions of the Merchant Shipping Act 1979.

The purpose of the new 1987 Pilotage Act was essentially to de-regulate the pilotage service – to replace the existing rigid and complex statutory structure with a straightforward flexible system administered by harbour authorities. In simple terms, if there were too many pilots, the ports would be able to sack some.

The ports would have a duty to decide on compulsory pilotage. The pilotage Districts were expected to shrink around the ports with a subsequent saving in cost. Whether or not pilots would be employed remained to be seen, but the CHAs had a responsibility under the Act to employ existing pilots, if that is what the pilots wished. While on the other hand the desire of the majority of the pilots to be self-employed, could be overruled by the ports. It is ironical that the Governments of Belgium and Holland were at this very time changing the status of their pilots from employees to self-employed status to reduce costs; an exercise the Germans did some years ago for the same reasons.

The negotiations were complicated – the ports in the main were without experience of running a pilot service. Certainly in the London District to the PLA a ship either had a pilot or it did not; how he got there or how he got home, the hours he worked, his arrangements for training, sickness and leave were to come as a complete surprise.

The CHAs each negotiated their own conditions with pilots separately. They needed the knowledge and experience of pilots to design a workable system but their opening offers of remuneration, designed to fit into their own port salary and status structure varied in most pilots' views, from the unacceptable to the downright insulting. It was hardly an atmosphere conducive to co-operation. Few professional people can have been asked to participate in the destruction of their own status and working conditions, as the pilots were being required to that year.

One of the real obstacles was of course the pay differential existing in practice between pilots and the senior staff of the harbour authorities. Senior marine staff of harbour authorities had never, up until then, been particularly well paid and in fact their earnings tended to be far less than those of the pilots. The reason for this was that there were always many applicants for each job as mariners sought shore employment and of course many were ex-Naval officers supplementing their pensions.

In the course of the debate on the Third Reading of the Bill in the House of Lords, Lord Brabazon of Tara indicated that the Secretary of State's guidance was likely to require the proposed arbitration panel to have regard to the previous earnings of pilots in the port, taking into account both actual earnings and the levels recommended under the former Letch agreement updated and of course the earnings, conditions of employment and working patterns of senior staff of the harbour authority, including those of marine officers, in comparison with the working condition and work patterns applied to pilots.

To most pilots the functions of a mainly desk-borne administrator did not appear particularly arduous; while I suppose to some Harbour staff the functions of the pilot look straight forward, particularly if the job was done well. The major difference was of course that each time a pilot went aboard a ship, he was well aware that through lack of skill he could lose his licence and even his Master's Certificate of Competency. Further provisions of the new Act were harsh. The pilot could be fined £1000, plus pilotage charges, if guilty of an offence of negligence. On summary conviction, go to prison for six months or on conviction or indictment, to prison for two years or a fine or both. He was also aware that while trying to climb an icy ladder on a ship making a bad lee, he could lose his life.

It was hard to visualize two more different jobs in the marine world in which to make comparison. To pilots, the CHA negotiators appeared to be interpreting the re-organisation to mean the pilots would be accommodated in their own poor salary structure, while ignoring the Secretary of State's guidance on the pilots' previous earnings.

There seemed to be a desire to take the pilots down a peg or two, but then one of the problems pilots have always had is a shortage of friends among others in the marine world, understandably I think, for two reasons. Firstly, jobs in the pilotage service had been scarce and particularly so during the preceding years; hence there have been many prospective applicants who had failed to get into the service, not because they were not first class applicants and quite good enough but simply because there were no vacancies before they ran out of time. The top age limit of 35 years of age left many disappointed, and even some quite embittered, men to find a career elsewhere in the ports, ship management or stay at sea under a foreign flag; at a time when our industry was being devastated.

The second reason was one of pure job satisfaction. It has always been to the frustration of some ship masters and particularly so to the masters of small ships to have to hand over the manoeuvring and berthing of their vessels to a stranger, a fact compounded at nearly every port in the world and one which I have already emphasized in earlier comments on the Master – Pilot relationship.

Now there had been many assurances from the Government on fair treatment for pilots in the Green Paper of 1984, then the White Paper of 1986 and in a letter from the Prime Minister to the Chairman of the UKPA (M) in 1986 when she wrote, "I am satisfied too that what we propose will deal fairly with the members of your distinguished profession." Sadly the way negotiations progressed and with the uncertainty over the years leading up to the Appointed Day, the pilot service became thoroughly demoralized. The majority of pilots able to leave with compensation left; fed up with the anxiety, the increasing work load and lack of appreciation or value. Some pilots, who the ports expected to continue just left, refusing to co-operate.

For those lucky enough to go out on compensation, the treatment might have appeared fair for although that compensation was very poor, it was argued that "self-employed people were not entitled to compensation". I wonder how other professions would have reacted if the Government were to decide by Act of Parliament their requisite qualifications were to be abolished overnight?

Ro-Ro Grimaldi entering Tilbury Dock

On the 1st October 1988 the Pilotage Act 1987 came into force; 330 pilots throughout the country were made redundant or failed the new medicals, a further 2 died in service and a further 89 left in the first four years mainly due to ill health and normal retirement; the total numbers in that period dropping nationally from 1171 pilots to 750.

My own service, The Cinque Ports London District Pilots with a proud tradition going back to the year 1525, ceased operation at Folkestone at Midnight on the 30th September 1988 with a last message to shipping on the VHF Radio. It was answered by Dunkirk Pilots, the Cap Gris Nez French

Coastguard and the British Ferry *Horsa*. A man arrived from Sealink to take the keys; the superb purpose-built weatherproof pilot station, built just 20 years before, was locked up and has remained unused as a pilot station ever since – Folkestone is not a designated CHA. Folkestone also lost a major tourist attraction, for the continual landing and shipping of pilots close off shore had become a familiar and interesting spectacle to residents and visitors alike and particularly so in bad weather.

The Trinity House Pilotage Service with centuries of experience of the practical operation of pilot cutters and management of pilots was replaced in the main by people new to the task. In the Thames Estuary this was to be The Medway Ports Authority and The Port of London Authority.

As a result of the Act, pilots were bitter and none more so than me. Those that could, happily escaped with compensation; one even went to New Zealand without compensation where his family settled down, successfully breeding horses and, I am told, at least one winner of the famous Melbourne Cup.

We all thought we had been very badly treated and although the Act stated that the CHAs had to offer employment to former licensed pilots, and negotiations on terms and conditions were underway throughout the country, a mere 48 hours before the Appointed Day few pilots had been actually contacted by the ports and knew whether they were to be authorised or not. Most pilots thought they had been kept scrambling for a job in order to weaken their negotiators; divide and rule appeared to be the name of the game.

Management simply were given too little time, they were not ready to take on the responsibility and could have done with another month. Their most difficult task was getting an employment package and working rosters agreed with the pilots. Prior to the Appointed Day, there was no long term plan for London; the aim was merely to get a system up and running that could be the basis for change as a result of experience and circumstance. Having decided to combine the three London Sea stations into one roster, management soon found it was not such a practical idea; separate pilot stations had initially been established in order to have pilots always available to meet the demands of shipping. That a workable solution was found reflects highly on the skill of the negotiating team and particularly that of the pilots who had to sell the package to their unwilling colleagues.

The helpfulness and assistance given to management by pilots probably depended on their number of years' likely future employment, but it varied enormously from open hostility to a genuine wish to help and set up a workable operation. Individually a great many pilots gave considerable assistance and much good advice, but when gathered together little assistance was apparent; the general feeling being that the PLA had the job of setting everything up – let them get on with it.

Despite a few pilots wishing to be obstructive, the service did survive those early months for which, according to management at the time, nearly all the credit must go to the pilots themselves who, for whatever reason – pride, professionalism, bloody mindedness or self-interest, made it work.

There had been a reduction from 311 pilots to 189 in the number previously manning the ports of the Thames Estuary and adjacent waters of the old Trinity House Pilotage District. By 1992 the numbers in London had dropped to 115, of whom nearly a half were newly recruited.

It was an interesting time, for while I saw nothing but gloom and depression and uncertainty, 49 young men found opportunity and the average age of pilots in London dropped dramatically from 58.6 years to 50.5 years.

The largest reduction in pilotage was achieved on day one by the closure of the Folkestone Pilot Station and the abandonment of the requirement for compulsory pilotage through part of the Dover Straits. The outer sea stations being established at the Sunk, off Harwich and the North East Spit off North Foreland. Further savings have since been made by the issue of pilotage certificates to quite large ships running daily into the Thames Estuary and by gradually increasing the size of the smaller ships, exempt altogether from pilotage. Just four years after re-organisation, 45% of ships using the Port of London were operating without pilots and I am sure that percentage has probably increased.

After a number of telephone calls I found I was to be offered employment with the Port of London Authority starting – tomorrow. I personally decided that with eleven years of pilotage before me before retirement I had better make the most of the new arrangements and soon discovered that of the two systems of work, I preferred the one I had not chosen but that which had been thrust upon me. As a salaried employee, no longer did I have to worry whether trade fell off and whether or not a ship might appear over the horizon or wait until one did. I was no longer responsible for arranging my transport home or back to my point of departure but was driven by taxi. Pilots worked a nine-day roster with six days off, a system which allowed one a better social life, as opposed to the uncertainty of the endless alphabetical sea roster of our self-employed Trinity House service. There was, for me, far more job satisfaction and berthing experience and particularly so when re-trained to pilot up the Thames as far as Crayfordness, working both inwards and out; one pilot sea to berth and vice versa. There was also the opportunity to boost my pension by working a considerable amount of overtime during my last three years' service.

Of course there were constant little irritations during those formative years, and one I personally found particularly annoying as certain members of management endeavoured to establish a superior role over a group of dedicated professionally qualified men with a lifetime of experience at sea. In the main, however, I found my own management in London increasingly benign and easy to work with once the initial few years of frustration and anger subsided. The pilots were consulted and recognised for their professional expertise, management were open to suggestions on risk assessment and improvement, and consultation improved as the disparate members gradually became a team – a team I felt part of and hence why I probably enjoyed working for the PLA.

Sadly, however, it seems that if anecdotal evidence is true (and the reader should be reminded that it is now eleven years since I took retirement and times bring continual change) considerable bitterness and division remains in a number of ports which can only be to the detriment of the customers, the stakeholders and safety.

Physical and Technical Changes

In addition to the political changes involving pilotage, there have been physical changes to the Thames Estuary since I was first licensed and even more since I retired. In 1967 the North Edinburgh Channel was deep enough for the largest ships from the south to enter, while outward ships in the main used the South Edinburgh Channel; although I do remember on several occasions entering via the South Edinburgh to race ahead of slower ships entering via the North Edinburgh. Sadly the South Edinburgh silted up through lack of use due to changing shipping patterns caused by the construction of VLCCs and the containerisation of cargo, and the sister channel began to close as more and more of these larger ships entered the estuary via the Sunk Pilot station. Following pilotage re-organisation, in 1988 the North Edinburgh Channel itself began to silt up and was finally closed when the depths in the Princes Channel and North Edinburgh reached parity. Since my retirement, a new Channel through the Fisherman's Gat has been buoyed and the Princes Channel dredged to 8 metres. The depths over the Diver's Shoal at the lower end of Gravesend Reach had been improved by the clever use of groyne deflecting the hydraulic flow of the river. A container terminal had been built on the river side of Tilbury Dock and subsequently extended, while roll-on roll-off terminals had been developed at Dartford and Purfleet. Currently the large Shell tanker terminal at Shellhaven is being re-developed into a container terminal, capable of receiving the largest container ships in the world. The shallow water off the North Kent coast is now saturated with large lines of wind turbines, generating electricity and much discussion as to the detriment and interference with radar images.

Ships have advanced technically, not just from a navigational view point with better radar and collision avoidance systems (ARPA), satellite navigation (GPS) and electronic charts (ECDIS), automatic identification systems (AIS), but with better propulsion systems, thrusters and azipods and bridge control systems capable of controlling many primary functions of the ships' activities from manoeuvring to cargo work, to fire fighting. Of course ships tend to be much larger now; always the pilot being pushed to the limit as they eventually outgrow the terminals built in an earlier age.

While in some ports, and for particularly large ships, the pilot will board by helicopter this remains in the main a rare and expensive operation. The one thing that really has not changed is the standard method of pilot boarding – the pilot ladder.

Chapter 35

Pilot Boat Code of Safe Practice

Sail off South Foreland

I am privileged to have in my possession the Pilot's notebook dated 1847, of a Cinque Ports Pilot by the name of William James Bowles, which was given to me on my appointment to the service some one hundred and twenty years after he began it. This fascinating record lists his earnings from 1847 to 1877, gives the names of the ships he piloted and the names of their Masters, together with detailed navigational leading marks throughout the district and to Flanders and Holland. It also gives a list of pilots drowned in service of which there were a good number: Messrs James Pascall, I. Daverson and H. Griggs all dying in 1850/51 alone. Over one hundred years later the death toll continued as the sea claimed the pilot victims of incompetence, poorly rigged, designed and maintained equipment and the risks inherent in the pilots' transfer from a violently rolling ship via a wet and slippery rope ladder, to or from a small pilot boat bouncing about on a dark and wild dangerous night.

Undoubtedly the luckiest escape from drowning was that of a colleague, Jim Francis, who fell into the ice-strewn sea off Ramsgate on the day the North East Spit pilot boat had been suspended from service due to pack ice, in the severest winter for many years; weather certainly worse than any we have had since then. The black forbidding sea appeared to be almost completely covered with contrasting white large pudding-shape plates of ice, shiny in the glow of the ship's floodlights on the night of the accident. However there were black leads in the outer harbour when Jim arrived early to join the German ship, MV *Weserstrom*, to review the situation. He decided together with the Captain to sail as soon as and if, the dock gates could be opened at 03:00 hours on the 31st January 1963.

The most difficult challenge was to initially gain sufficient way on the ship, as she manoeuvred from the cut of the enclosed dock to the outer harbour on an easterly course before swinging around to starboard, passing through the narrow entrance, on a south-south-westerly course to meet the strong tide running north-easterly across the solid granite harbour entrance. There could possibly be a build-up of pack ice at the entrance and I certainly would not have been happy, so early in my piloting career, to be so brave; but the gates opened and all went well. Jim confidently swept through the narrow entrance, passed the fixed red tidal light on the West Pier Head shining brightly in the crystal clear night, swung hard to port to clear the Quern buoy and stopped the engines; swinging around to push a clear space in the ice pans for the boat which was following him to come alongside. The adrenalin must have been pumping hard when, saying goodbye to the Captain and Chief Engineer, he descended to the foredeck and began to mount the few steps of the portable bulwark steps allowing him easy access to the pilot ladder. He perhaps sighed with relief that all had gone so well, oblivious to the trauma about to unfold.

Reaching the top step, he swung around, holding the stanchion attached to the steps, to prepare to descend the rope pilot ladder hanging down the ship's side. The combination of steps and attached stanchion were not secured, with the result that they pivoted with his weight over the bulwarks, tipping Jim into the sea on that dark bitterly cold morning. Immediately swept by the force of the tide out of the area illuminated by the harbour lights, he was never lost to sight of the vigilant Bob Cannon, the coxswain of the pilot boat, who skilfully manoeuvred the boat to have the casualty alongside. Unfortunately, being on his own, Bob was unable to recover the deadweight of Jim in his heavy wet clothing and boots into the icy boat; while Jim was rapidly losing consciousness, unable to use his frozen and quite useless limbs. Thinking and reacting quickly, Mr Cannon secured a rope under the pilot's armpits and lashed him to the side of the boat, towing the by now frozen body of Jim, literally freezing to death slowly and carefully the half mile into Ramsgate Harbour through the pack ice before he was safely recovered with help on the steps of the East Pier and removed to hospital. Sound and appropriate treatment of this obviously healthy and very tough young pilot meant that he was soon to be re-united with his wife Mary, mother of his two children with a third on the way, who had remained quite unaware of all the drama until later in the morning a very tired individual turned up at home in a taxi, wearing a hospital dressing gown and pyjamas while clutching a bag full of wet clothing which left a puddle in the hallway.

Jim was spurred into action, subsequently working hard and successfully challenging the Board of Trade, with the help of the United Kingdom Pilots Association and finally with the help of the Honourable Albert Costain MP for the constituency of Folkestone, to tighten up and improve on the Pilot Ladder Regulations; setting a standard which eventually received international recognition. However, initial response was, to say the least, unhelpful and almost obstructive; none of the improvements being finally achieved until tragically several more casualties occurred – two of them off the Port of Dover and Jim had re-enacted before the television cameras his accident, by falling off another German coaster into the Granville Dock.

On the 3rd August 1967, shortly after I was first licensed and joined the Cinque Ports Pilot service, I took the little ship *Robato* out of Ramsgate Harbour south through the Downs, past Dover to land at Folkestone for the very first time; it was a pleasant run there being hardly any wind and only a slight sea running on that warm sunny summer's day; life was looking up but little did I realise just how tenuous life as a pilot could become. The innocent weather was no harbinger that day to the incident that would claim the life of the Shaw Savill choice pilot Captain James H Pearson, who fell into the sea off Dover while landing from one of his company's ships the *Afric;* when again an unsecured aluminium step ladder, designed to allow access across a high bulwark rail, tipped with his counterweight over the side – he was drowned.

The findings of the subsequent Coroner's Inquiry (incidentally held with the Lord Warden of the Cinque Ports, the late Australian Prime Minister Sir Robert Menzies in attendance beside the Coroner Mr James A Johnson, taking a keen interest) was to greatly enhance the argument for change and strengthen the indomitable determination of Jim Francis and his colleagues to have steel stanchions fitted to pass through the bulwark rail, rather than the reliance on a flimsy light aluminium set of steps with attached handles, employed for the convenience of the crew rather than the safety of the pilot.

Sadly, although seen by the Captain of the *Afric* to be swimming breaststroke after entry into the water, Captain Pearson, who was a fit and very healthy 63-year-old man with thirty years piloting experience, had at some stage come into contact with the propeller of the pilot boat, he put up an arm to take a lifebuoy from the crewman but that was the last movement he was seen to make. He had injuries to his back consistent with having been struck by the propeller and next day dark blue clothing, like a pilot's uniform was found to be fouling the propeller of the pilot boat *Ocean Prince*.

Just a year earlier, a Deep Sea Pilot named Captain Leslie Hassel, who lived in the Gateway— a large block of flats on the sea front at Dover — had been drowned tragically off the port virtually in sight of his home.

Sadly yet another colleague, Cyril Neaves was drowned in Rotterdam when boarding a container ship where the accommodation ladder had not been landed properly on the quay and he slipped between ship and quay; attempts by a gallant Dutch Stevedore who without hesitation jumped into the dock to save him, were in vain. Visitors to the ship had been stepping from the quay all day onto a quayside bollard, in order to reach the ship's accommodation ladder when Cyril arrived and lost his footing. Unfortunately when the matter came to Court, compensation was diminished for, as a Master Mariner, he was held partly to blame. The argument was that he should have known better and refused to board this large Blue Star container ship, until the ship was moved sufficiently to land the accommodation ladder firmly on the quayside. By a strange coincidence, not long after the findings of the court were in the public domain, I was to attend the very same ship in Zeebrugge. Once again the accommodation ladder was obstructed by a quayside bollard — I refused to board — cargo was stopped and the ship was moved sufficiently to land the accommodation ladder. I was not popular when I boarded; sufficient to say that after the Master and I exchanged opinions, the Master/Pilot relationship suffered irreparable damage.

It was about this time and into this kind of atmosphere that I was asked to join the UKPA (Marine) Technical Committee where under the inspired leadership of a Tees Pilot, Mike Irving FNI, we were in the early stages of developing a dedicated high visibility Pilot Coat complete with automatic inflation, automatic lighting, reflective panels, helicopter strop and even a radio location beacon. Mike spent a lot of time jumping into the cold North Sea of the Tees Estuary testing various pieces of kit in the daylight and dark before reporting back to the committee; he deserved a medal and in fact I recall was awarded a silver medal by the European Marine Pilots' Association. When I subsequently took over as Chairman in 1996 the coats were general issue in London and many other ports.

The original drive to get pilots out of a plain navy Burberry type uniform raincoat, into more suitable and safer heavy weather clothing, was started by the late Stan Coe a Trinity House Pilot based at Gravesend. He set up a company called Seasafe to manufacture and develop a high quality coat to meet the ever changing Technical Committee requirements. The need for better clothing having been recognised with the development in the early 1970s of the lively, wet and fast GRP built pilot boats which replaced the small slow boats previously used, merely for the short distance between the large pilot cutters and the lee of the ship being served. The ability to use new materials and produce much better equipment had been demonstrated by the RNLI and the pleasure boat industry. The Seasafe Company, now with new owners and with an international market is the current lead manufacturer of pilot safety clothing. Stan who sadly passed away some time ago would be proud to see how his contribution to the safety of pilots has been such a story of success. I vividly remember the look of relief on his face when he finally produced a prototype for the committee which received our general approval and I promptly bought it for £75, which was in those days quite expensive – it was bright red and led me to suffer some leg pulling and incredulity and sniggering among my more conservative colleagues, a number of whom undoubtedly being more concerned with the price.

The coats were not the only safety equipment we were investigating and testing at that time. We also looked at different kinds of recovery equipment for retrieving a casualty from the water, for which there were a number of different davits and stern ramps being developed. We looked at a method for securing those moving along the deck of a pilot boat, using a traveller which hooked onto the guard rails. In our search for the most effective equipment we received a great deal of help and co-operation from Stuart Welford, the Research Officer of the RNLI, exchanging ideas and conducting trials to meet the mutual challenges of our respective operations. Like Mike Irving, Stuart was a human dynamo, the two together fired up with enthusiasm were full of ideas; it was a pleasure to work with them.

Some of the new pilot boats working the estuary had been fitted with a stern ramp on the transom which could be lowered, in order to raise the casualty horizontally to avoid the dangers inherent with dragging somebody suffering from hyperthermia vertically out of the water. Regular exercises had been carried out using a life-size dummy but I always felt, and still do, that such a method of recovering might be difficult in anything but a good to moderate sea because of the need to bring the casualty close to the turning propellers of the launch; albeit that they might be shrouded.

One summer's day in 1995 I persuaded the pilotage manager to allow me to carry out a training exercise with a group of newly authorised pilots, in order to demonstrate the equipment and incidentally the automatic inflation of the new pilot coat. The day was deceptively warm and the sea calm and ultramarine against the pale cerulean sky, as we ran north of the Broadstairs Knoll buoy at a moderate to slow speed, the twin diesels purring and the smooth water tumbling away excitedly under the forefoot. With George Harrison, the ex-Trinity House coxswain with years of experience firmly in control of the situation, all was going well as he looked for a nice clear area of water to carry out the exercise without interference from the odd fishing boat or yacht moving through the area; I on the other hand was looking for movement in the water where the ground swell tended to build up on the north side of the shallow water as the sea bed sought the deeper darker sanctuary of the southern North Sea.

Looking at me quizzically as I stood there, 62 years old in an old uniform battered cap and Seasafe coat, my spectacles in my hand, George suddenly asked me;

"What are you going to wear for this exercise, Mr Russell?"

"Well, George, I'm planning on going in just as I am."
I replied, hoping to fully test the coat.

"I would rather you wore a survival suit,"
came his instant response and he was right of course and he was in charge.

I reluctantly but grumpily pulled on a large survival suit over the Seasafe coat with some help and, asking someone to record the evidence on my newly acquired and invented digital camera, I jumped quickly over the side with the pilot boat still running ahead. My idea was to surprise the crew in order to properly exercise their responses and those of the passage pilots – I had quite a surprise myself.

I hit the water face down as I had intended but with a far greater impact than I expected. Bang – the life jacket inflated and I was rolled instantly on my back. The water was freezing and this was mid-summer, but thanks to the survival suit I remained dry inside. Deciding to get the maximum acting experience and drama out of the exercise and play the part to the full, I lay back and waited for rescue. The boat seemed a long way off before eventually turning and slowly bearing down on me, as I squinted in the dazzling sunlight through half closed eyes, it loomed enormously over me until suddenly all went black as I came into the shadow under the bow. I lay pretending to be comatose and felt the gentle nudge and prod of a boat hook on my floating body as I was worked towards the stern and the lowered recovery platform.

As the boat dipped her bows into the gentle swell the platform of course was raised clear of the water at the stern but skilfully my supposedly inert body was manoeuvred on to the steel platform, once the platform was submerged, without a great deal of difficulty and the platform hoisted to bring me horizontally to deck level with no more than a few bruises from the initial contact with the securing tackle on the stern hoist.

George had successfully rescued me, but I seem to remember the trainee pilots were reluctant to participate in the thrill of personal experience of rescue by stern recovery. George, by insisting on the survival suit, had probably saved my life for within six months I was subjected to a triple heart bypass at Guys Hospital suffering from a 98% percent blockage of the three arteries and could have gone at any time from what I was told was called sudden death syndrome. Luck has played a considerable part in my life and undoubtedly was with me on that occasion, as it was earlier in that year when I went Para ascending off Florida and carried out a breathing apparatus course in a smoke and flame filled container at Gravesend Sea School, quite unaware I had a problem.

In 1991 following the death of yet another UK pilot, the Department of Transport wrote quite correctly to the United Kingdom Pilots Association (Marine) Technical Committee, suggesting that there was a need for a

Code of Safe Practice to cover the boarding and landing and the operation of pilot boats rather than the boats themselves and their hardware. It was suggested that the draft code should be prepared by the experts – the pilots and the pilot boat crews – and commented on by the Department. I say this was the correct approach in the light of the subsequent petty furore which evolved. The Technical Committee, which was not a political animal but a purely professional adjunct to the UKPA, had been dealing directly with the Department for many years on all matters dealing with pilot ladder legislation and pilot safety equipment; most of the pilots in the country were self-employed, many owning their own boats prior to re-organisation.

It never occurred to the committee members that the request was anything but sensible, for who after all had any practical experience of this quite unique operation apart from the pilots and boat crews who had developed techniques and improvements over hundreds of years in the cauldron of bad weather, poor equipment and ship-borne apathy. I did express the view at the time that perhaps we were being asked to devise a set of rules that one day may bite us in the backside if there were found to be breaches in the way a particular operation was performed resulting in injury; not imagining that I would eventually be called upon to act as the Single Joint Expert in just such a Court case – but that's another story.

The Technical Committee took on the work and I was tasked by Mike Irving the Chairman to write the first draft; an unpaid job which needed to be done in my spare time between ships and my other interests, as I worked for the Port of London Authority. It was an interesting challenge as I sat here at my desk with a blank sheet of paper, thinking of the sequence of the boarding and landing process but not a difficult undertaking once I set down the paragraph headings logically; for by the year 1991 I had twenty-four years experience of boarding and landing to and from all sizes of ship in all kinds of weather to call upon.

Completing the draft (See Annex 1) the day before I was to go on annual leave, it occurred to me that the work was purely my own effort, work which I had not shown to my own colleagues or pilot boat crews or pilot boat operators; and that before it was discussed further, perhaps it should be viewed by at least some of my own colleagues to see if there were any glaring omissions that could be identified or if there was any serious criticism forthcoming. Naively possibly, unwisely undoubtedly, I had not even considered the consequence of requesting help from the new management with circulating the draft for comment. I quickly wrote a note to the PLA Pilotage Manager and sent him the draft asking him to circulate it to pilots and boat crews.

I came home to a furore – the Pilotage Manager had, it seems, circulated my draft to the ports instead, people who took great exception to the fact that the Department of Transport had asked the pilots "Union" to produce a draft code, when they the ports were now "in charge" of the operation of pilot boats. They, being new to the scheme of things and unaware of the existing history of the relationship between the Department and the UKPA Technical Committee, felt neglected; I suppose in retrospect it was understandable but the whole episode seemed extremely childish at the time and remains so as I think about it today. I asked the Pilotage Manager who in the CHAs had the experience to write such a code and who in fact he would ask to write the code? He replied with the benefit of my draft already in his hand;

"Probably you."

I was not invited to any further meetings to discuss the content or original draft and was therefore annoyed when some months later a glossy copy of a code was published, as being prepared by the British Ports Federation and issued to every pilot in the country. Apart from a couple of minor changes and the omission of something they obviously did not understand, it was identical to my original draft. Having been treated like a naughty school boy, I was furious at this blatant plagiarism and exploitation of my intellectual rights and it was further aggravated when, at an unrelated social function shortly afterwards, one of these so-called managers from another port boasted to me that he had actually drafted the code for the BPF himself.

I seriously thought for a while about suing for plagiarism but soon calmed down, recognising that I had volunteered for the task and been only too pleased to prepare the draft in my own time for the Technical Committee. To make a fuss about ownership of the intellectual rights now, when the original draft had obviously found favour amongst my peers and been accepted, was to lower myself to the level of the petty-minded individuals who raised the objections to the exercise in the first place. The important outcome was the production of the first Code of Safe Practice for the Boarding and Landing of Pilots and the successful conclusion of the idea for such a code conceived by Alistair Struthers, Principal Nautical Surveyor, at the Department of Transport. Amusingly I was able to thank the Pilot

Manager responsible, for saving the UKPA the considerable expense of printing the code.

The BPA code was subsequently used as a basis for a number of different editions as the CHAs produced their own individual codes, as part of their risk assessment procedures; but the debate continued long after I retired, my only involvement being when acting as the Single Joint Expert for a Court case involving injury to a pilot, I identified a part of the code which I felt I could have better drafted and an area which I had omitted.

After some sixteen years, a new version of the Code has finally been prepared jointly by the Marine/Pilotage Working Group of the British Ports Association (BPA) and the UK Major Ports Group (UKMPG) and the Technical & Training Committee of the United Kingdom Maritime Pilots Association (UKMPA). Much has been added including paragraph 4.5 which is relevant to my Court findings.

The current version can be found as (Annex 2) and on the web at:

www.britishports.org.uk/public/news

It was pleasing that the Working Group asked me to write the Foreword to the latest Code of Safe Practice, thus giving recognition of my earlier efforts and I can only hope that use of this work will further enhance the safety and the working environment of Pilots and Pilot Boat Crews internationally.

In these days of growing litigation and the need to cover every eventuality in the workplace and even the simplest task by Risk Assessment, it is too easy to dismiss and become irritated by much of the mountain of paperwork generated as statements of the obvious – just plain common sense – are written by so-called teams of experts. While I appreciate that many of my older colleagues who spent a lifetime safely boarding and landing from ships without the benefit of written advice but learning from their own experience and using their common sense, may consider such a code perhaps unnecessary, it was conceived at a time when yet another pilot had lost his life and nearly half the pilots in the United Kingdom were new to pilotage as a result of re-organisation. It is in that context that the original draft was produced and, as a result of that code, that much new equipment has been fitted to pilot boats together with appropriate training; I like to think that my humble contribution has helped to make the pilots' world a safer place.

Chapter 36

My Pleasure in Painting

I was asked recently where I learnt to paint, a question which I found flattering for it implied a certain standard of developed achievement, but to be honest I have had little tuition but have read a number of books on watercolours. I have always drawn and did quite well at school even as far back as 1942, where records show that I achieved *Honours* at Preparatory Level in a submission to The Royal Drawing Society together with nine other small boys; hardly a significant achievement I imagine, for the award appears to have been given to my whole class at Bethany. Certainly at school art was a strong subject; even in my worst school term report I achieved a high mark in art, when every other subject that particular term was abysmal.

My first real tuition came from a colleague of my father who, although a real artist, was serving in the National Fire Service during WW2. He taught me the rudiments of oil painting, starting with the preparation of a palette and finishing with a small still life of an orange balanced alongside a blue tumbler, on an open book. I remember as a young boy the cold north-facing garret heated with a one-bar electric fire, in a tall old building long since demolished to make way for an Asda supermarket and the long time the picture took to me to paint. As a small boy I became distracted by the painting of a nude lady stacked against the wall bearing a distinct likeness to the lady I occasionally caught a glimpse of around the house and with whom I now shared a secret. My progress was too slow, materials were difficult to obtain and I was to leave with just the one picture but I understand that my tutor went on to become the Head of a large Art College in the West Country in the years following the war.

I did little painting while at sea apart from the occasional pen and ink sketch, my main achievement being to design and paint the company logo around the bow of the *Peter Dal II,* a somewhat pedestrian effort but striking for all that.

Coming ashore into the Cinque Ports Pilotage Service my first paintings were probably the ones I did on large pieces of hard board outside my garage, while bearded and humming Rolf Harris style and using a large decorating brush, I splashed on emulsion while a little group of small excited children danced excitedly around shouting encouragement in the warm morning sunshine. I was painting background scenery for the 1st Dymchurch Brownies pageant floats, depicting "One Hundred and One Dalmatians", "The Sound of Music" and the like for Folkestone Carnival and the Hythe Venetian Fete – they were happy days.

The Tree at West Hythe (oils)

Most of my painting was done in my piloting days when I attended the local Adult Education Centre for tuition. I had been painting at home in oils the occasional landscape and took one along, a picture of a tree at West Hythe to show the Principal of the centre to ask at what level of tuition he felt I should join. I was flattered that he felt fit to put me into the advanced section and I was privileged to join some very talented local amateur artists and learn with them under the instruction of Peter Lucas a gifted painter and tutor who greatly encouraged us all. We painted landscapes in oils on large pieces of hardboard; often four feet long by three feet deep and soon I had enough to fill the house. It was great fun to be painting such large pictures but a little impractical, although it gave my father a great deal of pleasure as he retired and took up picture framing.

I was soon conscious however that like many artists under tuition, I was beginning to acquire the pallet of my tutor Peter Lucas, which pleased me in one way for I admired his work tremendously but at the same time I felt I was losing my originality, crude as it may have been. We exhibited our work within the college but I never managed to produce sufficient work to hold an exhibition of my own. Not long after L.S. Lowery died in 1976, I painted a large oil of a canal barge, horse-drawn wagons with a background of factory chimneys and grey terraced houses and pink sky which I submitted for the Rotary District Art Competition in 1977 and much to my surprise, it won. Undoubtedly the Loweryesque subject and colouring had some influence but I think it also had something to do with the fact that it was the largest picture and therefore dominated the competition.

Folkestone Harbour 1978 (oils)

The next thing that happened was for me to be visited by the owner of a local art gallery who, selecting from my collection a very large personal favourite picture of mine depicting Folkestone Harbour at low water, said he would undoubtedly be able to sell it. I did not want to sell but, intrigued to know what he thought he could get for it, I enquired as to his expectations. When he replied, I was astonished as to his valuation and immediately succumbed to the monetary inducement. It was a mistake which I bitterly regretted for the picture was only in the front window of the gallery a week before it was sold to I know not who, disappearing from my life. I had lost part of that life, a work and joy which I had spent hours patiently developing and enjoying, as it gradually came into existence and I carefully balanced the tones. I had by then learned to look at all pictures with one eye through a tunnel in my hand, made between my fingers and thumb to check the tonal balance. I was often surprised how much I had successfully achieved when viewed the next day or disappointed when immediately seeing imbalance with a fresh eye.

The Village of Postling, Hythe, Kent

My paintings are very personal achievements which continually give me more pleasure than they probably do to other people, some of course I like better than others but I cannot resist when visiting the family or owners of my pictures, sidling up in admiration to an old friend hanging on the wall and wondering just how I managed to achieve a particular effect or illusion. Sometimes I come across work I have completely forgotten about but usually I am delighted to be reminded of those enjoyable hours, hours when a subject will completely take over one's world, when the stresses and strains of modern living disappear and one can be completely absorbed in creating an effect with brush, colour, fingers and sandpaper. I remember many years ago when one summer's evening I was getting on so well with a picture that I completely lost all sense of time and was very surprised when Sally appeared to enquire if I had any intention of coming to bed – it was two o'clock in the morning!

It is easy of course to become discouraged and when not long after the gallery owner asked for more work and even suggested subjects, size and general colouring; I promptly stopped painting and refused to get onto the treadmill. I still bitterly regretted my earlier loss and it was easy to find an excuse – large wet oil paintings smelt of turpentine and were difficult to store taking weeks to dry, there was work to do on the house and garden, I was becoming very involved in my professional extra-curricular activities, I was Honorary Secretary to the Cinque Ports Pilots and was writing a paper for a seminar on the subject of navigational problems in the Dover Strait. I put away my oil paints, a great mistake in retrospect, for there is no doubt that like any human achievement one really needs to continually practise in order to improve from experience. I did a couple of cartoons to illustrate my paper which at the time was very critical of the situation in the Dover Straits but really did not paint seriously again for a number of years.

I had, in preparation for a large painting, always drawn on site in pen and ink or pencil to establish the tones, noting and writing on the colours I could see and sometimes using watercolours to get the feel for a picture. When following the Falklands campaign in 1982, I listened enthralled to an old friend Captain Shane Redmond OBE RFA as he told of his experiences with RFA *Tidespring*. I sat down next day and painted in watercolour my impression of his ship in company with HMS *Antrim* and HMS *Plymouth* on passage to retake South Georgia. I was encouraged by the result and over the following nine days I completed a set of ten watercolours depicting the Royal Fleet Auxiliary Service in action in the South Atlantic, as a tribute to my old colleagues who had distinguished themselves so courageously in the face of real danger. I put the paintings in a local exhibition and was surprised when they were picked up by Southern Television and I was interviewed together with my work. Very much tongue in cheek I offered the set on loan to the RFA and was delighted to be warmly received and privileged when some of them were hung for the memorial service held aboard an RFA Landing Ship at Marchwood, Southampton to those lost on RFA *Sir Galahad*. Subsequently the set which had been framed by my father hung for a number of years in the RFA Headquarters at Earls Court, London until I asked for their return following his demise and hung them at home.

Cartoons for Dover Strait Seminar 1978

RFA Blue Rover South Atlantic 1982

In March 1995 as a Vice President of the Nautical Institute I was asked to go out to Dubai at very short notice to be the stand-in guest speaker at the Dubai Branch Annual Charity Dinner, a prestigious black tie affair which included a Charity Auction normally raising thousands of pounds for maritime charities. In order to offset my travelling costs Mike Plumridge, the Deputy Secretary, suggested I might donate a couple of my RFA Falklands pictures to the auction and I readily agreed; picking out a painting of the Hospital Ship *Uganda* fuelling from an RFA tanker and the picture above of RFA *Blue Rover*. The auction was a stunning success and the two pictures made sufficient money to pay the return air tickets for both Sally and the guest speaker whose dinner jacket and baggage went onto Colombo but that is another story.

Since that time I have painted mainly in watercolour, trying my hand at old sailing ships and a multitude of holiday pictures painted in the Canary Islands, none however give me the satisfaction of those large earlier oils or the set of ten painted as a tribute to the bravery of those men of the RFA.

Chapter 37

Epilogue

When I first mentioned to one of my elderly pilot colleagues that I planned to write my autobiography he laughed and asked;

"What are you going to leave out?"

Another dear friend remarked;

"Autobiography you say, I never read them, too many I's".

Sitting here in my office in the long slopped roof of our share of an old converted Kentish tithe barn, looking out westerly through the Velox window across the fields and the small lake busy with mating ducks and moorhens; *Pent Farm* where Joseph Conrad once lived and wrote for some years is just visible, where the sun sets behind the new leaves of spring beginning to adorn the bare tree poles of winter. It is perhaps impudent of me to mention the name of this acclaimed literary genius in my own humble contribution of seafaring tales, but some of his most marvellous stories of fact and fiction were drafted long hand within sight of my desk here in this quiet secluded village of Postling, nestled in the lee of the North Downs. Thinking about it, this tithe barn was here and old, even when Conrad sat quietly remembering his own experiences on the River Congo and at sea as a Master Mariner; much as I have done. He, of course, did not have the benefit of a computer to recall the date of an event quickly or as I have been able to trawl, an almost daily record of my seagoing life of fifty years; although I believe his wife Jessie George, did at one time work for the American Writing Machine Company and undoubtedly helped produce some of his manuscripts on one of their new machines.

There even the vaguest similarity ends for he was obviously a gifted author, a giant in the literary world who achieved an ambition to go to sea to broaden his horizons; while having spent a lifetime at sea, I am the amateur scribe trying to record what for me was personally an exciting and fulfilling life.

Evening at Dungeness

Joseph Conrad on the one hand managed to produce many outstanding mostly fictional stories from what was in fact, a relatively limited seagoing career to some exotic at that time unknown places; while my efforts are to merely record factual anecdotes – amusing and serious – of a full lifetime at sea in the known and ever shrinking world of the last half of the twentieth century. My experience of four years sea time as an apprentice before written examinations, with some subjects repeated at Second Mate, Mate and Master, would probably be more familiar to men of Conrad's era than those of the last few decades, for much has changed as the world's shipping has become standardised.

During this endeavour I have been surprised how my memory has on occasion played tricks and how, having written of one particular voyage around Africa clockwise, I discovered in the attic some old saved letters written home to my parents, which clearly indicated the voyage had been anti-clockwise and therefore had to be re-written. My memories and dates of the RFA days are verified by my Seaman's Discharge Book and also by letters, while my Pilotage experiences are taken from my virtually complete record of pilotage accounts. Poor old Conrad has been criticised and had serious doubt cast about some of his memories of times and places but he, poor chap, only had those precious shaky memories of past adventures and lacked the facilities of our age to store and research information.

However we both have a number of aspects of our lives in common, apart from living for a long time in this lovely village – we both qualified as Master Mariners – both spent considerable time in the Far East – both at periods in our lives were bearded and both have a Japanese connection in our lives. I spent a considerable part of my early career on the coast of the Japanese Islands. The Japanese interest in Joseph Conrad is current and has been for at least the last several decades; encouraging Japanese students of English Literature to be very well read of his works and interested enough to be seen occasionally stopping to photograph his old home, *The Pent, Postling, Kent.*

Towards Lympne Castle from Palmarsh

I finally retired from Pilotage and seagoing on the 31st October 1999, after fifty years and had planned to come down river on the morning of my 65th birthday, driving the P&O Containership *Pegasus Bay* with the tugs giving me the traditional send-off with displays of projected water fire jets, while I grandly said my farewells to anyone that would listen on the vhf radio; but unbeknown to me my lovely Sally had been planning and saving for over a year and hired Lympne Castle for a secret retirement party and even invited the Chief Harbour Master and Pilotage Manager to ensure I would not work on that final day. My initial disappointment that the *Pegasus Bay* had been delayed in fog soon turned to sheer joy when I discovered the castle full of old friends and family, fine wine and victuals prepared by my old friend Robert Spicer and I am sure nobody in the world could have ever had a better retirement party in such a superb setting overlooking the Romney Marsh.

As for leaving out parts of my story – well of course I have. I hope that I have ignored anything that may have caused embarrassment to family, friends or colleagues both ashore and afloat and that which I have related is accurate and factual. Over the last few years I have been privileged to meet and dine, among others, with some very important public figures and been privy to some fascinating conversation – some of which I would dearly love to repeat but will not, for such conversations are I think sacrosanct.

Hopefully the reader will not have been put off by the number of references to the first person singular but enjoyed sharing with me this personal unplanned passage through the very full and very lucky life of this simple sailor.

Peter J D Russell

Portrait (photograph)

ANNEX 1

THE ORIGINAL FIRST DRAFT
THE SHIPPING & LANDING OF PILOTS BY LAUNCH
CODE OF PRACTICE

INTRODUCTION

1.1 A draft Code of Practice has been prepared by the Technical Committee of the United Kingdom Pilots' Association (Marine) at the suggestion of the Department of Transport in a letter dated 1 July 1991 (Tech. Com. Ref 33/7).

1.2 At this stage of drafting Pilots, Coxswains, Launch Crews and Launch Operators are asked to comment on any omissions they feel should be included in the draft. Professional criticism as to the content is welcomed but in making comment it should be remembered that the code is for general use of all those involved in the shipping and landing of pilots, the particular special needs of individual pilot stations may therefore only be covered in the most general terms.

1.3 Paragraphs have not been listed in order of importance.

1.4 The need for the Code is to bring to the attention of the many new personnel involved in the pilotage service, common safe practices to be used when making the relatively hazardous transfer from pilot boat to ship or vice-versa. It should also serve to remind those of long service of the need to avoid complacency through over familiarity.

CONTENT

3   THE PILOT LAUNCH

3.1   The pilotage Authority must ensure that the launch on service, in all ways, meets the requirements of the current national Pilot Boat Legislation.

3.2   Prior to leaving harbour or at least once per watch, the coxswain should check that his launch is in all respects ready for sea.

3.3   On joining and prior to leaving harbour, the coxswain and crew should familiarise themselves with the stowage and positions of the safety equipment fitted to that particular launch

3.4   On joining in harbour or at sea, the pilot should also endeavour to familiarise himself with the positions and stowage of the safety equipment fitted to that particular launch.

3.5   Because 3.4 above is not always easy when landing on a dark night, pilots should ensure that they are familiar with the normal positions of stowage for such equipment. Or where several different classes of launch are in operation, the normal stowage for such equipment in that class of launch.

3.6   Arrangements should be made for pilot launch mooring ropes to remain at the pilot launch berth, in order to avoid accidental loss or accident while underway.

3.7   The decks of the launch should be clear of all obstruction to the passage of pilot and crewman.

4   LEAVING HARBOUR

4.1   The launch should not leave harbour unless in all respects ready for sea.

4.2   The launch should be fully manned with a minimum of one coxswain and one able seaman.

4.3   The launch should not leave harbour unless all pilots and crew members on board can be seated (i.e. the number of persons should not exceed the boat's licence).

4.4   On leaving harbour, the launch should not be tasked to exceed its full complement by landing pilots into an already full or partially full boat.

4.5 Additional mooring ropes carried (see 3.6) should be safely stowed.

4.6 Radio VHF communications with Port/Pilot Station should establish that the launch is leaving harbour on task.

5. THE SHIPPING & LANDING AREAS

5.1 CHAs & Pilotage Authorities should ensure that areas chosen for the shipping and landing of pilots, allow sufficient sea-room for manoeuvre, depth of water and where possible shelter from the more exposed elements of the predominant wind and weather.

5.2 Where possible such areas should be clearly defined and clear of through routes used by non-piloted vessels (see paragraph 6.4).

6. APPROACHING THE SHIP

6.1 VHF Radio contact should be established between pilot launch and ship as soon as possible, after which both launch and ship should remain on a dedicated VHF Channel.

6.2 The position of the ship should be established by the coxswain of the pilot launch and where there is more than one vessel, their relative positions.

6.3 The pilot launch coxswain should decide on which side the ship, should rig her pilot ladder in order to give the best lee for his approach & communicate this information the ship.

6.4 The pilot launch coxswain may instruct the Master of a ship on the best course to steer in order to make the best lee for the safe shipping of a pilot. Such advice does not relieve the Master of the vessel of his obligations to avoid other shipping under the requirements of the Regulations for Prevention of Collision at Sea (1976). Masters receiving such advice should be aware that the coxswain of the pilot launch may be in a position where vessels on the weather-side of the ship he is serving, are obscured from his visual or radar view.

6.5 During the approach to the ship, both pilot and assisting crewman should remain inside the launch cabin until the launch is at reduced speed and in the lee of the ship.

6.6 At night the pilot boat deck lights should be turned on before anyone goes on deck.

6.7 During the final approach the pilot boat searchlight should be turned on to illuminate the pilot ladder and foredeck of the launch.

6.8 Before the pilot leaves the cabin the coxswain should advise him of his approximate position. This is particularly important in fog and in large shipping and landing areas.

7. THE SHIP

7.1 Upon establishing contact with the pilot station/pilot launch, the ship should rig a pilot ladder or combination on the lee side as requested and in accordance with the International Convention for Safety at Sea (SOLAS 1974) Chapter V Reg. 17 & IHO Resolution A667 (1991).

7.2 During the transfer of pilot between launch and ship, the officer supervising the embarkation at the pilot ladder should be in direct contact with the bridge of the ship. On large ships or when the embarkation point is not visible from the bridge, the communication should be by portable radio.

7.3 During the transfer the ship should maintain steerage way with the engines going ahead at a speed compatible with the ability of the launch to remain comfortably alongside. For the modern fast pilot launch this means a minimum speed of about 6 Knots.

7.4 The vessel should not be stopped or her engines put in reverse except in an emergency.

7.5 A vessel at anchor unable to manoeuvre to make a lee should get underway before taking the pilot.

8   PILOT BOARDING

8.1 When leaving the cabin once in the lee of the ship, both crewman followed by the pilot, should pass along the outboard side of the cabin to the boarding position which is normally the foredeck of the launch, in full view of the coxswain. This is to prevent injury and entrapment between cabin superstructure and hull of ship.

8.2 Both crewman and pilot should be wearing buoyancy aids.

8.3 When possible the crewman should be secured to the launch by a traveller clipped to the guard-rails.

8.4 Providing the ladder has been rigged at the correct height, the crewman should lift the end clear as the launch comes alongside. It is important that the ladder does not become trapped between ship and launch, causing damage and excessive strain on the ladder.

8.5 Where an adjustment to the height of the pilot ladder is required, this should be communicated to the bridge of the ship by the coxswain and the pilot and crewman recalled to the protection of the pilot launch cabin.

8.6 Before the pilot steps onto the ladder, it should be established that it is secure by communication with those at the top of the ladder. This is best done by the simple query – "OKAY?" " The reply being "OKAY" or "NO". It should be remembered that from the launch it is impossible to see the securing arrangements and that the word "OKAY" is understood internationally. If there appears to be nobody on deck at the top of the ladder, it is unwise for the pilot to attempt to embark.

8.7 The timing as to when to step from launch to ladder is important, particularly with the launch rising and falling alongside in heavy weather. The more experienced pilot will usually step onto the ladder at the top of the largest wave, thus leaving himself with a shorter climb and virtually little chance of being trapped. The pilot should try to avoid stepping onto the ladder when the launch is in the trough of a wave, for he will almost certainly find his legs trapped as the launch rises quicker than he can climb. It should be remembered that even in the poorest of weather conditions there is usually a lull between the largest waves. If unsure the pilot should wait for that lull and then climb quickly or abandon the attempt to board.

8.8 Faced with boarding a rolling ship the technique is to step onto the ladder as the ship completes her roll towards the pilot boat, climb quickly as the ship rolls away and then hold on as she rolls back again, resuming the climb as she rolls away.

8.9 When the pilot only has a reasonably short climb, it is better for the launch to remain alongside while the climb is completed to ensure the launch does not foul the ladder when leaving the ship's side.

8.10 With a long climb, the pilot may prefer the launch to move away from the ship's side in order to avoid serious injury in case of a fall. Such a decision should be made as a result of consultation between pilot and coxswain prior to the pilot leaving the cabin. If the launch leaves the ship's side, particular care must be made not to foul the ladder.

8.11 When boarding by hoists, it should be checked that a ladder is rigged adjacent to the hoist and available for immediate use in the event of possible mechanical failure (IMO Resolution A667 para4.7.3.).

8.12 When boarding by hoist, the pilot should climb the flexible short pilot ladder into the rigid upper section before indicating it is "OKAY" to hoist him.

8.13 The launch should move away from the ship once the pilot enters the hoist "cage".

8.14 The decision as to whether to attempt to put a pilot launch alongside a ship when faced with heavy weather, poor visibility, a large rubbing band or other obstruction to the task is the responsibility of the coxswain

8.15 The decision as to whether to attempt to board under adverse weather conditions must remain with the pilot.

8.16 During embarkation/disembarkation of pilots, the pilot launch radar should be switched to "standby'" as he climbs past the scanner.

8.17 When boarding with a combination accommodation ladder / pilot ladder, the accommodation ladder must lead aft.

8.18 The accommodation ladder must be rigged sufficiently high enough to allow the pilot launch / tug to lie alongside the pilot ladder section.

9   PILOT LANDING

9.1   As with shipping, communication should be established between ship and pilot launch and arrangements made in advance.

9.2   The pilot should ensure the pilot ladder is properly secure before disembarking.

9.3   The crewman should be at the bottom of the ladder ensuring that the ladder is rigged at the correct height and clear.

9.4   Before stepping onto the ladder the pilot should check that the launch is laying alongside in a comfortable lee and has not fouled the pilot ladder.

9.5 Before reaching the launch the crewman should advise pilot how many steps further to go and when to step backwards off the ladder, giving physical help when required.

9.6 Both pilot and crewman should be wearing buoyancy aids.

9.7 The crewman should be secured by traveller to the launch guard-rails when possible.

9.8 Pilot should make his way to the launch cabin via the outboard side of the launch followed by the crewman, once he has seen the launch clear of the ladder.

10 LEAVING THE SHIP

10.1 Before leaving the lee of the ship the coxswain should ensure both pilot and crewman are safely seated inside the launch cabin

10.2 Should the launch have difficulty leaving the side of the ship due to the effect of wind setting the ship to leeward. The coxswain should indicate his problem to the master and request the vessel either turns into or away from the wind until the launch can break away.

11 HEAVY WEATHER

11.1 Launches should proceed at a moderate speed in heavy weather compatible with sea conditions and launch design.

11.2 In fast GRP launches maximum use should be made of sprung seating for crew and pilots, together with seat belts.

11.3 To avoid injury on passage the stowage of ancillary equipment should be designed to be clear of seating areas, with particular emphasis on the space around head and shin.

11.4 Loose equipment or stores should not be carried.

11.5 Paragraphs 8.7, 8.8, 8.14, 8.15 and 10.2 also refer to *heavy* weather.

12 POOR VISIBILITY

12.1 The pilot launch must be allowed extra time on task in order to proceed at a moderate speed in poor visibility.

12.2 Launch radar must be operational.

12.3 Launch fog signal must be operational.

12.4 Paragraph 6.7 also refers to poor visibility.

13   MAN OVERBOARD PROCEDURE

13.1 In the event of an "over the side" accident, the first essential is to locate the casualty, to which all crew and pilots on board must devote their whole attention.

13.2 Once found and as the pilot boat is positioned, retrieval equipment can be prepared as per established drill.

13.3 Coastguard, Port authorities and shipping should be informed as soon as possible but long conversations must be avoided. Speed of sighting and recovery remain the priority.

13.4 Recovery should be made as per well-practised drill. The method will depend on the equipment carried and the weather conditions.

14   TRAINING FOR RETRIEVAL OF CASUALTIES

14.1 The success or failure of the rescue relates directly to the expertise of the launch crew and pilots and their familiarity with recovery equipment fitted to their launches and to training in the treatment of hypothermia, and artificial resuscitation training.

14.2 Retrieval drill for launch crews and the checking of recovery equipment should be carried out weekly with an appropriate log book entry.

14.3 Pilots should all be familiar with the recovery equipment of their launches and during their initial training should receive actual "over the side" training.

14.4 All seagoing pilotage staff should receive training in resuscitation and the treatment of hypothermia.

End

Drafted 12/9/91
P.J.D. Russell FNI

ANNEX 2

THE EMBARKATION AND
DISEMBARKATION OF PILOTS

CODE OF SAFE PRACTICE

The latest official new version of the Code has been prepared jointly by the Marine/Pilotage Working Group of the British Ports Association (BPA) and the UK Major Ports Group (UKMPG) and the Technical & Training Committee of the United Kingdom Maritime Pilots Association (UKMPA) in March 2007.

However being a living document subject to amendment it has not been printed but the latest edition can be found online at the following sites:

<u>www.ukmpa.org</u>

<u>www.britishports.org.uk/public/news</u>

ANNEX 3

Indentured to the Dalhousie Steam
& Motor Ship Company

ANNEX 4

Master's Certificate Of Competency

ANNEX 5

Trinity House Pilot Licence

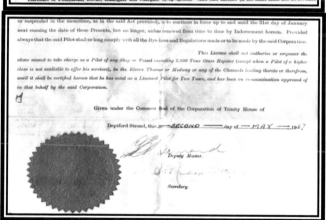

ANNEX 6

Annual Renewal on Re-examination

DESCRIPTION of the Person to whom this Licence was
granted on the 2ⁿᵈ MAY 1967

PETER JOHN DAVID RUSSELL, aged 32 Years, 6 Feet — Ins. high,

of a FRESH Complexion, has BROWN Hair.

Add in writing any very special or particular Mark, &c., which the Party may happen to have.

Renewal	24th	day of	JANUARY	19 68	R J Francis	for Secretary.
Renewal	8th	day of	JANUARY	19 69	R J Francis	Secretary.
Renewal	10th	day of	JANUARY	19 70	R J Francis	Secretary.
Renewal	6TH	day of	JANUARY	19 71	R J Francis	Secretary.
Renewal	5th	day of	JANUARY	19 72	R J Francis	Secretary.
Renewal	30th	day of	JANUARY	19 73	R J Francis	Secretary.
Renewal	28th	day of	JANUARY	19 74	R J Francis	Secretary.
Renewal	15th	day of	JANUARY	19 75	R J Francis	Secretary.
Renewal	22nd	day of	JANUARY	19 76	R J Francis	Secretary.
Renewal	28th	day of	JANUARY	19 77	R J Francis	Secretary.
Renewal	23rd	day of	JANUARY	19 78	David	Secretary.
Renewal	3rd	day of	JANUARY	19 79		Secretary.
Renewal	24th	day of	JANUARY	19 80	Mason	Secretary.
Renewal	14th	day of	JANUARY	19 81		Secretary.
Renewal	14th	day of	JANUARY	19 82		Secretary.

Renewed	14th	day of	JANUARY	19 82		Secretary.
Renewed	19th	day of	JANUARY	19 83		Secretary.
Renewed	13th	day of	JANUARY	19 84	Mason	Secretary.
Renewed	23rd	day of	JANUARY	19 85		Secretary.
Renewed	19th	day of	JANUARY	19 86		Secretary.
Renewed	29th	day of	JANUARY	19 87	Mason	Secretary.
Renewed	28th	day of	JANUARY	19 88	P J Mason	Secretary.
Renewed		day of		19		Secretary.

ANNEX 7

Endorsements on re-examination

LONDON   PILOTAGE DISTRICT

ENDORSEMENT TO LICENCE No. 2566 ———— ISSUED ON THE 2ᵐᵈ MAY —— 19 67.

TO PETER JOHN DAVID RUSSELL

This is to certify that the above named has acted as a FOURTH Class Pilot for a period of TWO years and has on re-examination as to his competency to take charge of ships and vessels exceeding 2000 tons gross register been approved of in that behalf by the Corporation of Trinity House and is promoted to the THIRD Class, but he is not authorised or empowered to take charge as a Pilot of any ship or vessel exceeding 4500 tons gross register (except when a Pilot of a higher Class is not available to offer his services) until it shall be certified that he has acted as a THIRD Class Pilot for ONE year and has been on re-examination approved of by the Corporation as a SECOND Class Pilot.

By Order of the Corporation,

TRINITY HOUSE,
LONDON, E.C.3
2ᵐᵈ MAY 1969.

FOR Secretary.

———— LONDON   PILOTAGE DISTRICT

ENDORSEMENT TO LICENCE No. 2566 ———— ISSUED ON THE 2ⁿᵈ MAY   1967

TO PETER JOHN DAVID RUSSELL ————

This is to certify that the above named has acted as a THIRD Class Pilot for a period of ONE years and has on re-examination as to his competency to take charge of ships and vessels exceeding 4,500 tons gross register been approved of in that behalf by the Corporation of Trinity House and is promoted to the SECOND Class, but he is not authorised or empowered to take charge as a Pilot of any ship or vessel exceeding 12,000 tons gross register (except when a Pilot of a higher Class is not available to offer his services) until it shall be certified that he has acted as a SECOND Class Pilot for ONE year and has been on re-examination approved of by the Corporation as a FIRST Class Pilot.

By Order of the Corporation,

TRINITY HOUSE,
LONDON, E.C.3
2ⁿᵈ MAY, 1970.

Edward Dobbs
FOR Secretary.

LONDON ———— PILOTAGE DISTRICT

ENDORSEMENT TO LICENCE No. 2566 ———— ISSUED ON THE 2ⁿᵈ MAY   19 67

TO PETER JOHN DAVID RUSSELL————

This is to certify that the above named has acted as a SECOND Class Pilot for a period of ONE years and has on re-examination as to his competency to take charge of ships and vessels exceeding 12,000 tons gross register been approved of in that behalf by the Corporation of Trinity House and is promoted to the FIRST Class

By Order of the Corporation,

TRINITY HOUSE,
LONDON, E.C.3
3ʳᵈ MAY, 1971

FOR Secretary

Deep Sea Pilotage Certificate

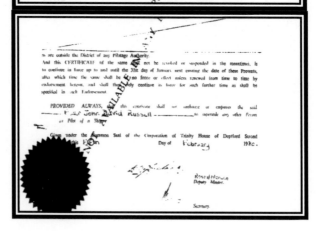

DEEP SEA PILOTS

(2370)   No. 692

To all to whom these Presents shall come: WP The Trinity House, Send Greeting, KNOW YE, that in pursuance and by virtue of the powers given us by The London Pilotage Order 1913, and of all other powers enabling as in this behalf, WE, the Trinity House, having *next duly examined* ———— Peter John David Russell ————— *of* ——— 7, Hinds Close, Dymchurch, Romney Marsh Kent ——————— Mariner, (the Bearer hereof, whose description is endorsed on these Presents) and having upon such Examination found the said ——— Peter John David Russell ———— to be a fit and competent Person, duly skilled to act as a Pilot for the purpose of conducting Ships or other Vessels, Sailing, Navigating, and passing on the Seas and Channels within the limits hereinafter mentioned. DO BY THIS CERTIFICATE, SPECIFICALLY APPOINT and LICENSE the said ———— Peter John David Russell ————— to act as a Pilot, for the purpose of conducting Ships or other Vessels sailing, navigating, or passing upon or through such of the Seas or Channels From Cong-and to the London Pilotage District and from Sheervess to heandam to the London Pilotage District ———————

... are outside the District of any Pilotage Authority.
And this CERTIFICATE (if the same shall not be revoked or suspended in the meantime), is to continue in force up to and until the 31st day of January next ensuing the date of these Presents, after which time the same shall be of no force or effect unless renewed from time to time by endorsement hereon, and shall then only continue in force for such further time as shall be specified in such Endorsement.

PROVIDED ALWAYS, that this certificate shall not authorize or empower the said ——— Peter John David Russell ————— to supersede any other Person at Pilot of a Ship.

Given under the Common Seal of the Corporation of Trinity House of Deptford Strond this 8th On   Day of   February   1980.

Ronald Marwick
Deputy Master.

Secretary.

ANNEX 9

Chart of Trinity House London Pilotage District 1967

ANNEX 10

Chart of Port of London Authority Compulsory Pilotage District Post 1988

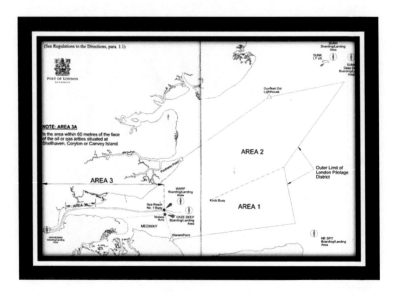